UNDERSTANDING HOW OTHERS MISUNDERSTAND YOU

Ken Voges & Ron Braund

MOODY PRESS

CHICAGO

ABOUT THE AUTHORS

Ken Voges (B.A.) is president of In His Grace, Inc., which provides believers and the church with behavioral tools and training. He is the author of *Understanding Jesus: A Personality Profile* and the *Biblical Personal Profile*. In addition to his writing and training work with Christian organizations, Mr. Voges is a consultant to medium and Fortune 500 corporations on human resources issues.

Mr. Voges and his wife, Linda, are active in the Spring Branch Community Church in Houston, where he teaches an adult Sunday school class and is chairman of the elder board. They have two children, Randy and Christy.

Ron L. Braund (M.Ed., D.Min.), has served individuals and couples for more than seventeen years as a licensed marriage and family therapist. Dr. Braund is a clinical member of the American Association for Marriage and Family Therapy (AAMFT) and directs AlphaCare, an expanding network of Christian counseling centers in the southeast. He has been instrumental in leading and developing the International Congress on Christian Counselling, a forum for the ongoing integration of theology and psychology among mental health professionals and pastors.

In addition to his clinical work, Dr. Braund is president of Discovery Resources, which offers consultation and training to universities, corporations, and churches across America.

Moody Press, a ministry of the Moody Bible Institute,
is designed for education, evangelization, and edification.
If we may assist you in knowing more about Christ
and the Christian life, please write us without obligation:
Moody Press, c/o MLM, Chicago, Illinois 60610.

ISBN 0-8024-1106-1

11 13 15 17 19 20 18 16 14 12

Printed in the United States of America

We would like to dedicate this book to our families:
Linda, Randy, and Christy Voges
and
Ginger, Rich, and Adam Braund

And to our parents:
Amy Voges and Don and June Braund,
who provided for our needs
and shaped our values

CONTENTS

ACKNOWLEDGMENTS

We would like to express our gratitude to the people who have made special contributions to our lives and to this book:

Ken would like to thank:

Dr. Joe Wall, who was the first to share with Linda and me the idea that differences are normal

John DeVito and Lou Bonelli, who made it possible for me to leave my position with General Electric and pursue this project

Pat MacMillan, for his support in providing the resources of Team Resources, Inc.

Sherry Davis, for reading and editing the first manuscript

Dr. Mike Kempainen, Pastor Tom Hovestol, and Pastor Brian Myers for their insights into the Scriptures

Ron would like to thank:

Charles and Jackie Ellis, for their Christlike love and encouragement through my years of spiritual development

Patricia Zier, for insight and support while the writing of this book was under way and for her tireless dedication to our counseling ministry

David Kline, for helping to shape and edit the last two revisions of the manuscript

The therapists and administrative staff of the AlphaCare Therapy Service.

FOREWORD

I was speaking at a church seminar in Raleigh, North Carolina, regarding D-I-S-C behavior, which is the topic of this book. I was about halfway through my presentation when a healthy, vivacious, elderly lady shouted out loud, *"I see it! I see it!"*

Well, she startled me! I stopped, looked at her and asked, "Are you all right?" (I thought she might be having a heart attack since she had "blurted out" so loudly!) She replied, "Yes, yes, I'm fine . . . but *I see it!"*

I asked, "Would you like to share something with the rest of us?" She replied, "I sure would!" I knew we were in for a good story!

She explained, "My husband and I, God rest his soul, were married for 38 years before he went home to be with the Lord. He always helped all the neighborhood children when they had school projects or sales. He always bought whatever those children were selling! But not me! I always told him it was a bunch of junk and he was just being a sucker! But he would just smile and say, 'I know . . . but I like to help!'

"Now I see it! We were married for all those years and I never really understood his personality or what made him tick until now! I am a "high D," and he was a "high S." It all makes perfect sense now! *I see it . . . I see it!"*

Then she did something really bold and unusual. She looked upward and said, "God would you tell him "I'm sorry?" We felt like a "connection" had occurred. It was a touching moment for us all.

As I thought about it, I was amazed. This was a Christian woman who loved God, believed the Bible, and I'm sure, wanted to enjoy a good relationship with her family and friends. Yet, because she lacked these insights about personality styles, she had never really known or understood the person who was closest to her own heart. Actually, this woman's story is not uncommon. Time and again, I have heard people tell how they never really "saw the light" regarding understanding people until they understood the D-I-S-C material.

So in writing *Understanding How Others Misunderstand You,* my good friends Ken Voges and Ron Braund have opened an important door for you. They reveal God as the Master Architect behind this D-I-S-C information. He is the One Who has designed us all. This is why we are "fearfully and wonderfully made" (Psalm 139:14). The more we know about God's plan, the wiser we will become. Through Ken and Ron's book, you will meet Bible characters in a brand new way—you will see them as human beings, just like you and me. You'll see them as flesh-and-blood people, rather than as stained-glass saints. Most importantly, their walk with God will become *understandable.*

Since all the things in the Bible were written to help us (Romans 15:4), then surely, the more we understand, the better off we will be. This book will be of great benefit in achieving that end.

—*Robert A. Rohm,* Ph.D.
President
Personality Insight, Inc.
Atlanta, Georgia

PREFACE

Some twenty years ago, I (Ken) was introduced to a behavioral model that identified different personality styles. It was extremely helpful to my wife, Linda, and me in understanding that differences are normal. Up until that time we were doing what many other married couples were doing: trying to change our partner to be like us. It wasn't working.

These new concepts helped us accept one another as we began viewing differing styles as strengths rather than weaknesses. Shortly thereafter, I began teaching adult Sunday school classes, integrating some of this information into my presentations. The reactions I received were generally positive. Participants began to focus on personal needs and to accept personality differences as being normal. New levels of understanding developed for most. Unfortunately, for others greater insight created a potential for misuse. Some class members used the information as an excuse for their behavior or as license to label others with negative tags.

This development disturbed me because I knew the information had much positive potential, if presented properly. I believed the key to overcoming the problem had to lie in using the Scriptures alongside the material. I began to analyze the behavior of personalities found in Scripture. That became a useful approach for helping others to associate their behavior with positive biblical models. The main focus of my teaching shifted to the Scriptures, which also helped overcome negative uses of the information.

In 1979, Betty Bowman introduced me to Dr. John Geier's DISC model of behavior and the instrument he developed, *The Personal Profile System.* I spent the next five years testing these concepts against the unique behavioral styles of biblical characters. It was a fascinating study. The characters came alive from the pages of Scripture. I was given the opportunity to modify the secular instrument to include biblical characters, and in 1984 the *Biblical Personal Profile* instrument was published. Currently over 200,000 instruments have been used with church groups, in counseling sessions, and for staff team building. In 1990, I left the General Electric Company to begin writing the *Understanding* series for Moody Press. I continually am encouraged to see the positive benefits others experience as they discover how to love one another.

One afternoon in 1985 I (Ron) was talking with Bruce Edwards, the youth minister of a church our counseling organization serves in Atlanta, Georgia. He showed me a copy of the *Biblical Personal Profile.* As a licensed marriage and family therapist, I had used several assessment tools with clients in order to help understand their personalities. I had even developed a seminar using a temperament analysis as the foundation for improving communication. Upon exploring the *Biblical Profile,* I recognized it as a valuable tool for understanding one another.

This version of the DISC material gave insight into how others are motivated and how misunderstanding tends to surface between people. Relating different behavioral styles to personalities like Peter, Paul, Moses, and Abraham made available powerful metaphors for integrating biblical truth with psychological principles.

Not long after beginning to use these instruments, I was encouraged to call Ken Voges, the author of the first edition of the *Biblical Profile.* Ken invited me to meet with him, and several weeks later I flew to Houston and received training at the home of Ken and his lovely wife, Linda. Out of that experience, a close working relationship developed. Since that time, I have traveled throughout the United States training others to use the *Biblical Profile* and have been involved in developing additional material with Ken. We have different behavioral styles and have had the opportunity to apply the truths contained in this book.

Our study of this material has showed us that the God of the Bible is far more personal than we had ever realized. He clearly understands the needs of each one of us and has modeled the way to understand and love one another rather than to react and reject each other. The purpose of this book—and the workbook that accompanies it—is to help you understand how others may be misunderstanding you and to give you an understanding of how your unique behavioral style relates to a positive biblical character. This discovery can reinforce the truth that God has a special purpose for your life. In addition, our desire is that you will be able to devise specific love strategies for improving the quality of your relationship with your partner, your children, your friends, and your associates. Your reward will be to experience personal fulfillment and become more effective in serving Christ.

ONE

PEOPLE ARE DIFFERENT

It is 7:30 A.M. Sunday morning in the Johnson household. The family begins its weekly routine of getting ready for church. Each member understands that getting to Sunday school on time requires leaving the house by 9:00 A.M., but how they respond to that information differs a good deal.

Dad hops right out of bed, does his exercises, showers, dresses, and goes directly downstairs, where he sits peacefully, sipping a cup of coffee as he reads the morning paper.

Jack, the teenage son, doesn't stir. He lies in bed, getting that last minute of shut-eye from staying up late on Saturday night. When Dad shouts upstairs for him to get up and get dressed so that the family can leave for church on time, he mumbles that he will be ready when it's time.

His sister, Suzie, is already up. Soon she has her bed made and is busily fixing her hair and putting on the outfit she picked out the night before.

In the master bedroom, Mom is having a tough time deciding what to wear. Add to this the fact that on Saturday she said she would make a nice breakfast for the family—but now she realizes she won't have time for that. She knows, too, that Dad is downstairs expecting her at any minute to come down to prepare the bacon and eggs she promised. She hollers, "I don't think I'm going to be able to fix breakfast. Can you guys get something on your own? Then we can go out for a nice lunch after church. Will that be OK?" Without waiting for an answer, she goes back to the task of trying to look her best.

It is now 9:05 A.M. Dad and Suzie are already in the car and have backed it out of the garage and halfway down the driveway. Jack yells, "Mom, they're in the car. We better go." He pulls on his shoes as he heads out the door. Mom is right behind him, but she has to run back into the house to get her Bible. Now they are on their way. It is 9:09 A.M.

There is a strained silence in the car. Finally the quiet is broken. "Is everything all right?" Mom asks.

After a few moments, Dad says matter-of-factly, "I hate walking into our Sunday school class late every week. Don't you think that just once you could be ready to leave on time?"

Mom responds, "The class doesn't begin on time anyway, so why should we be there early?"

Then Suzie says softly from the backseat, "But my class begins on time and I go in late every Sunday. I would rather not go at all than to have to be late. Everyone looks at me, and I don't like that."

Finally Jack speaks up. "Hey, I like it just the way we're doing it. You only need to be there for the last fifteen minutes. I don't like hearing that Sunday school teacher go on and on anyway." As he speaks the car pulls into the church parking lot. So begins another worship experience for the Johnson family.

WE ARE ALL DIFFERENT

Maybe you can identify with the Johnsons. Maybe your family, too, gets upset because different individuals in the family fail to meet the expectations of the others or because different individuals fail to respond to a situation the way the others wish they would.

Each member of the Johnson family had his own routine for getting ready to leave for church. No one deliberately set out to upset the others. But the way each person responded to the task made it likely that a tense environment rather than a loving one would develop.

It didn't have to be that way. Yes, people do respond in completely different ways to similar situations. No two people and their reactions are exactly alike. And yes, though we are distinctive, we have predictable ways of responding. Conflicts do indeed develop when the natural preferences of one person clash with the natural preferences of the other. But that does not mean that conflict will necessarily result when individuals with different preferences are together. No, we can improve our awareness and acceptance of differences, and we can learn to respond to others in a positive rather than a negative way. It is the chief message of this book to show how this can be done.

But before we deal with the specifics of learning how to respond to others in a loving way, we need to understand some basic facts about perception, motivation, needs, and values.

PERCEPTUAL DIFFERENCES

Colors. Suppose you were color blind and could only distinguish objects in terms of black or white. On the other hand, your partner had functional eyesight and had no trouble distinguishing colors. Let's imagine the two of you were shopping for a new car, and the salesperson directed you to a bright red sports car. From your color-blind perspective, the car would look black, not red. Your partner, however, would see the car in its true color, bright red. Which of you would be right? In terms of perspective, both of you. You would "see" the car as black. Your partner, whose eyes could distinguish red from black, would "see" it as being red, its actual color. Here the difference in perception would be tied to a difference in physiology. Your eyes would be physically unable to make a distinction your partner's eyes could.

A glass. Some perception-based differences are based on projection, the attributing of one's own ideas, feelings, and attitudes to external sources. Consider figure 1. How would you describe the glass? Give your initial, spontaneous reaction.

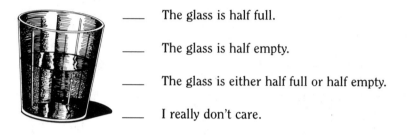

_____   The glass is half full.

_____   The glass is half empty.

_____   The glass is either half full or half empty.

_____   I really don't care.

Figure 1

Some people see the glass in terms of fullness and some see it in terms of emptiness, but strictly speaking, even though it could be said that they are projecting onto the glass an inner assessment of things, there is no "wrong" response to the question. For what is being asked for in this instance is a person's *initial* response to the glass. All four responses can be normal within a group. In fact, the danger to the personality lies in denying people the right to an honest, candid reaction to what they see.

Yet because there is such a tremendous pressure in modern American culture to see things in terms of fullness—the presumed "positive" response—when a group of Christian psychologists was asked to give its response to the picture 100 percent chose the "half full" response.

A report card. A similar kind of projection occurs with report cards. How would you assess the report card in figure 2? Give your *initial* response. When this report card was shown to forty-four middle class high school students and they were asked to give their initial response to it, the results were most interesting. More than 85 percent noticed the B in biology. This response was revealing and somewhat bothersome. Were the students reflecting as their own response a performance requirement their parents had for them, or were they simply reacting to the fact that one grade was different from the others? A follow-up seemed in order.

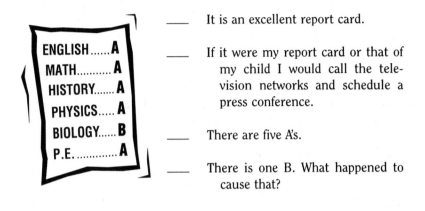

It is an excellent report card.

If it were my report card or that of my child I would call the television networks and schedule a press conference.

There are five A's.

There is one B. What happened to cause that?

Figure 2

In the follow-up, the students were asked to express how they would feel if they brought the report card home to their parents. They could check off more than one response. The questionnaire and the results:

Record how you would feel if you brought the following report card home.

15	1. Personally, I could bring this report card home and know that I would be encouraged by my parents.
13	2. My parents would want to know why I made a B in biology.
9	3. I would expect a reward from my parents if I brought this report card home.
14	4. I would be comfortable with this or any report card if I knew it was my best and I know my parents feel the same.
5	5. I would personally see this report card as a failure.
10	6. I would call NBC news and schedule a press conference.

It was good to know that fifteen students believed they would be encouraged by their parents and that fourteen felt it did not matter what their grades were if they gave their best effort. It was good to know also that nineteen students felt free to check the humorous options, ten creative souls considering the press conference an appropriate response to the report card and nine young capitalists opting for a reward. It was disheartening to see that thirteen students believed they would have to explain the B, and that five actually considered themselves failures.

The five who considered themselves failures were not necessarily surprising, however. Students who expect perfection judge themselves critically when they do not achieve it. For them, the reaction they had to the report card was normal, though if feelings of failure persisted and were not dealt with, their reaction could lead to problematic behavior.

A mother in one of our seminars came up after a session with tears in her eyes. "One of my children is just like that," she said. "She cannot stand making anything less than A's! If she doesn't have a perfect report card, she makes life miserable for everyone around her. How can I change her?"

Our response: "You cannot change your child. You can accept her and seek to understand what motivates her." All children are partially motivated by their personality styles. A parent needs to realize the uniqueness of his child's behavioral style and seek to guide him within that style.

A picture. In his book *Seven Habits of Highly Effective People*[1] Steven Covey uses a famous picture to illustrate the power of perception. Take a few moments to look at figure 3. Now turn and look at figure 4. Do you see a woman? How old would you say she is? Doesn't she seem fashionable and intriguing?

What if you were told that you are mistaken—that the woman in the illustration is really quite old and sad looking and that she has a large nose and a grim face? Would you agree?

1. Steven R. Covey, *Seven Habits of Highly Effective People* (New York: Simon & Schuster, 1989), p. 127.

Figure 3

Look at the picture again. Can you see this woman that we say exists? If you cannot see the old woman, you are in a position to believe or not believe that what we are describing is accurate. Until you actually see the old woman you must trust that our description is true.

Turn now to the end of the chapter and look at figure 5. It should be easy to see the old woman we have been describing. Keep looking until she becomes clear. We advise that you not read further in the chapter until you can see images of both the young woman and the old woman.

If you are like most people, this experience graphically reinforces the idea that prior conditioning influences how we perceive events. If we had shown you the older woman first, you would have had difficulty seeing the younger woman, for your perspective would have been affected by the first picture. There is a parallel in the realm of behavior. You will have difficulty understanding another person's behavior until you understand the needs that shape his frame of reference. The combined effect of our unique personalities (needs) and character (values) affects our personal perceptions. Until we experience life the way another person does, it is difficult to relate to the way he behaves.

MOTIVATIONAL DIFFERENCES

I (Ron) once had the opportunity of conducting a team-building training session with the University of Alabama football coaching staff in Tuscaloosa, Alabama. The offensive and defensive coaches were in the conference room adjoining the office of the head coach. During the introduction for the day's training, I made the following statement: "It is impossible for a coach to motivate his players to perform up to their potential." Needless to say, the head coach looked up with an expression that said, *What in the world are you talking about?* After all, mounted on the wall behind him was a portrait of one of the greatest motivators in all of football coaching history, Paul "Bear" Bryant. Some explanation of the seemingly absurd statement was necessary.

I pointed out that for a football player to be motivated to play his best he needs to accept personal responsibility for taking specific actions—but that it is also the responsibility of the coach to create an environment where those actions are likely to take place. To sum it up:

1. You cannot motivate other people.
2. However, all people are motivated.
3. People become motivated to action for their own reasons—not the reasons others have for them.
4. The very best a motivator can do is to create a healthy environment that allows others to motivate themselves into action.

Too often we assume the responsibility for creating change in others, when in fact true change can only come from within each individual. A football coach cannot motivate his players, but he can understand the motivational environment the different players on his team will respond to.

Bear Bryant knew how to do this. He was a master at taking players with different degrees of talent and bringing out their best effort. He would take an average player and understand what would motivate him to perform at an improved level. He would take a good player and encourage him to work on the skills he needed to bring his performance to an exceptional level. The combined improvement of his individual players created consistent winners as a team. How did coach Bryant motivate his players? Was it through speeches or some form of intimidation? No. It was because he took the time to understand the needs of each player on his football squad. Then he would work with his assistant coaches to create the environment needed to make his players want to make the effort required to improve the level of their performance. My statement wasn't so absurd after all!

More will be said about environments later in this book, but for now it is useful to mention that Bryant's attention to environments has application to marriages and to raising children. Psychologist Larry Crabb writes, "During literally thousands of hours spent trying to keep couples together, it has occurred to me more than once that if husbands would more strongly involve themselves with their wives and if wives would quit trying to change their husbands, most marriages would really improve."[2] A husband's spending more time with his wife may be the very environment she needs to be motivated to change in the ways her husband desires. A wife's refraining from giving the little advice he so dislikes may be the very environment he needs to change in the way she desires.

Put another way, marriage and family therapists can testify that efforts to change a partner's behavior consistently create resistance and resentment, whereas efforts to create the environment that makes the partner *want* to change open up the possibility of change and growth. Similarly, parents who try to change their children without understanding the distinctive perspectives and motivations of their children will end up frustrated at the same time their children struggle with feelings of discouragement and failure.

NEEDS VERSUS VALUES

Because differences in perception, motivation, and needs sometimes get mixed up in our thinking with differences in values, it is useful to distinguish between *needs* and *values*. Personal needs are basic to our existence. They can be divided into three levels: physical, relational, and spiritual. Physical needs relate to our survival in terms of food, sleep, shelter, and security. Relational needs involve a deep desire to belong and to experience affection and love. Spiritual needs consist of a drive for fulfillment and purpose. These needs are ones every person must address if he is to be healthy.

Personal values are the standards that guide one's life. They have to do with the beliefs that influence the choices a person makes. These values are clustered together into an organized way of thinking. The clothes a person wears, the place he lives, the politician he votes for, the work he chooses, the church he attends—all these are influenced by a clustering of values.

2. Lawrence J. Crabb, Jr., *Understanding People* (Grand Rapids: Zondervan, 1987), p. 18.

Figure 4

Needs-motivated behavior has to do with *how* a person acts. It has to do with what is most natural and easy for an individual to do. One person might have a need for being involved with a variety of social activities. Another person might prefer to spend time alone rather than with other people. Two different people with different kinds of needs. Neither involves a choice of right or wrong, just a difference.

Values-motivated behavior has to do with *why* a person does something. Values are standards of right and wrong and meaningfulness. Values-motivated behavior is tied to the ethical internal guidance system that influences the choices a person makes.

Not all people have the same values. However, few persons would actively disagree with these values statements:

"Honesty is the best policy."

"If at first you don't succeed, try, try again."

"Anything is possible through faith, commitment, and action."

But it is more difficult to arrive at a consensus with these values statements:

"Walk the straight and narrow."

"Live and let live."

"I'll do it my way."

"Let your conscience be your guide."

Different opinions about those beliefs might raise a values conflict.

Values have to do with "oughtness." They have moral and ethical weight. You can make discriminations on the basis of values that would be entirely inappropriate when merely needs were in question. This point is an important one in this book because people often interpret needs-based differences as having values-based significance. A person with a different personality style gets judged as wrong or inferior, when in fact all that is involved is a stylistic personality difference.

Needs-based problems need to be dealt with differently than values-based problems. Suppose a worker fails to meet an assignment deadline despite working hard and giving it his best effort. This is a needs-based problem. But if the worker's supervisor sees it as a values-based problem, a conflict between the worker and his supervisor will immediately develop. Resolving the problem may require only minor adjustments in the work schedule. On the other hand, suppose a Christian education director alters his Sunday attendance report to the pastor in order to give the impression that an attendance goal has been met. This is a values-based problem, and not to recognize it as such is to fail to respond adequately to an ethical dilemma. There will necessarily be a conflict between the pastor and the Christian education director, and it will be a difficult conflict to resolve. The job of the education director may well be in jeopardy.

At times a person's values conflict with his needs. Let's say a person believes in the importance of spending quality time with family. This is thought of as a value. Then he is invited to a golf outing with friends on a day he has promised to spend with family. He is faced with a choice between his desire to participate in the golf outing and the value he places on spending time with his family and living up to his promises. The golf activity represents a legitimate *need* for social interaction and physical activity, but it conflicts with *values* he also considers important.

This book is about understanding the basic differences in our needs-based behavior as opposed to differences in our values-based behavior. It focuses on the common differences in our behavioral styles that relate to personality rather than to character. We believe it is important to understand our differences in needs first before we address and integrate our differences in values.

PERSONALITY DIFFERENCE IS BY DESIGN

Personality differences are influenced by both heredity and environment. The influence of heredity is evident in many ways. According to *U.S. News and World Report,* "Scientists are turning up impressive evidence that heredity has a greater influence on one's personality and behavior than either one's upbringing or the most crushing social pressure."[3] The article goes on to observe that "new results from studies of identical twins are leading many scientists to conclude that genes not only control such physical characteristics as eye color and height, but also profoundly influence human behavior and personality."[4]

James Dobson has a similar view. In *Parenting Isn't for Cowards* he says, "It is my supposition that these temperaments are pre-packaged before birth and do not have to be cultivated or encouraged."[5] In Dobson's opinion, genetics plays a significant role in determining a person's temperament. From birth a child has a set of needs that is unique to his makeup.

Corroboration of this position can be found in the evidence of simple common sense. Any mother of more than one child will tell you that her children were behaviorally different from birth. From the very first, the second or third child showed a distinctive personality style. A university psychologist who studied how parents mold a child's character and ability had this to say: "Every parent of one child is an environmentalist, and every parent of more than one becomes a geneticist."[6]

Although genetics plays a major role in the formation of personality traits, the environment present during the development of the child from infancy through adolescence is also critical for healthy adjustment. Responsible parents help prepare their children to face life by being in harmony with their unique behavioral styles.

In Proverbs 22:6 Solomon observes, "Train a child in the way he should go, and when he is old he will not turn from it." Though this verse is usually interpreted to refer to teaching a child a specific body of moral absolutes, it may also refer to training a child in harmony with his natural bent ("the *way* he should *naturally* go"), or, to put it another way, it may refer to

3. "How Genes Shape Personality," *U.S. News & World Report,* April 13, 1987, p. 58.
4. Ibid.
5. James C. Dobson, *Parenting Isn't for Cowards* (Waco, Tex.: Word, 1987), p. 24.
6. "How Genes Shape Personality," p. 59.

creating a healthy and understanding environment in which the child can mature in accordance with his individual personality profile, or temperament. Training of this kind, it is asserted, is the type of training most likely to help a child develop into a responsible adult.

The Bible tells us that each person is unique physically, emotionally, and spiritually, and that God shaped the integral parts of us all.

> O Lord, you have searched me and you know me.
> You know when I sit and when I rise;
>   you perceive my thoughts from afar.
> You discern my going out and my lying down;
>   you are familiar with all my ways.
>   .   .   .   .
> For you created my inmost being;
>   you knit me together in my mother's womb.
> I praise you because I am fearfully and wonderfully made;
>   your works are wonderful, I know that full well.
>
> (Psalm 139:1-3, 13-14)

The psalmist who wrote this beautiful text, King David, recognized that God is intimately acquainted with all aspects of our development. Verse 13 of the psalm strongly suggests that God's personal involvement in the creation of man has to do with more than just his physical makeup.

In his letter to the Galatians, the apostle Paul proclaims that even while he was in his mother's womb God set him apart to reach the Gentiles. God was aware of Paul's personality before his conversion and knew that his particular behavioral style would be useful in completing the mission designated for him: "God . . . set me apart from birth and called me by his grace, [and] was pleased to reveal his Son in me so that I might preach him among the Gentiles" (Galatians 1:15-16). When one studies Paul's personality traits, it is clear that he was indeed ideal for the ministry God called him to fulfill. He was a creative, dominant individual well-suited to proclaim the doctrine of grace to a new group of people, the Gentiles, and to show in an aggressive way that salvation is not obtained through works. He was exactly the type of person who could effectively debate those who opposed the doctrine of salvation by grace through faith.

Paul's dominant style was present in his early life also. Before his conversion to Christianity, he was a strong and aggressive persecutor of the church and committed to ending its existence. Only after his encounter with Jesus Christ on the Damascus road did he use that same "driver" style as an effective builder of the church. Paul's personality profile, both before and after his conversion, did not really change . . . only his motivation and capacity for growth.

A LOOK AHEAD

As you can see, our differences are complex. Each person has a distinctive set of needs and values. Each has a distinctive perception of the world, a distinctive set of motivations, and a distinctive personality structure. That is how God intended it to be.

The purpose of this book is to help the reader
    know his own personality style
    know how to grow and mature within that style
    know how to be understanding of persons whose styles
        differ from his
    know how to create environments in which persons
        whose styles differ from his can flourish.

We want to provide our readers with a common language for explaining needs-based behavior so that they can learn more about themselves and how others see them. The next chapter of this book introduces that common language for relating to different styles of behavior and gives biblical examples of individuals who illustrate those styles.

Figure 5

TWO

A COMMON LANGUAGE FOR UNDERSTANDING BEHAVIOR

Jim sat in the back of the classroom with his arms folded, acting as though someone had forced him to be there. Sarah, his wife, sat next to him with a smile on her face, eager to get started. She noticed her friend Mary in front of the room, and before the seminar started she went up to say hello. Over to the side sat a couple whispering quietly to each other. Those who were late coming in began to make their way to their seats as the host introduced us. Each couple had come to participate in a seminar titled "Understanding How Others Misunderstand You."

The brochure promoting the seminar had promised help in improving communication skills so that those who attended could discern the needs and expectations of family, friends, and close co-workers. It also guaranteed that they would gain new insights into developing successful conflict resolution.

As we were about to begin, Jim spoke out from the back, "What's this study about anyway? My wife said it was something about behavior."

It was obvious from the question that Jim had not read the material describing the seminar. He was probably there to fulfill a promise to his wife. The unstated thought in his direct manner and assertive tone was *This better be good, or I'm out of here.*

Although Jim's question had a somewhat hostile tone, it got us right to the point. We began by stating the purpose of the seminar—to help those who attended understand the uniqueness of personality styles. We told the participants also that we intended to provide them with a language to describe the behavioral tendencies they and others had. From this understanding, we hoped to help them begin the process of constructing a plan to improve the quality of their interpersonal relationships.

We began this book in a similar way—by asserting that personality styles are distinctive and important and by distinguishing personality styles from behavior that is grounded in moral and ethical choices. With this chapter we want to begin to map out the language we have found useful in describing the behavioral tendencies people have. But first we need to talk about the potential we each have for a rich life and how that potential can be deflected.

THE POWER OF POTENTIAL

God desires for each person to realize his greatest potential. In Philippians 1:6 Paul writes, "[I am] confident of this, that he who began a good work in you will carry it on to completion until the day of Christ Jesus." Understanding ourselves and others is a prerequisite for reaching our God-given potential. Yet many of us spend more time avoiding our fears than focusing on our future. Fear comes in many forms and with different levels of intensity. We all have had moments when anxiety and depression attacked us. Being dominated by negative emotions can lead us into a pathological pattern of thinking and acting.

Pathology is a clinical word used in the medical profession and among mental health professionals to describe disease or dysfunction. When dysfunction goes unchecked, it leads to unhealthy levels of unusual, or "abnormal," behavior. Achieving our potential involves always moving toward healthier and healthier levels of functional, or "normal," behavior. In today's negative climate, we need encouragement in order to achieve our greatest potential.

In one of our seminars, a seminary graduate asked, "How can you justify from the Scriptures the need to study personality styles and self-esteem?" He went on to admit that he was skeptical. His question was a valid one. Does God encourage a healthy self-image? Let's let the Bible answer.

Matthew 22:34-39, which refers back to Leviticus 19:18 and Deuteronomy 6:5, gives a clear explanation of the importance of self-esteem. The main characters involved in the passage in Matthew are Jesus and a lawyer who is representing the Pharisees. Their interchange goes as follows (the italics are added):

> Hearing that Jesus had silenced the Sadducees, the Pharisees got together. One of them, an expert in the law, tested him with this question: "Teacher, which is the great commandment in the Law?"
>
> Jesus replied: *"Love the Lord your God with all your heart and with all your soul and with all your mind.'* This is the first and greatest commandment. And the second is like it: *'Love your neighbor as yourself.'* All the Law and the Prophets hang on these two commandments."

The intent of the lawyer's question was to trick Jesus into controversy and thereby discredit Him. In reality, the Sadducees and Pharisees themselves could not agree, so in their minds there was no right answer.

To the lawyer's surprise, Jesus did not quote directly from any of the Ten Commandments. Instead, He emphasized a personal relationship with God as being most important (v. 37), and a relationship between ourselves and anyone who comes into our area of influence (v. 39) as being next in importance. The word Jesus used for love was *agapao,* which refers to a level of love that is not only self-sacrificing but is attached to meeting the needs of others. Jesus' position was that if you practiced these two commands, all other laws would be fulfilled.

Christ's second commandment, "Love your neighbor as yourself," is the cornerstone verse to this book. The best way to start loving others in a sacrificial way is to understand them. We need to understand their physical, emotional, and spiritual needs so that we can seek to serve them by meeting these needs.

The Lord assumes that we are already "loving ourselves." The command is to "love our neighbor" in the same way we already love ourselves. (In the same way we already seek to meet our own needs.) Paul makes that same assumption in Ephesians 5:29), where he states, "For no one ever hated his own body, but he feeds and it cares for it, just as Christ does the church." The point in that verse relates to the husband's responsibility to meet the needs of his wife.

There is much discussion these days about going too far in meeting the needs of others, and neglecting ourselves. It is a condition called "codependency," which presumably makes a person neurotically dependent on the approval of others by an obsession with meeting their needs. There is no doubt that a person can become "unbalanced" to the point of self-neglect. However, writers on codependency must be cautious not to lose sight of the biblical attitude of sacrificial love and commitment to meeting others' needs. Warnings against codependency can become out of step with Paul's instructions to the Philippians, where he states, "Do nothing out of selfish ambition or vain conceit, but in humility consider others better than yourselves. Each of you should look not only to your own interests, but also to the interests of others" (Philippians 2:3-4).

It is natural for us to meet our own needs and neglect others'. That is why Jesus said, "Love your neighbor as yourself" (Matthew 22:39). He didn't mean, "Love yourself, then love your neighbor," but "Love your neighbor as you already love yourself." The Lord said to His disciples that the way to be the greatest in His kingdom is to be the servant of all (Matthew 20:25-28). To some, that would sound like very "codependent" behavior. It is simply the meeting of others' needs by a supernatural display of God's love working through one's supernaturally redeemed life.

There is a warning that must be sounded against self-degradation. In some Christian circles it has become popular to degrade oneself as a "sign" of one's spirituality. That is not what God intends. We must not denigrate ourselves as worthless, horrible individuals. On the contrary, we need to recognize our own wonderful individual creation (Psalm 139) and the fact that we are created in the image of God (Genesis 1:26; James 3:9). The reality that Christ died for us makes us very valuable

Relationship of Behavioral Styles and Representative Patterns

	Dominance predominant (High D)	Influencing predominant (High I)	Steadiness predominant (High S)	Compliance predominant (High C)
Dominance secondary	**Director Driver (*)** (Primary D)	Persuader, Promoter (*) (I/D)	Investigator, Administrator (*) (S/D)	Analyzer (*) (C/D)
Influencing secondary — On a par with Dominance	Organizer (D/I) Developer (*)	**Affiliator Networker (*)** (Primary I)		
Influencing secondary — With Steadiness	Motivator (D = I)		Advisor (S/I) Harmonizer (*) (S/I)	Cooperator(C/I/S)
Steadiness secondary — With Dominance		Encourager, Encourager (*) (I/S)	**Persister Supportor (*)** (Primary S)	Adaptor (C/S) Cautious Thinker (*)
Compliance secondary — With Steadiness		Negotiator (I/C) Performer (*) (I/C/S)	(Primary C)	Analyst (C/S/D)
Compliance secondary — With Dominance	Pioneer (D/C) Strategic Thinker (*)		Strategist, Researcher (*) (S/C/D)	**Perfectionist Deep Thinker (*)**

Table 1

Terms used by *Personal DISCernment*® *Inventory,* Team Resources, Inc.

(*) Terms used by *Personality Analysis Work Survey,* Christian Financial Concepts, Inc.

to God. He is looking forward to inheriting us for eternity. But we must not see ourselves as more valuable than "our neighbor," or we will fail to love him as we do ourselves. We need to have a healthy self-image as a result of being "in Christ," but also realize that our being "in Christ" has a goal of serving others. We can do that most efficiently by understanding the needs, goals, and motivation of those we are seeking to "love as ourselves." That is why it can help us to understand the temperament traits of others. It allows us to "love them" (to meet their needs) with a more thorough understanding.

To some extent, if we are involved in a love relationship, we all manifest some degree of codependence. The extremes at each end of the behavioral spectrum are independence and dependence. A healthy goal for each of us is to arrive at a balance between the two. Some call this interdependence. Interdependence is possible by taking care of the physical, emotional, and spiritual needs in one's own life in order to be in a positive position to understand and respond to the needs of others. Loving God, ourselves, and others in a healthy way is a worthy goal for each of us.

This book, which focuses on understanding normal, needs-based behavior, will help us to love God, ourselves, and others. When we can do that, we will be at much less risk of developing dysfunctional or codependent behavioral patterns and will lead much richer lives.

A LANGUAGE FOR DISCUSSING PERSONALITY: INTRODUCING DISC

In the 1920s and 1930s, a psychologist named William Marston developed the DISC model, a trait-based description of four behavioral styles into which he believed all persons fall. This system has gone through five generations of refinement, resulting in the development of a common language to describe normal human behavior. The system is based on aligning behavior traits on four continuums: D (Dominance), I (Influence), (Steadiness), and C (Compliance).

Various DISC suppliers have devised instruments that measure the intensity of individuals on these four DISC continuums. The model can become even more refined by adding specific categories to individual combinations. The specific profile tables used in this study offer the following information:

1. Primary drive of this style is
2. Personal giftedness of this profile is
3. Potential spiritual gifts of this pattern
4. The instinctive fear of this style is
5. The strength of this profile out of control is
6. Under stress this style becomes
7. The blind spots of this profile are
8. This style needs to work on
9. The best complementary team members are
10. The biblical model that best represents this style
11. Bible study references on strengths and weaknesses

The four general behavioral styles Marston had are divided into sixteen *Representative Patterns* (see table 1) and two *Special Patterns*. One, Jesus' Profile, is discussed in chapter 14. The other, the Level Pattern, can be found in the *Understanding How Others Misunderstand You* workbook. Each of the sixteen Representative Patterns, generally speaking, are combinations of two of the main behavioral styles and are immediately useful to individuals who fill out the instrument found in the workbook, beginning on page 115. The Representative Patterns in the self-scoring DISC instrument parallel behavior with positive biblical models. The instrument does not identify behavior with good or bad, just different.

In contrast to the *Minnesota Multiphasic Personality Index (MMPI)* and the *Taylor-Johnson Temperament Analysis (TJTA)*, discussed later in this chapter, the DISC instruments have as their purpose the measurement of "normal," or functional, behavior. Persons taking this instrument make selections within twenty-four sets of panels containing four descriptive adjectives. It requires individuals to make a "Most" and "Least" response based on a specific focus. The instrument can be self-administered and self-scored, with the interpretation being given by someone trained in its use.

The letter *D* in the DISC language stands for people with a behavioral style described as Dominance. People with this behavioral style tend to shape their environment by overcoming opposition to accomplish results. Persons who are described as D's (or as High D's, the term *High* having the meaning of "intensely" or "primarily") prefer being in control and getting results. Four Representative Patterns make up this behavioral style.

- *Director* (both the main and secondary aspects of this pattern are dominance-oriented; abbreviated as D)
- *Organizer* (Dominance combined with Influencing; abbreviated as D/I)
- *Motivator* (Dominance and Influencing in about equal strengths; abbreviated as D = I)
- *Pioneer* (Dominance combined with Compliance; abbreviated as D/C)

The letter *I* stands for *Influencing* of others. Those manifesting this behavioral style (the High I's) emphasize shaping the environment by bringing others into alliance to accomplish results. These personalities prefer a focus on relationships with people rather than on performing tasks. The four Representative Patterns in this style are the:

- *Affiliator* (primary Influencer; both the main and secondary aspects of this pattern are influencing-oriented; abbreviated as I)
- *Persuader (*Influencing combined with Dominance; abbreviated as I/D)
- *Encourager* (Influencing combined with Steadiness; abbreviated as I/S)
- *Negotiator* (Influencing combined with Compliance; abbreviated I/C)

The letter *S* stands for *Steadiness*. This behavioral style has an emphasis on cooperating with others to carry out a task. Those who show *S* tendencies (the High S) prefer being a part of a team rather than working alone, and they usually have the natural ability to handle repetitive functions. The four Representative Patterns in this style are the:

- *Persister* (primary Steadiness; both the main and secondary aspects of this pattern are steadiness-oriented; abbreviated as S)
- *Investigator* (Steadiness combined with Dominance; abbreviated as S/D)
- *Advisor* (Steadiness combined with Influencing; abbreviated as S/I)
- *Strategist* (Steadiness combined with Compliance and Dominance; abbreviated as S/C/D)

The letter *C* stands for *Compliance*. Persons who manifest *C* traits (the High C's) are driven by quality control and usually prefer structure and order. They like working with groups that emphasize quality in products or service. The four Representative Patterns in this group are the:

- *Perfectionist* (primary Compliance; both the main and secondary aspects of this pattern are compliance-oriented; abbreviated C)
- *Analyst* (Compliance combined with Steadiness and a midline Dominance; abbreviated C/S/D)
- *Cooperator* (Compliance, Influencing, and Steadiness; abbreviated C/I/S)
- *Adaptor* (Compliance combined with Steadiness and a midline Influencing; abbreviated C/S)

Integration of DISC and Biblical Characters

For some time before being introduced to the DISC model, I (Ken) had used a four-temperament model (*Choleric, Sanguine,*

Phlegmatic, and *Melancholy*) that had its roots in the observations of Hippocrates in the first century.[1] This model was updated and is currently being used by Tim LaHaye,[2] Florence Littauer, and Gordon Van Rooy, among others. But when I came into contact with John Geier's refinement of the DISC material which was originally published by William Marston, it was evident that Geier and Marston had come up with a more imperial explanation of personality traits than the four-temperament model. Since others had done some initial association of temperaments with biblical characters, I cross-referenced that material to the DISC materials and carried out my own inductive study of the Scriptures.

In 1984, the *Biblical Personal Profile* was published as a result of my studies, using the same basic terminology but applying the biblical characters to each of the styles. The following shows the DISC model's similarity to the traditional four-temperaments model of LaHaye, Littauer, and Van Rooy:

Greek Terms	*DISC*
Choleric	Dominance
Sanguine	Influencing
Phlegmatic	Steadiness
Melancholy	Compliance

For each biblical character I studied, I tried to use at least three separate Scripture passages that described that character's personality before I assigned that character to a particular personality profile. The key to the research was finding a description of each individual's ministry and how he or she reacted

1. Gordon Van Rooy, *Family Relations Seminar Manual* (Houston, Tex.: Institute of Human Enrichment, 1975), p. 1.
2. Tim LaHaye, *The Spirit-Controlled Temperament* (Wheaton, Ill.: Tyndale, 1966).

under different circumstances. In some cases, not enough behavioral information was available in the text to make a match of a particular style with a specific character. Unfortunately, this was particularly true of most of the women. However, I made my best judgment in correlating the character's response with behavior tendencies as described in the DISC model.

A methodical and inductive study of the Scriptures vividly portrayed Peter as an Influencer, Paul as Dominance, Moses as Compliance, and Abraham as Steadiness. Not only did each of those four characters fit one of the four major personality styles, but each also matched one of the sixteen DISC Representative Patterns. Further exploration of Scripture identified other personalities that amplified the DISC model. Eventually biblical characters were found for every one of the sixteen Representative Patterns (see table 1).

PETER, THE "HIGH I"

The first character I looked at was Simon Peter. LaHaye characterized his behavior as SanChlor,[3] which translates in the Geier DISC model to a D/I Profile, or Persuader Representative Pattern. The gift of this pattern is the ability to communicate with illustrations, pictures, and colorful stories so that a group of people personally relate to whatever the Persuader is selling. Persons with this profile also have the gift of bringing a group to the point of making a decision based on the information the Persuader has presented; that is, they have the "closer skills" useful in selling. The events in Acts 3 record Peter using his verbal skills to communicate the connection between the healing of a lame man, Jesus the Messiah of the Jews, and the God of Abraham, Isaac, and Jacob. The Jewish crowd understood his message, and about five thousand people made a decision for Christ.

The downside of this profile is that these people are likely to give in to social pressure. When they must make a decision between an agreed-upon principle and social rejection, Per-

3. Tim LaHaye, *Understanding the Male Temperament* (Old Tappan, N.J.: Revell, 1977), p. 99.

suaders will generally lean toward compromising the principle in order to maintain relational acceptance. In Galatians 2:11-12, the Scriptures record that Peter ate with the Gentile Christians until his orthodox Jewish brothers arrived. Those orthodox brothers evidently raised the issue regarding eating or fellowshiping with non-Jews. Peter, the High I, drew back from associating with Gentiles. Paul, the High D, confronted Peter to his face in front of his peers for bowing to pressure from the Jews. Paul did not understand the reality of Peter's problem, but was more interested in the principle Peter had compromised.

Another tendency of High I's is that in a negative environment they will use their verbal skills to deny responsibility. Recorded in the gospels are Peter's three denials of Jesus. That event will be discussed in more detail in later chapters.

PAUL, THE HIGH D

The next character I studied was Paul. LaHaye writes, "There is little doubt in my mind that the Apostle Paul was a ChlorMel."[4] The cross-reference in the DISC system is to the D/C. The gift of this pattern is an ability to pick out the flaw in a position or philosophy, change it, and give it a new level of meaning or understanding. D/C Profiles have the ability to organize their thoughts in writing so that a clear, corrective plan of action is communicated. They are also excellent debaters. So a word of caution applies in dealing with them: *never* debate this style on his home turf—unless, of course, you are working on humility.

It is my opinion that God used Paul's D/C Profile skills to communicate the gospel of grace. The first-century Jewish church had difficulty separating itself from the burden of the law as it related to salvation. The concept of "by grace through Christ" required breakthrough thinking. Paul, the D/C Profile, clearly saw the problem and confronted Peter in Antioch with these words:

4. Ibid., p. 103.

> We who are Jews by birth and not "Gentile sinners" know that a man is not justified by observing the law, but by faith in Jesus Christ. So we, too, have put our faith in Christ Jesus that we may be justified by faith in Christ and not by observing the law, because by observing the law no one will be justified. (Galatians 2:15-16)

Paul, a former Pharisee, and Barnabas travel to Jerusalem, where this position is debated before the council (Acts 15)—and win. In the letter to the Galatians Paul recorded this position, inspiring Martin Luther centuries later to be at the forefront of the Reformation. Today Galatians remains the cornerstone of the doctrine of grace.

A negative tendency of this profile is to be extremely critical and condescending toward others when they do not measure up to the D/C's personal standards. When Barnabas decided to take John Mark on the second missionary journey, Paul would not hear of it because Mark had deserted them in Pamphylia during the first journey. The exchange of words between Paul and Barnabas indicates that they almost exchanged blows over the issue.

ABRAHAM, THE HIGH S

At this point in my study, I felt fairly confident that the three resources—the recorded actions of the biblical characters, LaHaye's cross-reference of behavioral terms, and Geier and Downey's Classical Patterns—were compatible and consistent with one another in explaining behavior. However, I ran into major problems in my study of Abraham because the Representative Pattern that should have described his tendencies did not match his behavior. LaHaye classified Abraham as a Phleg/Chlor,[5] which translates to the S/D in the DISC system. The best terms to describe this style are *determination* and *tenacity*. Once an S/D sets his eyes on a goal he never gives up. But that was not Abraham's style, though it fit Jacob's. Jacob worked for free for fourteen years in order to marry Rachel, and he wrestled with

5. Ibid., p. 113.

God all night until he received a blessing. In Genesis 32:28 Jacob was told, "Your name will no longer be Jacob, but Israel, because you have struggled with God and with men and have overcome."

I was discouraged by the results I was getting and put the material aside. Shortly thereafter, my wife and I went on a seven-hour car trip to a convention in New Orleans. As an after-thought I took along some of Geier and Downey's work on the four Steadiness Personalities: the S/C/D, the S, the S/I, and the S/D. When I read the material on the S/I Pattern, I realized that it described Abraham to a "T." The primary characteristic of the S/I Profile is that he works to keep the peace and maintain harmony even if it means taking less for himself. These styles are excellent listeners. They make good teachers because they mix empathy and concern with the capacity for information and instruction. Abraham had all of these characteristics. When herdsmen of Lot and Abraham began to quarrel, it was Abraham who suggested that he and Lot separate in order to maintain peace. Abraham offered Lot first choice in the selection of land. Later, in Genesis 24, Abraham instructed his servant in the procedure he should follow in finding a wife for Isaac. Understanding the servant's concerns about the uncertainty of completing the mission, Abraham clarified his role and assured him that the issue of acceptance was in the hands of the Lord.

The negative side of this profile is that persons who have it are likely to want to keep the peace at any cost. S/I's avoid conflict and fear dissension. When Abraham went to Egypt, he lied about Sarah's being his wife so that he would not need to defend himself. When Sarah proposed the idea of producing an heir through Hagar, he agreed. Later, when there was strife between Sarah and Hagar, Abraham chose not to get involved.

MOSES, THE HIGH C

To complete the four-profile model, I chose Moses. LaHaye characterized him as a MelChlor,[6] which parallels the

6. Ibid., p. 109.

DISC OVERVIEW

focuses on
Change and Activity

Dominant & Decisive
Goal: Authority &
Action

emphasizes
Tasks &
Results

Influencing & Interactive
Goal: Persuasion &
Popularity

emphasizes
Ideas &
People

Compliant & Cautious
Goal: Conscientious &
Consistent

Steadiness & Supportive
Goal: Cooperation &
Caring

focuses on
Maintenance and Accommodation

Table 2

DISC C/D Profile. Persons with this profile are characterized by meticulous attention to details and a strong concern for quality control and the maintenance of standards. This pattern is also unique in its ability to work alone for long periods of time and still enjoy it. God chose Moses to spend forty days on a mountain alone so that His law could be recorded. Obviously, God intended for the law to be written down accurately. Later, in Exodus 32, Moses would confront the Hebrew people when they strayed from the teachings of the law. Moses spent another forty years with the people as together they wandered through the desert, and he wrote the book of Deuteronomy, which marks the regiving of the law.

Under stress, perfectionists have a tendency to be extremely cautious, ask a lot of questions, and refuse to accept change quickly. When God called him in Exodus 3, Moses asked five questions and then refused to accept the assignment the Lord gave him.

OVERVIEW OF THE DISC STYLES

Table 2 gives an overview of the DISC styles in relation to several components: goals, characteristic focus, distinctive emphasis.

VALIDATION OF THE DISC SYSTEM

Psychologists and other professionals in the human resource field commonly ask how valid the DISC instrument is to identify behavioral styles. Studies have been made to gauge this matter. In 1982 psychologist Sylvan Kaplan and his associates undertook to establish whether the DISC could be considered a valid instrument for measuring personality characteristics. Five separate instruments were administered along with the DISC: the *Wechsler Adult Intelligence Scale (WAIS)*, the *Myers-Briggs Type Indicator (MBTI)*, the *Cattell 16 PF*, the *Minnesota Multiphasic Personality Inventory (MMPI)*, and the *Strong-Campbell Interest Inventory (SCII)*. Kaplan and his colleagues concluded that the DISC correlated "significantly with the personality assessment instruments it was compared with."[7] The resulting *Kaplan Report* has been published and is available for further study along with subsequent reports. Information on how to receive this report is available by writing to The Institute for Leadership Development (the address is listed in the Resources section at the back of this book).

In addition to formal validation studies, the DISC system has also proved itself reliable in a rather unusual way. Several years ago I was invited to Guatemala by a missionary friend who had asked me to conduct a seminar on human behavior using the DISC. Although the instrument had been translated into Spanish, I didn't speak the language, and the people I was addressing didn't speak English. It was a long day as I conducted the entire seminar through a translator. Although the audience was most cordial, I felt the entire effort was a disaster. I gave the Spanish DISC and wondered what would happen. The audience seemed confused, and I couldn't seem to help them. As a last resort, I gave them the homework assignment of reading through the self-interpreting exercises in the instrument. But there was no way of knowing how well I was communicating with them. I went back to my room that evening quite discouraged.

My hosts were gracious people, and the next day they invited me to a church picnic in the mountains. I went along—feeling slightly less significant than a spare tire with no air in it. The food was great and the view marvelous, but I still felt frustrated with my inability to communicate with the audience the day before.

Then it happened. One by one persons who had been in that audience got in line with their wrinkled, marked-up profiles in hand and started asking questions through the interpreter. The questions gave me confidence that they had indeed understood the model and had personalized it. I answered their questions, but had to wait for the translation to determine whether they now understood me. They did! It was an eerie

7. Sylvan J. Kaplan and Barbara Kaplan, *The Kaplan Report* (Minneapolis, Minn.: Performax Systems International, 1983), p. 34.

feeling to answer a question and have to wait a minute or two before getting a grin or laugh or sometimes a tear. The smiles and the bear hugs of those people were unforgettable. We couldn't speak to one another, but we *did* communicate. I went away with a new appreciation for the DISC instruments.

INSTRUMENTS THAT MEASURE "ABNORMAL" VERSUS "NORMAL" BEHAVIOR

We need to do one other thing before we take up in the succeeding chapters of this book a detailed look at the system of understanding behavior as outlined in this chapter: discuss two psychological instruments that measure "abnormal" versus "normal" behavior, the *Minnesota Multiphasic Personality Inventory (MMPI)* and the *Taylor-Johnson Temperament Analysis (TJTA)*. These two instruments are in contrast to the DISC instrument used in this book, which has as its single purpose the measurement of "normal" or functional behavior.

THE MINNESOTA MULTIPHASIC PERSONALITY INVENTORY (MMPI)

The *Minnesota Multiphasic Personality Inventory (MMPI)* is one of the most popular in the category of objective personality assessment tools. It was developed in 1940 and consists of 566 self-reference statements. Persons taking this test are asked to give true-false responses to such statements as "I have never done anything dangerous for the thrill of it" or "My daily life is full of things that keep me interested." Concerning the interpretation of the *MMPI*, J. D. Matarazzo states that it is "a highly subjective art which requires a well-trained and experienced practitioner to give scores a predictive meaning in the life of any given human being."[8] In other words, use of the *MMPI* should be confined to licensed mental health professionals. Interpretations of the *MMPI* were designed to distinguish between normal, neurotic, and psychotic persons. The clinical scales were formulated from the testing of people who manifested

8. John R. Graham, *The MMPI, A Practical Guide* (Oxford Univ. Press, 1987).

pathological behavioral traits. Consequently, the *MMPI* is mostly used in clinical counseling settings.

THE TAYLOR-JOHNSON TEMPERAMENT ANALYSIS (TJTA)

In an attempt to provide information through personality tests less threatening than the *MMPI,* other instruments have been published comparing normal (functional) behavior and more abnormal (dysfunctional) behavior. The *Taylor-Johnson Temperament Analysis (TJTA)* is one of those instruments. It is a popular test counselors have used to offer clients a contrast between different behavioral traits.

The *TJTA* has nine scales measuring the following: nervous/composed, depressive/lighthearted, active-social/quiet, expressive-responsive/inhibited, sympathetic/indifferent, subjective/objective, dominant/submissive, hostile/tolerant, and finally self-disciplined/impulsive.[9] The test is most commonly used in premarital counseling as a means of determining the degree of differences between two people and their perceptions.

In the *TJTA* some traits are classified as "excellent to acceptable," whereas others carry the warning "improvement desirable to improvement urgent." Individuals often express dismay when they have scores that fall into those classifications. Consequently, the *TJTA* can be most helpful when problem traits are explored with a professional counselor or minister.

A WORD OF CAUTION

As you learn about the personality styles, you will learn the labels associated with each. Before one seminar, Mary tersely exclaimed, "I'm not sure I want to learn how to just label people." We agreed with her—it was not *our* goal either! The personality trait descriptions should not be used to typecast or label others or, conversely, to excuse ourselves for negative behavior. If a label helps to clarify differences, then it is useful, but if it is used to create barriers to communication, it is confining. Our intent is to clarify rather than confine.

9. Robert M. Taylor, *Taylor-Johnson Temperament Analysis Profile,* 1976.

A LOOK AHEAD

Understanding the behavior styles of biblical characters will become much clearer to you in future chapters as you better understand the different DISC personality traits. You will discover, as we have, how a simple common language for personality styles—DISC—can make the people God used thousands of years ago seem as real as if they lived today. And you will learn also how understanding the different personality styles of the persons God used can immeasurably help you understand yourself.

THREE

EXPECTATIONS AND ENVIRONMENTS

The expectations we place on ourselves and those around us have a dramatic impact on our behavior. Understanding the influence of those expectations helps us grasp how misunderstandings between people develop.

Let's return to the plight of the Johnson family whose story we told at the opening of this book. We left them traveling to church after a morning clash of personality styles. Their little Sunday family feud was an example of how unmet expectations can put stress on relationships.

The predetermined time for the family to leave for church on Sunday morning was 9:00 A.M. Dad assumed that meant that everyone should be in the car by 8:59 so that he could pull out of the driveway at exactly 9:00. On this particular morning he had the additional frustration of Mom's not preparing the breakfast she had promised. In all probability his frustration was not from the lack of bacon and eggs but from the lack of follow-through by his wife.

Mom had a different concept of the schedule. To her, leaving for church at 9:00 A.M. really meant leaving at "nine-ish." Moreover, she felt that she had a perfectly reasonable excuse for not fixing breakfast.

Suzie knew that Dad expected everyone in the car before 9:00, so her agenda was to make sure that she was on time. In addition, she did not want to be late in order to avoid calling attention to herself at Sunday school.

Jack was not concerned about leaving for church on time simply because he was not interested in going anyway. Had he been interested, you can be sure that he not only would have been on time, he would have made sure the others were ready too.

THE EXPECTATIONS WE HAVE

Everyone in the Johnson family had different expectations for themselves and the other family members. Each person expected the others to behave according to his or her own needs. Because there were so many unmet expectations among the family, conflict resulted.

The members of the Johnson family represent the four DISC personality styles introduced in chapter 2, and as such each member illustrates the different expectations of self and others those four personality styles have. Dad was a Compliance (High C) personality, the personality type having the highest level of expectations of self and others. He set a high standard of performance for himself and expected the same from others. Mom was an Influencing (High I) personality, the personality type having the lowest level of expectations. She did not have strict standards for herself or anyone else. Suzie represented the Steadiness (High S) style, the personality type having high expectations for self but low ones for others. Though she held herself to a high standard, she did not hold others to that same standard. Jack represented the Dominance (High D) style. He had high expectations for others to comply with his desires, but he gave himself freedom to alter personal expectations when he preferred it.

To sum it up, each of the four DISC Profiles uses a different set of criteria in formulating expectations (table 3) and has a different set of high and low expectations of self and others (table 4).

Relationships function better when our expectations are preferred rather than mandated. When we make demands on others, we are expressing an authoritative claim on their response to us. Preferences, however, give others the opportunity

Table 3

Criteria involved in understanding DISC Expectations

Dominance (High D)	Desires being in charge and setting own standards of achievement.
Influencing (High I)	Desires a friendly environment and the freedom and flexibility to make changes.
Steadiness (High S)	Works at being supportive and carrying out the expectations of others.
Compliance (High C)	Desires being right, fulfilling commitments, and having control of quality.

Table 4

Understanding Differences in DISC Expectations

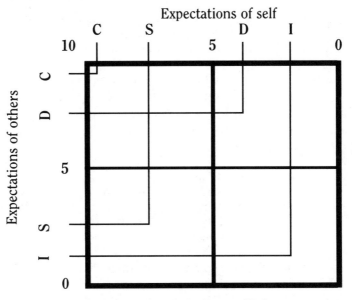

(The number 10 indicates high expectations; the number 0, low expectations)

to make choices for themselves. Once we understand the expectation levels of the various personality styles, we can replace harsh judgments of others with acceptance. Instead of trying to change one another, we need to seek better communication with others and a commitment to work together.

EXPECTATIONS THE COMPLIANCE PERSONALITY HAS OF HIMSELF AND OTHERS

People with the Compliance personality often have goals and expectations that go beyond even their own energies and time. If for some reason they fail to live up to their expectations of themselves, a steady and subtle erosion of self-confidence occurs. They also tend to downplay their ability to do a job well. As a result, they require support and reinforcement from others in taking on new responsibilities.

When God asked Moses to join His team and represent Him before Pharaoh in freeing the children of Israel from Egypt, Moses had this to say:

> But I'm not the person for a job like that! (Exodus 3:11, LB*)

> Lord, please! Send someone else. (Exodus 4:13, LB)

Jonah is another Old Testament example of a High C who was reluctant to take on an important assignment because of fear. The Lord called him to convey to Nineveh the message that He was intending to destroy the city because of its wickedness. What did Jonah do?

> But Jonah was afraid to go and ran away from the Lord. He went down to the seacoast, to the port of Joppa, where he found a ship leaving for Tarshish. He bought a ticket, went on board, and climbed down into the dark hold of the ship to hide there from the Lord. (Jonah 1:3, LB)

Jonah and Moses both felt inadequate to accept the calling of the Lord and initially declined to get involved. In their

*The Living Bible.

minds, what God was asking them to do was beyond their capabilities. Because each one doubted his ability to live up to God's standards he was hesitant to begin.

In addition to placing high expectations on themselves, Compliance personalities often project unrealistically high standards on family, friends, and co-workers. In the Johnson family, Dad expected himself and everyone else to be ready to leave for church not at 9:01 or 9:00 but 8:59! And there was no flexibility on his part.

Compliance personalities expect everyone to honor commitments—to the letter. Dad was not upset because he did not have bacon and eggs with his coffee. He was upset because Mom had not lived up to a commitment she had made. Certainly if he had been the one to promise making breakfast he would have *delivered,* and he expected no less from her.

Scripture records an instance where a Compliance personality criticized even God for not following through on a plan. In Jonah 3 we are told that after Jonah finally responded to God's call, he proclaimed to the city of Nineveh that God would destroy the city in forty days. The people of Nineveh responded to the message, asked for forgiveness, and pleaded for mercy. As a consequence, God did not carry out His judgment. But Jonah expected God to follow through with His plan of destruction. Even during this time of pouring out of God's grace, Jonah became angry:

> He [Jonah] complained to the Lord about it: "This is exactly what I thought you'd do, Lord. . . . I knew how easily you could cancel your plans for destroying these people." (Jonah 4:2, LB)

In spite of the fact that the lives of thousands of people were saved, Jonah was angry because the Lord did not follow through as he had expected.

EXPECTATIONS THE STEADINESS PERSONALITY
HAS OF HIMSELF AND OTHERS

Persons with the Steadiness style, like the Compliance personalities, have very high expectations of themselves. In fact, one of the expectations they place upon themselves is to live up to the expectations of others!

The Johnson's daughter, Suzie, is a good example. She had every intention of complying with Dad's standard of being in the car by 8:59 A.M. And if Steadiness personalities make a commitment, we can generally count on them to meet it. If Suzie had been the one to promise making breakfast for the family, Dad would likely have had his eggs and bacon and still been in the car by 8:59. Suzie's commitment to make breakfast would have been in addition to her personal expectation of being in the car by 8:59.

Two case studies in Scripture exemplify this quality of following through on expectations. In Genesis 14, the king of Sodom indicated to Abraham that he was entitled to the goods captured in his defeat of Chedorlaomer. "And Abram said to the king of Sodom, 'I have sworn to the Lord God Most High, possessor of heaven and earth, that I will not take a thread or a sandal thong or anything that is yours, lest you say, "I have made Abram rich"'" (Genesis 14:22-23, NASB*).

In true High S fashion Abraham turned down the king of Sodom's offer to take some of the spoils because he had made a previous commitment to God not to do so. He upheld his high standard of excellence.

In 1 Samuel 1-2, the story of Hannah illustrates how a High S woman followed through on a promise to God. Hannah had no children, and she became so distressed about it that she could not eat. After spending many long hours in prayer, she vowed that if God would give her a son she would give him up to His service. God answered her prayer, and Hannah did conceive and named the baby Samuel. True to her word, when Samuel was weaned, she gave him to Eli, the high priest, and dedicated him to a lifetime of service in the Lord's work.

Steadiness personalities tend to set standards for themselves that are not always realistic. Like persons with the Compliance style, their inability to measure up to self-imposed standards often requires that others offer supportive reinforce-

New American Standard Bible.

ment to offset the feeling of inferiority. If Suzie had been unable to get breakfast made as well as be in the car by 8:59, she would likely have needed emotional reinforcement to avoid feeling like a failure. A word of encouragement will usually help to resolve this problem.

Generally speaking, High S styles do not require the same standards of others as they require of themselves. Unlike the High C, individuals with a High S profile have a lower expectation of others. They tend to be more patient and accepting of others and typically operate from a friendly viewpoint. When Mrs. Johnson explained that she did not have time to fix breakfast, Suzie probably accepted that explanation without feeling frustrated—unlike her High C father.

WHAT THE DOMINANCE PERSONALITY
EXPECTS OF HIMSELF AND OTHERS

In contrast with the Compliance and Steadiness personalities, Dominance personalities have low expectations of themselves and high expectations of others. Their agenda is usually to be in control and make decisions that support their own goals. These goals are generally made within the range of their abilities and interests. Though they have high expectations of others, they reserve the right to change the rules if it enables them to achieve their desired results. In fact, they are the most likely to feel that the "end justifies the means." Jack, the High D son in the Johnson family, thought it was not critical to leave on time for Sunday school simply because he was not interested in going. Although Jack was not in a position to impose his expectations on his dad, he certainly had no intention of being the first one in the car, either.

Driven to achieve their own goals, Dominance personalities often expect other people to be disciplined and directed. They resist explanations of why projects are not completed. As mentioned earlier, if Jack had wanted to go to church, he would have expected everyone else to be on time. In fact, he probably would have been supervising the effort!

Rather than projecting expectations as preferences as opposed to demands, the High D style often shows such force of character that others view them as being harsh and unyielding. In Acts 15:36-41, for example, the apostle Paul was very demanding in dealing with Barnabas. Because John Mark did not live up to Paul's expectations on the first missionary trip, Paul refused to have him along on the second. Paul's expectations seemed unreasonable to Barnabas. The dispute between the two men was so sharp they ended up going separate ways on the second missionary journey.

WHAT THE INFLUENCING PERSONALITY
EXPECTS OF HIMSELF AND OTHERS

The lowest level of expectations, both of self and others, comes from those with the Influencing personality style. As we shall see in upcoming chapters, those who are High I's are more concerned with people and relationships than they are with tasks and objectives. Their desire for harmony among people inhibits them from expecting anything that would place a stress on a relationship.

Moses' older brother, Aaron, had an Influencing personality style. When Moses made his famous sojourn on Mount Sinai to receive the Ten Commandments (Exodus 20:1–32:7), he left Aaron in charge to watch over the restless Hebrews. Moses spent a long time with God on the mountain, and the people grew restless and insecure. They pressured Aaron to fashion a god of gold in order for them to have a tangible object to worship. Aaron gave in to maintain peace. His expectations of himself and of the people were low, and he compromised his convictions.

Moses, however, had a Compliance personality style, demanding much of himself and much of others. When he returned and "saw the calf and the dancing," he "threw the tablets [of the law] out of his hands, breaking them to pieces at the foot of the mountain," and severely rebuked the people (32:19-21).

It is difficult to understand Aaron's intentions unless you view them from the High I perspective. His primary goal was to maintain harmony among the campers. In his High I mind, he justified bending the rules to keep people happy. Aaron's hope for harmony was out of balance with his desire to obey God. Moses, the High C, put a halt to this line of thinking when he returned from being on the mountain with the Lord. Fortunately for Aaron, Moses came to his aid—but not before many people had lost their lives.

Similar to the Steadiness Pattern, the High I has the lowest level of expectations for others. The Steadiness personality does not want to place restrictions on others that might inhibit their own desires for freedom and flexibility. High I's generally accept others for who they are and desire to understand rather than to impose personal judgments.

SUMMING UP EXPECTATIONS

To summarize our understanding of each behavioral style as it applies to expectations, High C's expect perfection both of themselves and others. High S's are committed to doing things correctly but do not necessarily expect others to comply with their high standards. High D's have realistic expectations as they apply to themselves but can impose higher standards on others in order to maintain control. High I's have relatively low expectations of themselves and others. They prefer to focus on maintaining relationships rather than on accomplishing tasks.

THE ENVIRONMENTS WE NEED

Typically class members come and listen for several sessions and diligently record information—but true learning begins when that information connects with reality and has application to a person's life. It is common that the initial breakthrough in understanding the behavioral model comes in the discovery and confirmation of differences in expectations of the DISC Profiles. This type of breakthrough happened to an associate pastor in one of our training sessions. He was a youth pastor at a local church and had profiled out as a High C, Perfectionist Pattern. He had high expectations and high performance standards. He didn't understand why the senior pastor continually exhorted him to comply with detailed standards at the same time the senior pastor didn't meet them himself. Being a High C, the youth pastor expected that the senior pastor's standards applied to both of them, and he resented the fact that they obviously didn't. He was having difficulty understanding the senior pastor's management style.

As the concepts we presented in the seminar became clear to him, the youth pastor quickly recognized that his superior's profile was a High D, probably a D/I Profile. He now understood why the senior pastor responded as he did. But how was he to deal objectively with the stress the senior pastor's behavior was causing in the relationship? He and the senior pastor were opposite profiles and viewed and evaluated information differently. These differences set in motion natural conflicts for which there was no resolution other than to agree to disagree.

"I now understand the *why* part of our not seeing eye-to-eye, but not the *how,*" Jim said. "But how do we communicate with one another so that we can work together as a team?"

"Jim, it's both simple and hard. The next step in understanding his behavior is to realize that his need system is different from yours. If you are to be effective in communicating with him, you must know what motivates him and structure your messages around his needs. He must be committed to doing the same for you. For example, some profiles need short, direct messages, whereas others need complete explanations. It takes hard work to focus on the other person's needs rather than on your own, but it happens to be what the Scripture teaches."

We shared the following Scripture passage with Jim:

> Do nothing out of selfish ambition or vain conceit, but in humility consider others better than yourselves. Each of you should look not only to your own interests, but also to the interests of others. (Philippians 2:3-4)

Jim retorted quickly, "But what if he doesn't desire to meet *my* needs?"

"You're not off the hook. You are still responsible for loving him. Now that doesn't mean being a doormat. The strategy is to create the right environment, so that you effectively communicate your message and give the Holy Spirit the opportunity to work in his life. That's all you are responsible for, and that's all you can do. What you need to know now is what kind of environment to create so that progress can be made."

Jim's interpersonal conflicts are common and predictable. So long as people attempt to relate to one another from a "self" perspective, miscommunication will continue to be a major problem. My hope is that the following model—taken from 1 Thessalonians 5:14—will lay a foundation in your life for effectively dealing with differences, so that positive relationships can naturally develop.

In 1 Thessalonians 5:14, the apostle Paul uses a series of counseling terms to instruct the believers in Thessalonica in how to create the particular environments that are needed to encourage the different types of people. The terms Paul uses are diverse and are intended to be used as they apply to specific individuals in specific situations. In *Christian Psychiatry*, Dr. Frank Minirth uses this passage as the basis for his observation that a balanced approach is necessary in Christian counseling in order to meet the differing needs of patients. The DISC model likewise uses a similar method in advocating using different approaches in meeting the needs of persons with differing styles. In addition, we have found that Minirth's method, the DISC method, and 1 Thessalonians 5:14 exemplify the approach the Lord used in counseling and loving His people.

Here is the text of 1 Thessalonians 5:14 (the italics are added):

> And we *urge* you, brothers, *warn* those who are idle, *encourage* the timid, *help* the weak, *be patient* with everyone.

URGE

The word *urge* (*parakaleo*) means to beseech or exhort and is intended to create an environment of urgency to listen and respond to a directive. It is a mildly active verb used by Paul in Romans 12:1; 15:30; 1 Corinthians 4:16; and elsewhere. The model for responding to High D's includes providing direct answers and being brief and to the point.

WARN

The word *warn* (*nouthetheo;* "admonish," KJV*) means to warn and to confront at the same time. It is an "active" verb and refers to creating a confrontational environment for the purpose of producing a change in direction or behavior. It is meant to be used with an unchecked, strong-willed person who is running out of control. It fits with the High D model in that it has to do with creating a confrontational environment for the purpose of getting a person's attention.

Christ used this style with Paul on the road to Damascus. He also used this style in Matthew 16:23 when Peter, the High I, tried to prevent Him from going to the cross. In Exodus 4:14, God uses a similar approach to motivate Moses, the High C, to be His representative before Pharaoh. But here it must be noted that the Lord used this approach specifically when Moses discounted his own value as a person. The style is more commonly used on strong-willed styles as opposed to the typically compliant High C's such as Moses. The Scriptures seem to indicate that the Lord used this style with High C's only when they projected a "poor me" attitude.

ENCOURAGE

The word *encourage* (*parmutheomai*) means to console, comfort, and cheer up. The process encompasses an active environment that includes elements of understanding, redirecting of thoughts, and a general shifting of focus from the negative to the positive. In the context of the verse, it refers to the timid ("fainthearted," KJV) individual who is discouraged and ready to give up. This style is commonly needed by the High C when he is dealing with change and incomplete details. It is also an appropriate style to use in dealing with a High S when he is faced with confrontation.

God initially used this style with Moses (in Exodus 3-4) when He patiently and persistently answered all of Moses' questions regarding going back to Egypt. In Genesis 15, God reas-

*King James Version.

sures Abraham of His support following his victory over the four kings. It appears that Abraham was concerned with reprisals and was also discouraged about not having an heir. God gave Abraham the encouraging news that he would indeed have a son.

HELP

The word *help* (*antechanai*) primarily has the idea of "taking interest in," "being devoted to," "rendering assistance," or "holding up spiritually and emotionally." It involves a more passive approach, with the idea of coming alongside a person and supporting him. In the context of 1 Thessalonians 5:14, it seems to refer to those who are incapable of helping themselves and are in need of physical, emotional, or spiritual support from someone else.

In 1 Kings 19 Elijah flees for his life because Jezebel has sworn to kill him. He became so drained spiritually, emotionally, and physically that he requested that God take his life. Rather than exhort him to "shape up," the angel of the Lord came alongside Elijah and dealt first with his physical need for nourishment by offering food twice. He also gave Elijah an opportunity to rest. Later, when Elijah complained about being totally alone in serving the Lord, God corrected him by observing that there were still seven thousand in Israel who had not bowed down to Baal. Then God gave Elijah the assignment of anointing two new kings to carry out His work, and He raised up Elisha to become Elijah's replacement.

PATIENT

The word *patient* (*makrothumeo*) literally means "to be long-tempered." It is a universal tool of encouragement and good will. Patience is required in every aspect of our Christian lives. Though patience takes on different meanings for the various DISC models, it is an absolute necessity in dealing with a certain segment of believers.

THE LORD EXPRESSING PATIENCE

TOWARD THE HIGH D

Following the confrontational Damascus road experience, Paul immediately tried to lead his Jewish brothers to Christ. It wasn't the mission to which he was called, but he stubbornly went forward anyway. Not surprisingly, he encountered serious problems and was rejected. God graciously allowed Paul to work under his own power for about three years. He experienced failure twice and, under death threats, was removed from his ministry for about ten years. God patiently waited until He knew that Paul had the potential to serve rather than to lead. The thirteen-year exile was crucial in Paul's development as an obedient servant. God was committed to patiently waiting until Paul was ready.

TOWARD THE HIGH I

Peter's I/D Profile had the ability to overflow with optimism. When Peter confidently proclaimed that he would never deny Jesus, the Lord patiently explained that he would indeed deny Him three times. Furthermore, Jesus told Peter that Satan had sought permission to sift him like wheat. However, Jesus assured Peter He had prayed for him that he would be strengthened through the experience. The Lord allowed Peter to be broken so that he would follow Jesus' model of leadership rather than depending on his own instincts. Later, after Peter's denials, Christ graciously restored Peter to leadership by reconfirming him in front of his peers, the other disciples.

TOWARD THE HIGH S

God initially called Abraham in Ur of the Chaldeans. Part of the instructions included the request that Abraham leave his family. Abraham did not fully comply, and God patiently waited until his father died in Haran. Following this event, God recommunicated His instructions. Abraham obeyed, but took along Lot. In Genesis 13 conflict among Lot's and Abraham's servants caused Lot and Abraham finally to separate. After this separation, God again confirmed His promise. The Lord patiently allowed Abraham to process the idea of letting go of his family and putting his sole dependence on the Lord. Abraham was in his late seventies when he finally made that decision. In the meantime, God patiently waited on him.

TOWARD THE HIGH C

When God called Moses in Exodus 3, He outlined what He wanted Moses to do and then patiently answered all of Moses' questions with specific details. Later, He graciously allowed Aaron to be a spokesman for Moses until he saw and experienced what God intended for him to do. God could have destroyed Pharaoh in one plague but used ten so that Moses could formulate in his mind the true power of the Lord. During this internship, Moses came to understand his role within God's overall plan. Rather than rush ahead, God operated within Moses' ability to process information. Through exercising His patient style, the Lord gave Moses the opportunity to be the leader He intended him to be.

A LOOK AHEAD

Because of varying expectations of self and others, it is normal for individuals initially to interpret information differently. What is important to understand is that all of these perspectives are needed in order for balance to occur. Unfortunately differences are commonly viewed as threats to our personal need systems, and conflicts often occur. We "agree to disagree," and imbalance results.

If we are to take advantage of insights into personality differences, we must find a way to show that we respect contrasting views. We can do that by creating the environments that give others the potential to share how they really feel. The next chapter identifies different responses by each personality style in everyday situations.

FOUR

THE DISC PERSONALITY STYLES IN DAILY LIVING

What response can we expect from the four personality styles in various situations? That's important to know, for if we know the characteristic responses of each of the personality styles, we foster acceptance and keep ourselves from being surprised by the differences in the way the personality types respond to the same set of circumstances.

If you were to draw them, the High D individual would probably have an intense, no-nonsense look. He's forceful and direct. The High I individual would probably be a bit more casual, with an outgoing look on his face indicating his tendency toward openness and friendliness. The High S would likely look a bit more conservative and cautious. He is intent on being supportive. The High C individual is intense—he is like the High D in that respect—but he is also more analytical.[1]

APPROACH TO TEAMWORK

The successful completion of most projects usually requires the coordination of different people and their skills. That is teamwork. Although there is always the potential for conflict, when committed, all four of these personalities can work in harmony.

1. Drawings of DISC styles are shown in the *Understanding How Others Misunderstand You* workbook, pp. 32-28.

The High D usually wants the role of initiating the action and then taking charge. He sets the tone for moving out to reach a specific goal. The High I draws upon his wealth of contacts in order to gather the resources necessary to fund and promote the project. The High S is ever supportive and willing to offer his skills to work on the project. The High C prefers to offer design, technical skills, and quality control for the successful completion of the job. Which personality profile is the most important? By now you should realize that no one style is considered the most important. They are all necessary for a well-rounded team approach.

LEADERSHIP OR MANAGEMENT STYLE

Leadership has to do with influencing the behavior of others. Such influence takes many different forms and correlates nicely with the DISC personality styles.

A leader with a High D personality tends to take an autocratic approach with other people. In an organization with a High D person at the top, there is an emphasis on defining responsibilities, implementing action, and managing trouble. An hierarchy of leadership is usually installed so that there is a direct line of authority.

The High I leader, on the other hand, takes a more democratic approach to leadership. He will usually facilitate open communication and initiative by others in the organization. In spite of the increased freedom and delegation of responsibility, the Influencing leader usually prefers to have the authority to make the final decision after representative views are expressed.

A High S person in a leadership role tends to take a participatory approach to the job. Most of the daily decisions are delegated to others while the High S leader offers support by listening to others and allowing everyone in the organization the opportunity to follow through on individual assignments. This facilitating leader strives for peace and smooth operation in the company.

The High C personality usually leads with a more bureaucratic approach. He will emphasize establishing and following proper procedures for the successful completion of a task. As long as there is compliance to policies, people in the organization can have their own responsibilities and make their own decisions. The organizational system and not personality style tends to be in charge.

The autocratic, democratic, participatory, and bureaucratic leadership styles are different—as different as the leaders themselves. It was once thought that there was a "best" leadership style in business, but there is no reason to believe that to be true. In fact, responsible leadership often requires a willingness to adapt to a style that fits the needs of the particular moment.[2]

Management styles can clash. You can imagine the potential for conflict when a High D style and a High C style meet head-on, the autocratic meeting the bureaucratic. One way to deflect trouble and avoid misunderstandings and resentment when leaders with two styles must work together is to work out ahead of time clearly defined boundaries articulating where responsibility and authority begin and end.

SENSITIVITY TO THE FEELINGS OF OTHERS

Ever had a day when you wished you had stayed in bed? Ever had a day when you wished someone else had stayed in bed? Most of us have had both kinds of days. Every day of our lives we have an impact on others, and they on us. By the end of the day, we can be a bag of complex emotions. How others respond to us can help us or hurt us as we work through our emotional response to specific events. Predictably, each of the four personality styles have characteristically different ways of dealing with the feelings of others.

Because of the High D person's concentration on tasks and goals, he has a tendency to be insensitive to the feelings of others. Rarely is this deliberate neglect, but the intensity with which he strives to meet his objectives can cause him to consider emotional expressions as obstacles. The High D person is prone to see life as a battle during which any walls in his way

2. Kenneth H. Blanchard, *SLII: A Situational Approach to Managing People* (Escondido, Calif.: Blanchard Training and Development, 1985), p. 3.

must be torn down. Unfortunately, that approach is likely to result in emotional casualties along the way.

The High I person is much more sensitive to the feelings of others. He wants everyone to be happy and enjoying life, and he works toward that end—even if those about him don't necessarily share those goals. When someone is down, he is usually quick to offer encouragement and attempt to provide a practical solution for an emotional lift.

A person with a High S personality is also very conscious of feelings. He will make every effort to avoid hurting another person even if that means making personal sacrifices. He will avoid conflicts and stirring up controversy and will strive to smooth out problems that might cause dissension.

Just as High S people are similar to the High I people with regard to the way they handle emotions, High C personalities have a good deal in common with High D people, though with a different emphasis. Because High C people are task oriented, they have a limited supply of sympathy to offer others. The High C person takes a logical approach to feelings. He tends to view life in terms of black or white and thus is more analytical about feelings—if someone feels good, he sees that as the result of responsible choices; if someone feels bad, he sees that as the consequence of poor choices. Be more responsible next time and you will feel better, he says.

RELEASING STRESS

Have you ever been under intense emotional pressure? Likely you have. Pressure comes at us from every direction. Pressure on the job, at home, at church, even pressure from friends. It builds, and builds, and builds some more, until finally you just can't stand it anymore. In a dazed moment of stress release, you reach for your—pajamas!

If you can identify with that method of stress relief, you may well have a High S personality. Indeed, each personality style of the DISC model has a unique way of dealing with the build up of emotional pressure—stress.

Since people with a High D personality prefer to be in control of their environment, emotional intensity builds up in them when their personal goals are blocked. They will usually seek a physical stress release. Once their emotions are released, they will begin to respond better to the people around them. Unfortunately, they may have selected a stress release that looks to others like a personal attack, with the result that the High D personality will have alienated them.

People with a High I personality respond to stress by becoming even more talkative than usual. Their emotional release seems to be more of an attempt to express nervous energy. Even though this response may seem similar to the High D style release, it is a bit more channeled into a positive direction. Whereas we might be offended by the High D style of releasing stress, the High I's style merely tires us out.

The High S's style of stress release is the opposite of the High I's. When a build-up of emotion occurs, these people prefer to release stress by getting a little rest! Because of their intense dislike for conflict, emotional stress has its greatest toll on people with the High S personality. Sleep can be a great escape. You might say they would rather work stress out in their dreams than in person.

People with a High C personality prefer to tune out stress. This response is largely due to their dislike of chaos. When they are under stress, they need to be alone with their thoughts so that they can process a response. If you notice that a High C person is deliberately avoiding you, that may be a sign that you are the cause of his stress.

RECOVERY FROM EMOTIONAL STRESS

The release of stress isn't the end of the recovery process. Each of us has his preferred way of getting recharged to meet the challenges of daily life. Failure to take the time to recover can lead to emotional burnout, when one's life-purpose can get out of focus.

High D people usually need to get involved with physical activity as a way of working out the build-up of stress. Some High D people release their energy on a golf ball. One High D pastor we know takes his chain saw into the woods near his home and cuts down a tree. We don't ask who he might have on his mind as he saws the tree into little pieces.

High I people usually recover by seeking and spending more time with people. After all, they need others, lots of others, to listen to them talk! They are always willing to take a break and get away for some fun. They originated the saying "All work and no play makes Johnny a dull boy." When they do get tired, they need only a short amount of rest before they are ready to get back into action. Other people reenergize them rather than drain them.

As for the High S person, he usually needs to keep on sleeping. He needs the opportunity to break the routine of all mental stress with "nothing time." Watching television, working in the yard, or taking leisurely walks all qualify.

In contrast, the High C needs time alone to recover from emotional stress. Whereas the High S person reaches for his pajamas, a High C person reaches for a good book. He prefers doing something quiet, maybe pursuing a hobby, preferably alone, to recover from emotional stress.

Problems easily occur within relationships when these different stress-recovery needs clash. If a High D man has a High S wife, there will be an obvious difference in the way they prefer to deal with stress. The same applies when a High I wife is married to a High C man. Couples need to develop a workable strategy for coping with stress so that they can head off unnecessary disagreements. Giving understanding to your partner will help avoid misunderstanding. Being aware of each others' needs and allowing the other the freedom to recover from stress in whatever form he or she requires can keep relationships fresh.

Making a Spiritual Commitment to Christ

Our personality style may have an impact on the way in which we make a commitment to Christ. Just as each of the four styles in the DISC model is different in its characteristic way of dealing with people, so they are each different in the characteristic way they encounter Christ.

When a High D personality recognizes his need for accepting Christ, it usually happens after some traumatic event in his life. Something major usually has to happen to get his attention. The apostle Paul, on his way to persecute the Christians in Damascus, was temporarily blinded. Although most of us would not prefer such a drastic method of getting our attention, God is willing to let us encounter difficulty to wake us up, and High D people often report this to be necessary.

As you might expect, people with a High I personality style rarely hesitate to express their faith verbally and make a public commitment to Christ. Because they are people oriented, they look forward to telling friends and family about their new experience.

A professional fisherman I (Ron) know accepted Christ at one of the churches where we have a counseling center. The man was so excited about trusting Jesus that after he got home from church, he started calling friends all over the country. While he was talking to a close friend in Houston, Texas, the friend said he wanted a man visiting with him to hear the good news. That man was at the time the President of the United States, who was also on a fishing trip. An excited High I can get his message to the highest office in the land.

Steady and supportive High S people usually surrender their lives to Christ with a minimum amount of attention being drawn to themselves. Their commitment is solid and sincere but with a little shyness as well. Any reluctance to speak out is more than compensated for by their tremendous loyalty and years of faithful service to God.

The High C person approaches commitment to Christ with a dose of mental scrutiny. Because of his need for thoroughness and correctness, he may experience a period of internal struggle over whether or not he has done everything right. He may very well feel some performance must coincide with his faith. During evangelistic crusades and revivals, this is the one who battles the most with the issue of the security of salvation. Indeed, the High C may commit and recommit his life to Christ, just trying to be sure he has done the job right. It is important, yet so very difficult, for a High C to understand the sufficiency of God's marvelous grace.

THE MISSION OF THE CHURCH

Pastors and church leaders know how different people are when it comes to the work of the church. Just as the different personality styles vary in their approach to teamwork, leadership, sensitivity, response to stress, and making a commitment to Christ, so they vary in their approach to the mission and ministries of the church.

High D people usually have a strong desire for the church to provide comprehensive programs for all the people. They take an aggressive, goal-oriented approach to shaping the mission of the church. It is not uncommon for High D pastors to lead their churches in several building programs and work toward expanding the church's professional staff to provide a complete ministry for all.

High I people are interested in programs that will reach more and more people for Christ. However, they tend to avoid wanting to work in traditional ways on a project, opting for ministries that reach out in new and innovative ways. They tend to place greater importance on being emotionally expressive of faith. High I's can be excellent at eliciting passion for and participation in important causes.

Church members with a High S personality style are generally supportive of the church leadership and respect the hierarchical structures that direct the church's mission. As you might suspect, High S's prefer a church that is more traditional and working toward peace and harmony. They will tend to place more emphasis on social services and reaching their city for Christ through supporting community involvement.

High C members prefer a church that is operated "by the book. Of all the personality types, the High C tends to be more cautious regarding new projects, though he will get involved if proper planning and procedures are assured. The High C is willing to be stubborn and critical if that means preserving and achieving church goals. They place a strong emphasis on doctrine and following the proper procedures for accomplishing Christ's mission on earth.

A LOOK AHEAD

Some folks want to scream, others to sleep. Some want to talk, others prefer silence. People really are different, aren't they? And yet very predictable in so many ways. If we understand how that predictability can help us look beyond our own needs, we can begin to understand our misunderstandings and be more successful in serving each other rather than wanting to be served by others.

The following chapters break down each of the DISC environments in negative and positive models. The purpose of these models is to provide believers with a means through which they can love one another so that the Holy Spirit has the opportunity to build unity.

FIVE

UNDERSTANDING THE DOMINANCE STYLE

How would you feel if you were given the assignment of leading a small, ill-equipped army that had been inactive for forty years? What would be your response if you were ordered to march that army against an enemy who possessed greater strength and the advantage of fighting on familiar territory? What may create panic in and seem hopeless to most of us is well suited for some people—those persons with the Dominant (High D) personality style.

Do you have a goal that seems unobtainable? A task with insurmountable obstacles? Does a mountain you want to climb seem too high? Does a river look too wide to cross? The person with the Dominant personality style is the one you want to lead the way. That behavioral style is willing to accept challenges, create action, and obtain results. High D's can climb that mountain and cross that river.

After he has accepted a challenge, expect a High D to become focused on specific tasks and authoritatively manage trouble and solve problems. High D's are driven to overcome opposition in order to accomplish results. They possess an unusual ability to thrive in negative environments. Challenges give them the chance to create something better than was there before. In this chapter, we will show how the Lord used the High D's in Scripture to accomplish His purposes. Below is the list of the four High D Representative Patterns and the parallel positive biblical characters who represent those patterns.

High D Representative Pattern	Biblical Character
Director (primary D)	Solomon
Organizer (D/I)	Joshua, Sarah
Motivator (D = I)	Stephen, Lydia Apollos
Pioneer (D/C)	Paul, Rachel

What sets a High D apart from other people is his drive to solve problems, take authority, and make quick decisions. This drive often causes High D individuals to seek leadership roles where short-term goals and challenges exist.

GENERAL TENDENCIES OF THE PERSON WITH THE DOMINANCE STYLE

POSSESSES A STRONG SENSE OF PERSONAL WORTH

A High D demonstrates confidence that he can accomplish just about anything he desires. So pronounced is the self-assurance of a High D that others with equal or greater skills have a tendency to defer leadership roles to him. If a High D is chosen to lead a group up a mountain, he won't just *think* there is a way over, he will *know* there is.

As with any strength, this tendency toward confidence can be overextended. High D's enjoy talking about their accomplishments, but they seldom mention mistakes or failures. One revealing comment from a High D: "I don't make mistakes, but I have been known to change directions when one of my decisions doesn't pan out."

The High D's have a much greater tendency to project confidence than members of the other DISC Profiles (table 5).

Task-oriented leadership requires confidence. The army mentioned at the beginning of the chapter would need a High D to lead it. That is exactly the type of leader God chose when He selected Joshua to lead the Israelites in the conquest of Canaan following the exodus from Egypt.

Table 5

Confidence Continuum

greater -- lesser

D   I   S   C

D   Does not hide accomplishments
     Can easily become self-centered
     Has less interest in hearing another's opinion

I   Projects self-confidence, but reflects more of a "We"
     attitude rather than an "I" attitude

S   Prefers modesty
     Likes validation of accomplishments from others

C   Rejects outward expression of confidence from others

SOURCE: Adapted from Life Associates, Inc., The *DISC Model: Trainer and Consultant's Reference Encyclopedia.*

As general of the Israelite army during the time of Moses, Joshua well characterized how God uses a High D to accomplish a monumental task. The Israelites had wandered in the desert for a generation. Their ancestors had been brickmakers and slaves of Pharaoh. Now they were to march on an enemy with a strong, well-trained army. It was quite a mountain to climb, and God knew the man He could trust to lead the way.

In order to keep Joshua from becoming overconfident in his ability to lead, God gave him an important personal assignment: to meditate on "the Book of the Law" "day and night" so that he would be able to follow God's leading (Joshua 1:8). Joshua's success was dependent on his submission to the will of God on a daily basis.

At the end of his life, Joshua brought the people together and offered one final challenge. After generations in Egypt, many still served the gods of that land. Joshua gave the people a choice between serving the gods of Egypt or serving Jehovah.

In High D style, he was straightforward and to the point. "Choose for yourselves this day whom you will serve. . . . But as for me and my household, we will serve the Lord" (24:15).

History records that the Israelites continued to serve the Lord all the days of Joshua and the elders who outlived him. His influence on others carried well beyond his own life.

Joshua exerted a positive influence in his leadership style. Unfortunately, however, not all High D's have that impact. The Scriptures record the behavior of another D who had the same specific profile as Joshua but was guilty of responding selfishly to his own needs. His life shows how an ability to influence others can get out of control.

That individual was the pharaoh of Egypt before whom Moses and Aaron stood. Moses challenged that pharaoh to submit to God's authority and allow the Hebrew people to be set free. But Pharaoh saw the Hebrews as his personal belongings and slaves. To him, they existed on earth to achieve his personal goals, which included building monuments to himself. Since he considered himself to be a god, he had little hesitation in challenging Moses as to who Yahweh was. To his High D mind, he had no peers. His arrogant attitude would not allow him to accept submitting to someone else's authority and face the possibility of not completing his building program. In previous situations, his confident nature prevailed, but this time it destroyed him.

TASK ORIENTED

As the High D people pursue their goals, they sometimes view the opinions of others as obstacles rather than helpful insights. One High D manager said, "People are only a means to accomplish results and sometimes they get in the way." Some individuals would be offended by that statement, but it illustrates the degree to which High D styles think in terms of task orientation rather than people orientation.

The High D personality has a much greater tendency to produce results than do the other profiles (table 6). The High D

Table 6

Preference for Producting Results Continuum

greater --- lesser

| D | S | C | I |

D   Emphasizes task accomplishment over relations with people
     Tends to be aggressive in conflict situations

S   Adapts to a variety of work styles and seeks to maintain
     harmony in relationships

C   Prefers quality over quantity
     Resists involvement where conflicts exist

I   Higher people priority than task accomplishment
     Can deal well with abstracts
     Hesitates to push others

SOURCE: Adapted from Life Associates, Inc., The *DISC Model: Trainer and Consultant's Reference Encyclopedia.*

person goes for results above all else. He is perfectly willing to let relationships take second place. If a High D personality perceives someone as being a threat to his goals, he will do whatever it takes to meet the challenge that person represents, even if it means entering into conflict with him. To those who consider getting along with others as important, such as High I individuals, the High D person comes across as being cold and insensitive.

In Genesis 16, Abraham's wife, Sarah, demonstrates this tendency to fight the competition rather than build closer relationships. Sarah and Abraham deeply desired to have a son who could continue the family line, but Sarah had been unable to conceive. So she argued for a new approach to achieving their goal. Sarah's plan was for Abraham to have sexual relations with her maid, Hagar. If a son resulted, they would have an heir. To Sarah's High D way of thinking, it was a simple plan with a concrete goal. Abraham, the supportive S, cooperated, and Hagar was successful in conceiving a child.

Later on, when Hagar realized she was pregnant, she didn't respond graciously to Sarah but instead rebelled against her authority. In classic High D fashion, Sarah went to Abraham with a demand for action. But Abraham wanted no part of the conflict between the women, and instead of resolving the matter he gave Sarah total control of the situation. Sarah responded to the conflict between her and Hagar by treating Hagar harshly.

Sarah's bitterness against Hagar was so intense that Hagar could not stand up to the conflict. Eventually she ran away. She had discovered how difficult it is to stand up to the wrath of a High D who thinks you have jeopardized his or her goals.

But after she ran away, Hagar had an encounter with the angel of the Lord, who told her to return to Sarah and submit to her authority. Hagar obeyed, and the conflict was settled—at least until Sarah gave birth to Isaac thirteen years later.

MOTIVATED BY DIRECTNESS

Sandra spent weeks putting together a proposal for a new project the president of her company was considering. She pulled together all of the important data, organized it logically, and typed the proposal, then proofread it for errors and typed it again. Finally, she bound the proposal together, rehearsed her delivery, and went confidently to a scheduled meeting to present her plan.

Only moments into her presentation, the president reached over, grabbed a copy of the proposal, flipped to the back page and said, "Just where are we going to get the funds for this project?" The High D president was painfully direct and wanted to get to the bottom line. He completely overlooked the supporting data Sandra had prepared because he wasn't interested in the details at that stage in the project. The logical order of the presentation, the careful typing, the rehearsed delivery were wasted on him. What was it going to cost? What will be the return? That's what the High D president wanted to know: bottom line information.

Sound familiar? Like Sandra, you may have been nose-to-nose with a High D. High D's have a tendency to be direct (some would say blunt) and to expect others to act toward them with the same directness (bluntness does not offend them). They prefer that information be given to them in bites of ten words or less—or at least they want people to get to the point as quickly as possible. If they want more information, they will ask questions. You can generally tell whether a High D is interested in what you are saying by the directness with which he approaches you and requests more information.

Prone to launch into a project on his own, a High D figures out the details as he goes. Rather than read instructions, he wants to operate by his instincts. Only when all else fails will he try reading the directions. So when a High D tries to put together Johnny's model airplane, be prepared for a design other than the one pictured on the box! If you want an exact replica, get Grandpa (preferably a High C grandpa) to do the job.

And as for climbing that mountain, while the others are still standing at the base enjoying conversation and building rapport, the High D Profile likely has already begun to climb. Remember—ask a High D to lead you only if you're ready to move.

BLIND SPOTS OF THE HIGH D

MAY FEAR BEING TAKEN ADVANTAGE OF BY OTHERS

High D's quickly seize opportunities that allow them to assume control of their destiny. When others challenge their position, they become uncomfortable and seek greater control. Their fear of losing control often leads them to take offense at the aggressive behavior of others. Instead of responding in a patient and cautious manner, they see confrontation as the best method of dealing with challenges to their goals.

Solomon demonstrated how fears can lead to confrontation. In 1 Kings 2 David chooses him as his successor to the throne. By tradition, Solomon's older brother Adonijah should have been made king, but this did not happen. After Solomon was firmly established in his rule over the kingdom, Adonijah came to Solomon's mother, Bathsheba, and asked for a favor. Could he take a member of David's harem, Abishag the Shunammite, as his wife? On the surface, the proposal seemed like a harmless one, and Bathsheba spoke to Solomon on Adonijah's behalf about the request. But access to the harem was a royal prerogative, and if Adonijah had married her he could have laid claim to the throne. Solomon immediately perceived that threat and ordered Adonijah and his brother killed. Later, Solomon would also have Joab, one of David's generals, killed for joining in the plans with Adonijah. The moral of this story is to be careful if you find yourself in competition with a High D. High D's are quick to take the offensive against a challenger. Don't cross a High D unless you are ready for battle. And don't go to battle unless you know you can win! Harvey Mackay, the author of *Swim with the Sharks Without Being Eaten Alive: Outsell, Outmanage, Outmotive and Outnegotiate Your Competition* (New York: Morrow, 1988), offers practical advice for such situations.

TENDS TO BE INSENSITIVE TO OTHERS

The tendency not to be concerned with the views and feelings of others is often a blind spot of the High D. With their strong nature and objective skills, High D's consider their judgment to be sound, and they are unencumbered by other people's feelings. They are extremely self-sufficient and think they are right most of the time.

"Beating your head against the wall." That is probably the best way to describe how it feels when you try to get your opinions across to a High D. The self-confidence and task orientation of the High D can desensitize him to the feelings and thoughts of others. People who work around a High D for very long often report that they feel as though they've been used. It is not unusual for even an employer of a High D to sense that his views are not being considered. Sensitive people are often left bruised and bleeding in the wake of a High D on his mission. But the High D was climbing the mountain in the only way he knew.

Connie, a High S, felt abused by her husband, Dave, a High D. For more than fourteen years she had given in to his need for control. Being in the Army's Special Forces had taught Dave to view every problem as a mission to conquer. His take-charge style contributed to his being successful in business pursuits. Dave owned his own company and had achieved financial security by the time he was forty. But at home he had created an atmosphere of insecurity and unconditional surrender. Connie had long ago given up trying to match Dave's ability to prevail in disagreements. In fact, the only way she could end an argument was by admitting she was wrong and promising to change.

Dave didn't realize the damage his insensitivity did to Connie's need for support and encouragement. Being right and having an explanation for every problem made him feel in charge. Now, faced with his wife's nervous breakdown and the probability of divorce, Dave sought counseling to understand his insensitive ways. Dave realized that though his direct approach might work in business or war, it was proving disastrous in his marriage. His need for control had got out of control, and he wanted to learn how to change.

The High D needs to learn to listen to others and be sensitive to their needs. Failure to listen can prove costly. In the Old Testament record are many proverbs of Solomon, but often he did not heed his own advice. He warned in Proverbs 1:7 that "the fear of the Lord is the beginning of knowledge, but fools despise wisdom and discipline," yet toward the end of his reign, Solomon married many foreign women in order to bring about alliances as a means to keep peace. In time he felt obliged to worship the cultural gods of his wives. Ultimately, this practice affected his relationship with the Lord. Twice God personally confronted Solomon over the issue, but he remained insensitive to the Lord's voice and did not listen. Only because of God's promise to David did Solomon remain as king. However, the Lord made clear to Solomon that as a consequence of his unwillingness to change, the kingdom would be torn apart and given to a servant. And that is what happened. Following Solomon's death, the kingdom was split, and Solomon's son was left with only the two tribes, Judah and Benjamin. It was a great price to pay for not listening to the Lord's directives.

CAN BE IMPATIENT

Along with being insensitive, High D's can be impatient. We recall being in a High D's office in which a sign had been placed—a gift from his wife—that read, "Lord give me patience and give it to me NOW!" My High D friend explained how difficult it was for him to be patient and how he continually worked to overcome this trait. That is a common feeling for High D's. Usually, specific events or special people help teach them patience. In this man's case, the Lord gave him an excellent tutor —his High S wife, the most patient of the personality styles.

OVERVIEW OF THE ELEMENTS
OF THE REPRESENTATIVE PATTERNS

Thus far, except in a portion of chapter 2, our focus has been on describing the four major categories of DISC behavioral styles. In the following pages, and in the succeeding seven chapters, we will examine sixteen blends of the DISC model, which we will call Representative Patterns.

As we mentioned in chapter 2, each of the sixteen Representative Classical Patterns is a unique combination of high and low position points on the four D-I-S-C continuums. In each of the Representative Patterns, one of the four DISC styles is generally predominant in the personality along with secondary influences. Those secondary influences further distinguish a particular Representative Pattern from the others. Understanding the sixteen Representative Patterns will better equip us to relate well with others who have different personality styles from our own.

We will discuss the characteristics of the Representative Patterns in light of the ten components listed in the High Pattern tables starting on page 90. Additional information on these unique blends is available in the two DISC instruments that are a part of the *Understanding How Others Misunderstand You* workbook.

1. *Primary drive*. This category describes the basic uniqueness and character of the pattern.

2. *Personal giftedness*. This category describes the individual skills of a particular style.

3. *Group giftedness*. This category describes how a specific pattern can positively impact the efforts of a team.

4. *Potential spiritual gifts*. This category lists spiritual gifts that are naturally congruent with the skills of the style. However, one must always remember that God is sovereign and can choose to distribute a spiritual gift that *does not necessarily* align itself with an individual's natural bent and/or skills. When this happens, the *expression* of a particular spiritual gift will generally be different in a unique way.

5. *Internal fear*. This category describes the basic protector drive of the pattern and is often the negative motivator of a particular style.

6. *Strength out of control*. This category describes the typical overextensions of a pattern's skills and carried to an extreme the unique types of *sin* issues that pattern must deal with.

7. *Under stress becomes*. This category describes how the specific styles tend to protect themselves. This can be either a positive or a negative motivator.

8. *Blind spots*. This category describes the elements that individual patterns do not see and are unaware of. This category and the *strength out of control* component are generally the two areas that cause the greatest misunderstandings and interpersonal pain.

9. *Needs to work on*. This category lists key traits the individual patterns need to learn in order to overcome misunderstandings and develop a more balanced pattern.

10. *Best team members*. This category lists the patterns that possess complementary skills that are critical to the balance and development of a particular style.

Table 7
Primary High D Pattern

I. Distinctive tendencies of this pattern:

Primary drive	Very independent in seeking solutions to problems
Personal giftedness	Innovative problem solver
Group giftedness	Energy base to see that things get done
Potential spiritual gifts	Wisdom, Exhortation, Administration
Internal fear	Loss of control
Strength out of control	Focusing on goals without concern for people's feelings
Under stress becomes	Intense, active, and initiates action
Blind spots	Seeing the need to be accountable to others
Needs to work on	Empathy, understanding, and cooperation with others
Best team members	I/S/C, I/S, S/I

II. Biblical characters who represent this pattern:

1. Solomon
2. Rahab (*)

III. Further Bible study:

Strengths	Eccl. 2; 1 Kings 6; 9:1-9
Weaknesses	1 Kings 2:34-46; 11:1-13

*Not enough information to be absolutely certain of the specific style.

The following pages cover the four "D" Representative Patterns. They include the *Director, Organizer, Motivator,* and *Pioneer* Patterns. We have also included a brief description of selected biblical characters who represent the different patterns and amplify a few of the components. There are distinct differences between these four Dominance Patterns. For example, the Director projects the most pure tendencies of the High D style. The Motivator has equal tendencies toward directness and expressiveness. The Organizer individual tends to be driven by accomplishing goals but has the ability to influence others to his or her point of view. On the other hand, the Pioneer Pattern is restrained in speech but is most gifted in setting the pace in developing new systems. Recognizing these subtle differences can be helpful in understanding the uniqueness of these D styles.

THE DIRECTOR (PRIMARY D)

POSITIVE TRAITS

Of the four High D Representative Patterns, only the Director (table 7) is characterized with the primary drive for dominance (indicated by the reference "Primary D"). The remaining profiles have a secondary influence from either the I, S, or C. The Director is more of an individualist and tries to meet his own personal needs. He places an emphasis on seeking answers to difficult challenges without help from others.

In the book of Ecclesiastes, Solomon demonstrates the writing style of a Primary D by the way he searches for the answers to life. Throughout the book the pronoun *I* is used to characterize his individualistic method of thinking. The conclusion he came to at the end of his search for meaning was that indulgence cannot satisfy and is a manifestation of vanity. He also concluded that life can be enjoyed to the fullest through realizing that it is a gift from God. A wise man is one who lives his life in obedience to God, recognizing that God will eventually judge all men. As a Primary D, Solomon had to find these answers on his own. He did so by personal experience rather than by consulting the "experts." He was willing to take responsibility for his own failings as well as for his successes.

PERSONAL GIFTEDNESS

The major focus of people with a Director Pattern is to identify the problem and seek innovative methods of solving it. Directors disregard the norms of acceptable behavior and use whatever will work to meet the challenge at hand.

In 1 Kings 3:16-27, Solomon handles a very difficult problem involving two women who claimed to be the mother of the same baby. The women's heated argument before the court ended when Solomon proclaimed that he would solve the problem by cutting the baby in half. It was a quick, challenging, and brilliant response—and it brought forth the truth immediately. The true mother was identified by her willingness to give up the baby in order to save it. Her compassion was what Solomon looked for, and he awarded the baby to her. The story was heard throughout Israel, and all marveled at Solomon's wisdom. It was a classic case of a Primary D exercising his skill at solving problems through exercising a straightforward approach.

STRENGTH OUT OF CONTROL

Directors will use their ability to manipulate others as a means to promote their own causes. Though others might call the practice manipulative, they see themselves as merely being shrewd.

An incident in Solomon's life (1 Kings 2:36-46) provides an example of manipulation of information used negatively. Solomon had ordered Shimei, a member of Saul's family, to live in Jerusalem and not to venture across the Kidron Valley, saying that if Shimei violated this command, he would be killed. Several years later, Shimei traveled to a place called Gath in order to retrieve three runaway slaves. This trip was not directly against the rules Solomon had established, but because Solomon thought of Shimei as a threat to the throne, he insisted that his order was violated and had Shimei killed. Solomon's

Table 8
High D/I Pattern

I. Distinctive tendencies of this pattern:

Primary drive	Strength of character, gets results
Personal giftedness	Flexibility, self-motivated aggressively takes charge
Group giftedness	Acts as catalyst to carry difficult assignments
Potential spiritual gifts	Leadership, Exhortation, Faith
Internal fear	Lack of urgency in moving ahead in accomplishing a goal
Strength out of control	Pushes for action when patience is a better option
Under stress becomes	Emotionally reactive and demands action
Blind spots	Seeing where their actions contribute to negative consequences
Needs to work on	Not manipulating people and circumstances; not striking out toward others
Best team members	S/C, S/C/D, S/I, C/S

II. Biblical characters who represent this pattern:

1. Sarah (*)
2. Joshua

III. Further Bible study:

Strengths	Josh. 3:1-17; 24:1-33
Weaknesses	Gen. 16:1-6; 21:1-10

*Not enough information to be absolutely certain of the specific style.

excessive reaction came as the consequence of his interpreting his rules to accomplish a personal goal without regard for others.

ORGANIZER PATTERN (D/I)

POSITIVE TRAITS

The person with the Organizer Pattern (table 8) is driven mainly by dominance and secondarily by influencing traits (indicated by the abbreviation "D/I"). Persons with this Representative Profile display a gift for taking command of situations. These individuals are quick and decisive and give direct and forceful instructions. When they speak, few people will challenge the plans they have in mind.

As we have seen, Joshua was a good example of an Organizer. The word *command* is used more than forty-nine times in the book of Joshua. Joshua frequently used the word when he spoke to the Israelites. He spoke directly and to the point. The response of the people to his leadership is summed up in Joshua 1:16: "Then they answered Joshua, 'Whatever you have commanded us we will do, and wherever you send us we will go.'"

PERSONAL GIFTEDNESS

Organizer Patterns command respect, and others rely upon their strength and persistent character. They have determination and are willing to move forward no matter what the barriers. Others may falter when faced with obstacles, but the Organizer individual sees obstacles as challenges waiting to be conquered.

While under the leadership of Moses, Joshua was one of the twelve spies sent out to inspect the land God had promised His people. Ten of the spies returned with negative reports that focused on the reasons the land could not be taken. Only Joshua and Caleb brought back favorable reports. They saw the opportunities rather than the obstacles. Unfortunately, the people were influenced by the majority opinion and panicked. When order was restored, God promised the land to the next generation. Joshua's reward was to lead that new generation in the conquest of the Promised Land. Through Joshua's skillful leadership, this goal was accomplished.

STRENGTH OUT OF CONTROL

Under stress, Organizer Profiles have a tendency to be impatient and to use confrontation and intimidation as a means of gaining control. Pharaoh attempted to use this tactic in his dealings with Moses. Because the D/I Profile has a strong ego, the tactic normally works. But with God's help, Moses was able to handle Pharaoh's style and fulfilled God's plan for freeing the Hebrew people. Pharaoh's capacity for control ultimately became his downfall.

THE MOTIVATOR PATTERN (D = I)

POSITIVE TRAITS

Persons with the Motivator Pattern (table 9) are quick to identify the best way to motivate those around them. They have a keen sense of knowing what other people need or want. They do not mind confrontation and have the skills to dominate any debate through force of character. In the book of Acts, Stephen so effectively debated a group of Jewish clergy that they were unable to refute his arguments. In their efforts to discredit him, they brought him before the Sanhedrin. Stephen's speech to this body of seventy men is one of the longest sermons recorded in the New Testament. He communicated the gospel so effectively that they were convicted of personal guilt. Motivator Patterns do not use the tentative words *suggest* or *think*. Instead they forcefully claim, maintain, and allege. So powerful and convicting was Stephen's sermon, the leaders resorted to violence and had him killed to silence his message. Motivator Patterns are often willing to risk rejection.

PERSONAL GIFTEDNESS

Persons with the Motivator Pattern have equal measures of dominance and influencing traits (indicated by the abbrevia-

Table 9
D equal I Pattern

I. Distinctive tendencies of this pattern:

Primary drive	Strong drive to control by charm and persuasion
Personal giftedness	Talented at achieving goals through verbal skills
Group giftedness	Articulating a point of view
Potential spiritual gifts	Prophecy, Evangelism, Teaching
Internal fear	Not having authority to control events, complex relationships
Strength out of control	Overwhelming others with words and arguments
Under stress becomes	Intimidating and can tend to manipulate others
Blind spots	Understanding that their aggressive style often causes covert responses
Needs to work on	Not having to win every argument, slowing down
Best team members	S/C, S/I, I/S

II. Biblical characters who represent this pattern:
1. Stephen (*), Apollos (*)
2. Lydia (*)
3. Laban

III. Further Bible study:

Strengths	Acts 7:1-50; 16:14-15
Weaknesses	Acts 7:51-60

*Not enough information to be absolutely certain of the specific style.

tion "DI"). They have the ability to be both confrontational and entertaining. They are skilled with words and have no peers in their ability to persuade others of their point of view. In Acts 18, an evangelist named Apollos is characterized as "an eloquent man and mighty in the scriptures" (KJV). He inspired people with his message of the gospel and publicly refuted unbelievers by showing from the Scriptures that Jesus was the Christ. In addition to being persuasive, Motivators are usually tactful in getting their ideas across.

STRENGTH OUT OF CONTROL

Motivator Patterns have an ability to manipulate the rules to work for their personal advantage. They perceive what others want and withhold those rewards until the goals they seek are accomplished. Laban used the promise of marrying his daughter Rachel to get Jacob to work for him for a total of fourteen years. That was carrying manipulation a little too far!

Motivator Patterns often forgive themselves for their shortcomings and when failure occurs shift personal guilt to someone else. Laban used this tactic on Jacob in their final confrontation. But God had warned Laban not to harm him, and, with the Lord's help, Jacob successfully handled the situation and was able to return safely to Canaan with Rachel and his family.

THE PIONEER PATTERN (D/C)

POSITIVE TRAITS

Pioneer Patterns (table 10) are driven mainly by dominance and secondarily by compliance traits (indicated by the abbreviation "D/C"). Pioneer Patterns have a gift for analyzing a system and determining its shortcomings. They not only have the ability to see the big picture, but also see the details of the picture. They can quickly discern the solution to a problem and present it in such a way that it makes sense. The apostle Paul had a creative ability to understand that salvation was not possible by keeping the Mosaic law. He reasoned that the function

Table 10
High D/C Pattern

I. Distinctive tendencies of this pattern:

Primary drive	Being the front-runner in developing new concepts
Personal giftedness	Being the instrument to bring about change
Group giftedness	Critically looking at old systems and making them better
Potential spiritual gifts	Discernment, Wisdom, Prophecy
Internal fear	Not being influential, others failing to meet their standards
Strength out of control	Fixing things that are *not* broken
Under stress becomes	Sulky; condescending and critical toward others
Blind spots	Understanding that *grace* and *forgiveness* are critical elements in relationships
Needs to work on	Communicating warmth and patience, softening a judgmental, critical spirit
Best team members	I/D, I/S, I/S/C, S/C

II. Biblical characters who represent this pattern:

1. Paul
2. Rachel (*)

III. Further Bible study:

Strengths	Rom. 3:20-30; Gal. 3:10-29
Weaknesses	Gal. 2:11-14; Acts 15:36-40

*Not enough information to be absolutely certain of the specific style.

of the law was to show that all men were sinners and in need of a Savior. His creative writings formed the basis for the entire New Testament.

Pioneer persons influence others by setting the pace for communicating new ideas. God called the apostle Paul to deliver the doctrine of grace to the Gentile nations throughout the world. He was responsible for establishing most of the Gentile churches during the first century.

PERSONAL GIFTEDNESS

Pioneer Profiles impact relationships by their ability to initiate activities that bring about change. Paul's message of salvation by grace through faith in Christ alone created a great deal of controversy in the Jewish community. Throughout his ministry, Paul would effectively debate any issue that would uphold and advance the gospel. He spent his life and ministry working toward bringing about change in the thinking of both the Jews and Gentiles.

INTERNAL FEAR

Pioneer people fear not having sufficient authority to change a course of events or the lives of others. Their fear is multiplied if their work is unsuccessful or not accepted. Paul encountered many attacks on the legitimacy of his apostleship and suffered unbelievable physical and emotional hardships. Some of the attacks to his ministry must have been extremely painful, particularly the attempt to discredit his calling by Christ from those who opposed his methods. He effectively defended his apostleship and the doctrine of grace in the letter to the Galatians. His ability to handle his natural fears and answer his critics with grace is remarkable. His life is a testimony of submissiveness to God and of allowing the Holy Spirit to turn weaknesses into strengths.

A LOOK AHEAD

Now that we have examined the High D family of Representative Patterns we will take a deeper look into the uniqueness of this personality style. This is an important step in learning how to understand the ways in which we might misunderstand a Dominance personality.

Learning how to respond to the needs of persons with each DISC style will help us to create loving environments in our relationships. Practical suggestions for relating to each style are illustrated by events in the lives of biblical characters.

SIX

RESPONDING TO THE NEEDS OF THE DOMINANCE PERSONALITY

One of the activities we enjoy is getting some feedback on how the DISC material is being received by those who participate in our seminars. On one occasion I (Ken) met with Phil, a High D. He is a successful salesman for a major chemical company and had become a Christian late in his life.

Phil was straightforward in his comments. He told me he disagreed with one trait attributed to the dominant personality —the drive to win.

"It wasn't 'the winning' that drove me for many years," he said. "It was the 'fear of losing'! I couldn't face being a loser, so I drove myself to always be number one. In corporate America and sports, they preach that you must always win—or at least that's what I heard. I was extremely aggressive and intimidated everyone around me, including my boss. I had no rules except to be first."

Out of curiosity I asked, "Phil, if your motive was 'not losing,' how did you feel about winning?"

Phil smiled and replied, "Totally empty. I couldn't enjoy the victories. All they meant was that I had put off losing."

I probed further, "What happened when you lost or came in second?"

Phil shared the painful experience, "Awful. Internally I was terrified, and externally I expressed anger, which tended to keep people away. I wasn't much fun to be around!"

Fortunately for Phil, the emptiness of his victories drove him to search for a deeper meaning to life. This search ultimately led him to make a commitment to Jesus Christ.

After his conversion, Phil's high drive for excellence did not change, but it began to be channeled in a healthier direction. That came about as he learned to be guided and controlled by the Holy Spirit. He remained very goal-oriented but internally was able to relax more in his work—so much so that he reported feeling guilty for not being as aggressive and intense. When his yearly review came around, he was prepared for the worst from his supervisor. The feedback he got shocked him.

His boss commented, "Phil, I've never seen such an improvement in attitude! What's happened to you?" Phil couldn't believe it. In his mind, his relaxed attitude was a liability and a sign of weakness. He had expected a poor review, but instead he was being complimented as a valued team player.

As the years have passed, he still wins awards and remains one of the company's top salesmen. His drive to win is still there, but it is now under control. No longer does he fear to lose.

Other High D's have confirmed that this fear of losing is a very real part of their experience. Fear of this type usually means that a personal strength has got out of control and has turned into a weakness.

Nothing is wrong with striving to win. But when the pursuit of winning compromises values and relationships, it has gone too far. Someone has said that "unguarded strength can become double weakness." As long as our culture teaches a philosophy that only winning brings significance, this imbalance will continue. High D's naturally buy into the notion that winning is the sole thing of importance, only to find that they must pay a high price in stress and struggle to meet that goal. They are caught in a terrible trap. They must play the game, always being in control and always pushing forward. To relax would risk becoming vulnerable. Those who are around them, co-workers or family members, become nothing more than objects whose major function is to help the High D's achieve their goals. If they don't perform properly, they can expect an unpleasant reaction. This pressure often results in broken relationships.

Phil agreed with these observations and is currently working to prevent his driven nature from getting out of control again. Evelyn, his High S wife, confirmed that he has made significant progress and is much more sensitive to her needs and those of the family's. She smiled and quietly told me, "I can tell Phil is less uptight, and it really shows at home. However, we're still working on learning how to smell the roses." For a High D, controlling the drive to succeed is a never-ending process.

You may have already guessed that Phil's Representative Profile is that of the Pioneer Pattern (D/C). His biblical personality counterpart is the apostle Paul. Pioneer Patterns usually report that a war is continually being waged in their minds. One message says, "I must do this," whereas other mental tapes counter with, "I should not do it." An ongoing mental struggle takes place: action versus caution, good versus bad, right versus wrong. In Romans 7:15-25 the apostle Paul gives a description of this mental battle.

> I do not understand what I do. For what I want to do I do not do, but what I hate I do. And if I do what I do not want to do, I agree that the law is good. As it is, it is no longer I myself who do it, but it is sin living in me. I know that nothing good lives in me, that is, in my sinful nature. For I have the desire to do what is good, but I cannot carry it out. For what I do is not the good I want to do; no, the evil I do not want to do—this I keep on doing. Now if I do what I do not want to do, it is no longer I who do it, but it is sin living in me that does it.
>
> So I find this law at work: When I want to do good, evil is right there with me. For in my inner being I delight in God's law; but I see another law at work in the members of my body, waging war against the law of my mind and making me a prisoner of the law of sin at work within my members. What a wretched man I am! Who will rescue me from this body of death? Thanks be to God—through Jesus Christ our Lord!
>
> So then, I myself in my mind am a slave to God's law, but in the sinful nature a slave to the law of sin.

I asked Phil if he could relate to Paul's struggle.

Phil responded, "In stereo, hi-fi sound! I face this battle daily, but now, at least, I have been able to turn down the volume."

"So you still face the problem?"

"Absolutely!"

When I asked Phil how he was able to reduce the intensity, Phil said, "By claiming the verses of Scripture that follow Romans 7. Romans 8:1-4 offers a message of hope."

> Therefore, there is now no condemnation for those who are in Christ Jesus, because through Christ Jesus the law of the Spirit of life set me free from the law of sin and death. For what the law was powerless to do in that it was weakened by the sinful nature, God did by sending his own Son in the likeness of sinful man to be a sin offering. And so he condemned sin in sinful man, in order that the righteous requirements of the law might be fully met in us, who do not live according to the sinful nature but according to the Spirit.

After Phil and I read the passage together, I observed, "So you and Paul came up with the same answer—walk by the Spirit."

Phil confirmed, " You got it! But you must remember the battle goes on constantly. It's never over—just under the Spirit's control. And there's something else. People think that D's are tough and don't need other people. It's an image we may project, but it's a myth. Inside we desire relationships like anyone else. We don't have the natural skills to develop them, so we retreat to achieving our goals. We need your help, but that means risking failure and that's scary."

COMMON RESPONSES OF THE HIGH D UNDER STRESS

Over the years we have found that some people desire a more personal interpretation of their profiles and those of their family. At the beginning of each class teaching of the DISC personality styles, we set up the ground rules. They are simple— "dinner at your place." We find that comfortable surroundings are more relaxing and allow time to zero in on personal issues. It also gives a better idea of the dynamics of the family.

On one such occasion, an attractive middle-aged mother of two invited my wife and me (Ken) to dinner. The home we were invited to was large and tastefully decorated, and it had a backyard pool. Both parents were stylishly dressed, and the delicious candlelight dinner was served with great care in the formal dining room. The husband, Joe, was an oil company executive, and his wife, Mary, was a part-time interior decorator. From the appearance of their home, it was obvious she was talented.

Mary's profile was an I/S Pattern, and Joe's was a C/S Pattern. The daughter, Sally, aged nine, was an I/S Pattern, and the son, Jimmy, twelve, was a D/C Pattern. Mary's need system was satisfied by lots of expressions of affection, whereas Joe needed structure and order. It appeared that they had adjusted to one another's need system and had a loving relationship. The problem was Jimmy.

Mary and Joe perceived their son as being abnormal and had spent the last four years going from psychologist to psychiatrist trying to heal their son of his affliction. No therapy seemed to help. They were willing to try anything—including having their Sunday school teacher over for dinner. (It is always nice to know where you fit!)

I asked Mary to describe Jimmy's behavior. She said he was constantly in rebellion against any structure they put on him. Their relationship with him could be described either as a major or minor war. The parents gave a blow-by-blow, color account of some of their difficulties with Jimmy. I could tell things were getting tense, so I asked how he was when he was asleep. They laughed and told me how much they enjoyed those peaceful moments—and they told me how guilty they felt about not being able to do a better job of parenting their son. They wondered what they could do next in dealing with him.

The first issue we had to confront was their feeling of guilt. In *Parenting Isn't for Cowards,* James Dobson does an excellent job of dealing with the issues parents face in living with a strong-willed child. He makes a number of insightful comments on the subject, but two are particularly significant here:

1. You (the parent) are not to blame for the temperament with which your child was born. He is simply a tough kid to handle and your task is to rise to the challenge.
2. He is in greater danger because of his inclination to test the limits and scale the walls. Your utmost diligence and wisdom will be required to deal with him.[1]

As I gave Mary and Joe insights into the characteristics of High D children, and particularly of the Pioneer Pattern, Mary confirmed that behavior in Jimmy. I told the two parents that it was likely that Jimmy was a normal Pioneer Profile and that their need systems were incongruent with his. They couldn't believe Jimmy was normal, but we focused on what they could do to restructure their parenting strategy so that Jimmy had the best opportunity to grow. I also made sure they understood that even with the right strategy the possibility of continued conflict was assured. Pioneer Patterns thrive on disorder and they will create it even if it doesn't exist in their environment. Mary and Joe had much to challenge them as parents. It is never easy parenting a Pioneer Profile child, but I reminded them that the apostle Paul's profile was the same. That seemed to give Mary and Joe some hope.

CORE NEEDS OF THE HIGH D

In my conversation with the two parents I outlined the core needs of the High D and the impact of those needs on their relationships with others. The desire of the High D, I told them, is to be in total control of his environment. He will naturally challenge and rebel against any structure imposed on him. Also, High D's do not respond well to "touchy, feely" behavior.

As an Encourager Pattern, Mary felt it appropriate to hug and kiss her children on the cheek as they went off to school.

1. James Dobson, *Parenting Isn't for Cowards* (Waco, Tex.: Word, 1987), p. 24.

Sally, the Advisor Pattern, responded to this display of affection, but Jimmy would give his mother an "I-think-I'll-throw-up" look and walk off in disgust. His reaction would crush Mary. She was trying to communicate with Jimmy through her need system, i.e., by showing affection, but Jimmy's need system was for action and control. Add to that the fact that he was a twelve-year-old boy, trying to show he was grown-up and ready to conquer the world, and the potential for conflict was obvious. He would act out his need system by disagreeing with any rule that blocked his goal of doing whatever he set his mind to.

THE PATTERN OF CONFLICT WITH A HIGH D

Conflict with a High D follows a typical pattern (table 11).

Table 11

When a High D Encounters Stress

- Having to face submission to someone else's authority (issue: loss of control)

- Personal goal is being blocked or threatened

- Confrontive action toward the messenger(s)

- Confrontive reaction by the messenger (s)

- Jungle warfare syndrome: survival of the fittest

- Communication deteriorates to a messenger system

In the Old Testament the High D stress model is illustrated in a negative way through the confrontation of Moses, the High C, and Pharaoh, the High D. In the New Testament the High D stress model is illustrated in a positive way through the confrontation between the apostle Paul, a High D, and the Lord Jesus.

HIGH D REACTION ILLUSTRATED
IN THE ENCOUNTER BETWEEN PHARAOH AND MOSES

THE HIGH D BEING CHALLENGED

In Exodus 5, Moses and Aaron take up the task of convincing Pharaoh to allow the Hebrew people to leave Egypt.

> Afterward Moses and Aaron went to Pharaoh and said, "This is what the Lord, the God of Israel, says: 'Let my people go, so that they may hold a festival to me in the desert.'" (v. 1)

Moses was asking Pharaoh to submit to God's authority and let His people journey into the wilderness. The typical reaction of a High D to such a request is to reject the idea initially. God knew that Pharaoh would do this and had prepared Moses for that rejection:

> But I know that the king of Egypt will not let you go unless a mighty hand compels him. So I will stretch out my hand and strike the Egyptians with all the wonders that I will perform among them. After that, he will let you go. (3:19-20)

God understood that in Pharaoh He was dealing with a High D. He knew He was headed for a confrontation with Pharaoh. He advised Moses of His plan up front—though Moses did not appear to understand it.

THE HIGH D'S PERSONAL GOALS BEING BLOCKED OR THREATENED

Once a High D personalizes a goal, he normally expends all his energy into meeting that goal. Typically, he eliminates any obstacle in his path with whatever works the quickest and best. If the barrier persists, the High D builds up great amounts of energy, which is usually released in the form of expressing anger. He often resorts to an ends-justifies-the-means mentality, bending the rules in his favor to accomplish his goal. When an individual becomes the obstruction, the High D sees to it that life is extremely unpleasant for that person, even to the point of bringing emotional or physical pain upon him.

Pharaoh was being asked to give up his labor force, which in turn would force him to give up his building program. He was faced with having to submit to the authority of an eighty-year-old shepherd and his older brother.

HIGH D CONFRONTATION WITH OTHERS

It would have been unrealistic to believe that a High D like Pharaoh would willingly make such a concession. To the contrary, the natural reaction he had to their proposal was confrontational. Aaron and Moses and their God were hindrances to his goals and had to be eliminated. Observe Pharaoh's threat as he tried to deal with what Moses and Aaron presented:

> Pharaoh said, "Who is the Lord, that I should obey him and let Israel go? I do not know the Lord and I will not let Israel go." (5:2)

One can expect the High D to disagree with any plan that is contrary to his goals. He will also typically disagree if the plan does not allow him to be in control. Obviously, Pharaoh was experiencing stress on both these points, which is to say that he was faced with goals incongruent to his own and he was faced with a potential loss of control.

CONFRONTATIONAL RESPONSE OF OTHERS TO THE HIGH D

Moses, being a cautious High C, had Aaron articulate their response to Pharaoh:

> "The God of the Hebrews has met with us. Now let us take a three-day journey into the desert to offer sacrifices to the Lord our God, or he may strike us with plagues or with the sword." (v. 3)

Although there was nothing inherently wrong in Moses and Aaron's being firm, their approach only caused Pharaoh to move to the next phase of the High D's stress reaction.

ALL-OUT CONFRONTATION

Pharaoh's response to Moses and Aaron was heated:

> But the king of Egypt said, "Moses and Aaron, why are you taking the people away from their labor? Get back to your work!" Then Pharaoh said, "Look, the people of the land are now numerous, and you are stopping them from working." (v. 4)

Pharaoh then plotted to destroy the Israelites' spirit and will:

1. He refused to give them straw to make bricks.
2. He made them gather their own straw.
3. He maintained the previous quota of bricks.
4. He had the foremen beaten when the quota was not met.
5. He told the foremen that they were being beaten because of the plan Moses and Aaron had proposed—that of going into the desert and sacrificing to the Lord.

Pharaoh's plan was to discredit Moses and Aaron and make them appear as the enemy—a common High D strategy. It worked. When the foremen left Pharaoh's presence they said to Moses and Aaron,

> "May the Lord look upon you and judge you! You have made us a stench to Pharaoh and his officials and have put a sword in their hand to kill us." (v. 21)

Moses and Aaron went away discouraged, feeling they were victims caught in the middle of a conflict of which they desired no part. There was a total communication breakdown.

COMMUNICATIONS DETERIORATE TO A MESSENGER SYSTEM

Anyone facing a confrontation with a High D must understand and learn how to use the "messenger system" as a potential means of resolving conflict.

If a confrontation becomes unpleasant, High D's will typically close off communications except through a messenger of their choice. It is the High D's' way of maintaining control. Though this tactic can be infuriating, it can also be used to reestablish communications. To be effective, the messenger must have the gift of diplomacy under pressure while focusing on actions and tasks. Moses' Perfectionist Profile was ideally suited to passing on God's messages to Pharaoh. However, Moses did not understand the significance of the messenger strategy until the interchange of the third plague.

To counter the ego strength of the High D personality, and to give him the greatest assistance in growing and maturing, a tag-team system must be used. One individual in the team must be committed to wearing the black hat and the other individual must be committed to functioning as a diplomatic messenger who continually communicates the will of the confronter. The hope is that the High D will change directions over time. The important issue is to remain in communication. A real danger does exist, though. The High D may "kill" the messenger. After his first encounter with Pharaoh, Moses faced this issue:

> Moses returned to the Lord and said, "O Lord, why have you brought trouble upon this people? Is this why you sent me? Ever since I went to Pharaoh to speak in your name, he has brought trouble upon this people, and you have not rescued your people at all." (vv. 22-23)

Once the messenger system is used, all efforts must be made to support the messenger, if the strategy is to be successful. Observe the reassurances God gave Moses:

> Then the Lord said to Moses, "Now you will see what I will do to Pharaoh: Because of my mighty hand he will let them go; because of my mighty hand he will drive them out of his country." (6:1)

THE THREE R'S IN LOVING THE HIGH D

In order to increase our ability to relate to and love High D's, we must understand their need system. Remember, a High D often wants control, freedom to operate, limited supervision, variety of activities, challenges, and instructions in ten words or less with a bottom line.

Below are nine principles in knowing how to respond to, relate to, and reinforce the High D.

HOW TO RESPOND TO A HIGH D
- Be firm and direct
- Focus on actions and goals
- Caring confrontation may be necessary to get his attention

HOW TO RELATE TO A HIGH D
- Be brief and to the point
- Explain "How to achieve goals"
- Allow him time to consider your ideas

HOW TO REINFORCE THE HIGH D
- Have the messenger repeat the plan of action, focusing on goals, objectives, and results
- Give bottom-line instructions
- Get out of his way

An example from the life of the apostle Paul gives insight into the positive resolution to a confrontation with a High D. Before Paul's conversion to Christ, he was known as Saul, a Pharisee dedicated to his career and to the persecution of the first-century church. Though most people would consider Saul's behavior as a negative illustration of the High D personality style, our emphasis here is on describing High D traits in action, not in commenting on the rightness or wrongness of what Paul did. Our discussion will follow the outline of the nine guidelines given just above.

ACCEPT THE FACT THAT THEY ARE DRIVEN BY CHALLENGING GOALS

High D's are usually driven by challenging goals. If their environment prevents their achieving those goals, a negative reaction may result. Most D's, particularly Pioneer Patterns, fear not becoming as influential as they would like. This fear is often related to their personal goals being blocked or progress toward a future position or objective being challenged.

The apostle Paul was driven to become the best among his peers, the Pharisees. He was committed to doing whatever it took to advance his career. In Acts 22:3 Paul gives some background on his early life: "I am a Jew, born in Tarsus of Cilicia, but brought up in this city [Jerusalem]. Under Gamaliel I was thoroughly trained in the law of our fathers and was just as zealous for God as any of you are today."

Paul was from the tribe of Benjamin, bilingual in Hebrew and Greek, and a Roman citizen. At about the age of twenty, he attended the rabbinical school of the Pharisees and was tutored by Gamaliel, who, at that time, was the most respected teacher of the law. Paul had all the qualifications to ascend to the top —possibly even seeking the position of high priest.

However, on Paul's path to success, a new group emerged as competition—the followers of Jesus Christ. After the stoning of Stephen at the hands of the Pharisees, Paul saw the opportunity to advance his career and became a leader committed to eliminating the followers of Christ. His zeal made him extremely popular with the high priest. Obsessed with pursuing his goal, Paul, as a Pioneer Pattern, tended to see others as objects rather than people. In his thinking, it was no problem to bend the rules to eliminate the believers in Christ, even if that meant giving false testimony. Achieving the goal meant everything to him.

THEY PREFER BEING IN CHARGE AND RESIST BEING RESTRAINED

In their need for control, Pioneer Patterns prefer positions of power that provide unusual opportunities. Their drive for the unusual is further stimulated if the challenge includes something rare or different and causes them to go where no one else has gone. They also seek to be released from constraints that might block the achievement of their goal. They have the ability to methodically work within a system and secure total control.

In Acts 9:1-2, we pick up Paul's activities, "Meanwhile, Saul was still breathing out murderous threats against the Lord's disciples. He went to the high priest and asked him for letters to the synagogues in Damascus, so that if he found any there who belonged to the Way, whether men or women, he might take them as prisoners to Jerusalem."

A pastor and Greek scholar, Mike Kempainen, made a study of Paul's behavior showing how the Pioneer Pattern got out of control in Paul's case and how the Lord created the right environment for change to take place in Paul's life. Below are Dr. Kempainen's insights on Paul (Kempainen is using the *New American Standard Bible*):

> The background to this incident in Acts 9 is Saul's leading the persecution against believers in Acts 8:3.
>
> But Saul began ravaging the church, entering house after house; and dragging off men and women, he would put them in prison.
>
> "Saul," it says [in Acts 9:1], was still "breathing threats and murder" against any and every believer he could find. The "still" which begins the verse shows that some time had elapsed since the murder of Stephen, and Saul had not let up on his vicious attack at all. The Greek words used in this verse speak of "inhaling" these threats, which make it even more intense.
>
> The verb in verse 2 [of Acts 9] indicates that he asked the High Priest (as a favor to himself) for authority to do his "bounty hunting" of believers. Since Rome had given the Sanhedrin Council civil authority over Jews in foreign cities, he requested that this authority be given to him personally. He was asking for blanket permission to carry on persecutions with legal authority, and his intentions were toward both men and women, without distinction.

So intense was Paul's hatred for Christ and His followers that he (a Pharisee) asked permission from the High
Priest (a Saduccee) to render any and every believer he could
find helpless ("bound") and drag them back to Jerusalem for
trial and a sure death. Paul himself refers to this cruelty in
Acts 22:4, and [it] is probably a reason for his referring to
himself as the "chief of sinners" in I Timothy 1:15.

It is difficult to realize that this is the same person who
would later in life become such a strong advocate for Christ. A
significant event had to occur in Paul's life to cause him to
change so radically. It did—on the road to Damascus. By that
encounter Paul was given a chance for positive change.

CONFRONTATION MAY BE NECESSARY TO GET THEIR ATTENTION

The High D is interested in direction and action, rather
than relationships. Because he has high ego strength there is a
risk of this trait getting out of control. We will see later that the
High I responds best to a favorable, fun-loving environment.
But in the case of the High D, the best environment is straightforward and bottom line. There are times when backing away
from a High D is a viable strategy, but experience has confirmed that being willing to make a loving confrontation will in
most cases help a relationship with a High D.

In the case of Paul, God intended him to be a leader in
bringing the gospel to the Gentiles. He had become knowl-
edgeable in the Scriptures and could effectively teach the Word
to the non-Jewish world. In Galatians 1:14-15, Paul gives us
further insight into his background.

I was advancing in Judaism beyond many Jews of my own age
and was extremely zealous for the traditions of my fathers.
But when God, who set me apart even from birth and called
me by His grace, was pleased to reveal His Son in me so that
I might preach Him among the Gentiles, I did not consult
any man, nor did I go up to Jerusalem to see those who were
apostles before I was, but I went immediately into Arabia and
later returned to Damascus.

Before his conversion Saul sought to destroy the church totally, thinking he was doing the will of the Lord. He got reinforcement from his superiors and peers that his actions were justified. He reveled in the prestige and power that his new position of authority provided. As cold and insensitive as he appeared to be in dealing with the believers of "the Way," he could have actually enjoyed this assignment. His destructive activities were not what God wanted, and a confrontation resulting in a radical change in his direction was imminent.

Saul was on a mission to Damascus to arrest more believers and bring them back to Jerusalem. He had successfully obtained a letter from the high priest giving him complete power in dealing with the disciples of Christ. Then, during his journey to Damascus, there suddenly appeared a flashing light from the sky. The light was so bright it blinded him. Saul was stopped in his tracks, neutralizing his ability to proceed. But because his hearing was not affected, he had no choice but to listen. And it was at that point that Jesus worked an incredible change in Paul's life.

BE FIRM AND DIRECT AND FOCUS
ON HOW THEIR ACTIONS AFFECT YOU

Once a High D has been confronted, it is critical to focus on how his actions directly affect you rather than entering into a personality attack on him. Such an attack will usually yield an ego reaction rather than a productive response. Notice how Jesus confronted Paul directly about his actions: "Saul! Saul! Why do you persecute me?" (Acts 22:7).

BE BRIEF AND TO THE POINT

High D's want to get to the bottom line as soon as possible. Jesus dealt with Paul immediately and concisely.

After the confrontation, Paul had the presence of mind to ask a question in hopes of clarifying what was going on. "Who are you, Lord?" he asked. Jesus' response to the question is only twenty-eight words in the *New International Version,* but in that response Jesus communicated who He was, how Paul's activities were affecting Him, and what He wanted Paul to do first. He also promised him more information once he arrived in Damascus. "I am Jesus of Nazareth, whom you are persecuting. . . . Get up . . . and go into Damascus. There you will be told all that you have been assigned to do" (vv. 8-10).

ALLOW THEM TIME TO COOL DOWN
TO REFLECT ON YOUR IDEAS

The emotional shock of his blindness effectively limited Paul's physical activities. In fact, he was not able to eat or drink for three days. However, it appears that his mind was clear during this time to think, analyze, and ponder what might happen next. The Lord chose to leave Paul in this blindness until he was ready for redirection.

One of the questions we ask in a small group exercise is this: *As you reflect on the environment Jesus created for Paul in Acts, do you think He was too harsh in what He did?*

High D's consistently report that the Lord's confrontational approach was not too harsh. In fact, they think the direct approach that Jesus used was entirely appropriate. It is also noteworthy to add that in these small group discussions, High D's express the opinion that it is very useful to allow them time to analyze and reflect on their options.

THE MESSENGER

The benefit of the messenger system is twofold. First, it neutralizes the potential for further ego conflict between the confronter and the High D. Second, the messenger or arbitrator can reconfirm on a rational basis the goals and objectives of the confronter. The messenger is generally in a better position to communicate positive messages back and forth while allowing the High D's ego to remain healthy and the confronter's resolve to remain intact.

In Acts 9, Ananias, a local believer, is given the assignment of confirming his association with Jesus and his knowledge of Paul's encounter with Him. Ananias's message was brief; however, it included Paul's healing and the receiving of the Holy Spirit, a second messenger.

> "Brother Saul, the Lord—Jesus, who appeared to you on the road as you were coming here—has sent me so that you may see again and be filled with the Holy Spirit." (v. 17b)

Paul did regain his sight; he rose, was baptized, took food, and was strengthened. He fellowshipped with the disciples and immediately began proclaiming Jesus as the Son of God.

BE PREPARED FOR THEM TO MAKE QUICK CHANGES

High D's will commonly do an about face quicker than any other profiles. They can become as zealous for a new direction as they were for the previous one. Acts 9:20 states concerning Paul, "At once he began to preach in the synagogues that Jesus is the Son of God."

With this capacity to make rapid changes comes the tendency to begin the new crusade at an even higher level of intensity than the earlier one. This was the case with Paul, and it created additional problems for him. Paul's ministry efforts immediately after his conversion caused so much conflict that he had to leave Damascus secretly under death threats. Paul needed to learn how to be more patient before he could launch out in the new challenge to reach the Gentiles.

Because of these quick changes, it is often difficult for others to believe in the sincerity of a High D's new direction. Others need time to adjust. Surely that was true of the believers in Jerusalem. They needed time before they were convinced of Paul's conversion. Acts 9:26 confirms, "When he came to Jerusalem, he tried to join the disciples, but they were all afraid of him, not believing that he really was a disciple." God used the High I, Barnabas, to help the believers in Jerusalem adjust to and accept Paul into their fellowship. High D's would benefit from listening to the counsel and cautions of others before launching out in their newfound directions.

UNDERSTAND THEIR GREATEST STRUGGLES

Dealing with pride is probably the High D's greatest hindrance to spiritual maturity. The Bible indicates that often God's strategy for overcoming pride is to allow us to go through personal pain. The Lord used a discomfort referred to by Paul as a "thorn" to constantly remind him of his need for God. In 2 Corinthians 12:7-10, Paul records asking the Lord three times for relief from this "thorn in my flesh" before he understood its purpose.

The person with a Dominance personality has a struggle over turning weaknesses into strengths. It is not uncommon for a High D to develop a plan of action and offer a quick prayer to the Lord to bless it. Learning patience and allowing the Lord to lead in directing their activities is always a good indicator of maturity.

It is also difficult for D's to be part of a team and be in submission to someone else's authority. But if the quality of submissiveness is developed in them, they can become a valuable contributor to a team's success. The athletic arena gives us the best picture of how a team can become successful if individual stars are able to cooperate with the goals of the group.

The apostles Paul and Peter offered two additional principles that are excellent models for us all, but particularly important for the High D.

> Brothers, if someone is caught in a sin, you who are spiritual should restore him gently. But watch yourself, or you also may be tempted. (Galatians 6:1)

> Humble yourselves, therefore, under God's mighty hand, that he may lift you up in due time. Cast all your anxiety on him because he cares for you. (1 Peter 5:6-7)

The risk of humbling himself and losing control is a particularly difficult mountain for the D to climb. But if he does, the rewards can be magnificent.

Paul is the positive model of success through submission to God. Pharaoh is the negative model who shows us that rejecting a necessary confrontation can be fatal. The opportunity to grow and be blessed was available to both men. Paul chose to respond in submission after his first encounter. Pharaoh stubbornly refused and had to be subjected to ten difficult lessons. In the end, Paul won and Pharaoh lost. We have the choice of becoming submissive to God or an object lesson for others.

A WOMAN'S PERSPECTIVE ON THE DOMINANCE PERSONALITY

As we have seen in this chapter, confrontation is a strategy necessary to get a High D's attention. Susan, a Pioneer Profile, and someone familiar with the biblical material on the DISC model, agreed to comment on Acts 9 and how it related to confrontation. Below are her insights:

> You asked for my reactions to the transactions between Paul and Jesus on the road to Damascus. I do not see the encounter as a violent one. Rather it was an act of mercy—the quickest, kindest, and least painful means of bringing Paul to a place of godly repentance. In other words, it was an act of Godly redirection. It was the perfect confrontation for a High D. A fish fry wouldn't have done it [Susan's reference to the way Christ dealt with Peter in John 21]!
>
> I believe Paul thought he was upholding the law of God, but Jesus communicated to him that he was actually persecuting the Lord of Glory. What a shock! That one question—seven words—cut through all the rationalizations and preconceptions Paul had.
>
> This single, insightful statement ("Saul! Saul! Why do you persecute me?") cut cleanly, directly, and precisely to the heart of the matter, and we D's understand this sort of message.
>
> Then Jesus made another statement included in the King James Version. It comes directly after Jesus identifies himself and it reads, "It is hard for you to kick against the goads." From my perspective, I think that Jesus is looking into Paul's heart and saying, "I see your pain, Paul." So few people, including High D's themselves, see their personal pain. We are viewed as tough folks, but we have our pain, too. What Jesus does is identify Paul's vulnerability. What's more important, Jesus is willing to be there alongside him.

All this happens within a couple of minutes. I think it is significant that within the confrontation there is definitely an element of compassion. Paul needed both and so do I.

What Other People Had to Say About the High D

What do you consider to be most difficult when relating to the High D?

High D: "It's no problem for us to become confrontational; however, our body language and tone of voice sometimes becomes a catalyst for escalating events into an all out war."

High I: "Providing short answers, sticking to their plan, and being committed to a goal without a relationship is hard for me to relate to."

High S: "Using confrontation and having to respond quickly is so out of character for me."

High C: "Being brief! . . . You have to be kidding. We feel a compelling need to give out all the details.

What can you do to build a better relationship with the High D's?

High D: "Continue to talk straight with them, but know when to back off."

High I: "Modify our need for a totally unstructured environment."

High S: "Be willing to risk change and security."

High C: "Be willing to modify the rules and structure if it doesn't sacrifice quality."

Where do you most need the talents of the High D?

High D: "Knowing and feeling their commitment to goals."

High I: "Their energy and ability to complete the job."

High S: "Their ability to stand up for a commitment."

High C: "Their ability to be decisive at a critical point in getting a project done. We High C's have a tendency to want to continue to do more planning. However, D's have the inner confidence to say, 'Quit researching and just do it!'"

REACTIONS FROM THE MEMBERS OF THE HIGH D FAMILY

High D's have a special gift for discerning problems and devising strategies to correct them. They cause things to happen and work well in an unfavorable environment. As with any profile, excessive reactions can and do occur. The example we have covered involving Jesus' interaction with Paul in Acts 9 is intended to give insights into helping the High D work through stressful times.

The following comments are from other High D's who were willing to give us their insights on how to love them through tough times and respond to their needs.

When you are under stress, what is the most responsive thing we can do for you?

High D Pattern: "Talk to me about what you want me to do and not about abstract feelings."

High D/I Pattern: "If I need correction, give me affirmation, then correct the action . . . but don't make it a personal attack."

"In the home, I desire emphasis on relationships and not perfection in decor, food, or table settings."

"Depends . . . sometimes I need to talk, while at other times I just need to go out and beat up on a golf ball."

D equal I Pattern: "Listen to me and then ask questions. If I get too loud, it's OK to hit me with a 2 x 4. I need it sometimes!"

"I oftentimes am forceful and loud. I may express some radical options that I really don't mean, so don't take me too seriously."

High D/C Pattern: "Give me the opportunity to think through issues before expecting me to react."

"Leave me alone to mull over my options. When I'm ready to talk, I'll let you know."

It must be understood that High D's are motivated by achieving goals and objectives, unlike the High I's, who are motivated by interacting with people. D's desire to be in control as they achieve their goals. When communicating with them, it is good strategy to do so on those terms. Confrontation is often necessary to get their attention, but it would be naive to expect them to thank you for it. At best, you might see a change in direction.

A Look Ahead

It is encouraging to know that following Paul's conversion to Christ, his negative drives were transformed into a positive force. Paul had grown up in a society dominated by a works-oriented religion. God selected Paul for the unusual assignment of presenting something new—a grace-oriented faith—to the Gentiles. Paul's submission to God helped evangelize the world for Christ. Without his obedience and commitment to follow through on the challenge, we might not have had the opportunity to trust Christ ourselves. High D's have an important place in God's plan.

SEVEN

UNDERSTANDING THE INFLUENCING STYLE

Whereas the Dominance personality style sets his sights on leading an army, others are needed to inspire the troops to give their all. Whereas the High D strives to set the pace, the Influencing personality initiates with poise and persuasion. High I's have the ability to provide practical insight to assist and encourage others to carry on, especially when they are discouraged.

Within team sports, blending different personality styles helps to balance successfully reaching goals and achieving team unity. For example, a head coach of an NBA team described the strategy his coaching staff used to build his team into a consistent play-off contender. Put into the terminology of this book, the coaching staff combined the dominance abilities of the High D with the influencing abilities of the High I.

The head coach was a High D. He led the team of mostly High S (steadiness) players in a fashion similar to a Napoleon general. He gave emphatic directions and demanded discipline when carrying out team goals on the court. The assistant coach was a High I influencer. When players got tired or discouraged, his job was to offer understanding and inspiration. He was always optimistic and developed personal relationships with individuals on the team. If the head coach was harsh in dealing with a player, the assistant coach came alongside with encouragement to press on. As coaches, these two men complemented each other's style and were successful in accomplishing the mission of building a strong basketball team.

Throughout history, God has used High I's to accomplish His mission. Who helped Moses persuade Pharaoh to release the Israelites? Who was appointed king of the Hebrew nation at a critical time its history? Who helped establish the first-century church? Who encouraged discouraged disciples? The Influencers—Aaron, David, Peter, and Barnabas. These were leaders God called who had the High I style of working with others. They were concerned not just with results in a mission but with relating to the people who carried out the missions.

High I behavioral styles generally have a positive outlook on life. They are expressive, enthusiastic, and the life of any party. Being adept at conversation, they seldom have difficulty meeting people. Because of their social skills, they have a strong ability to move others to agree with them in a friendly manner.

Out of the sixteen Representative Patterns described in our DISC model, four are identified as High I Patterns. They are listed below, followed in parenthesis with the abbreviations indicating the primary and the secondary styles that make up the pattern. In the next column are names of the positive biblical models that represent each pattern.

Classical Pattern	Biblical Character
Affiliator (primary I)	Aaron, King Saul
Persuader (I/D)	Peter, Rebekah
Encourager (I/S)	Barnabas, Abigail
Negotiator (I/C)	David, Mary Magdalene

GENERAL TENDENCIES OF THE INFLUENCING PERSONALITY

HAS A STRONG CAPACITY FOR
TRUSTING AND ACCEPTING OTHERS

Because of their emphasis on people and relationships, High I's have an unusual capacity to trust others and project unconditional acceptance toward a wide range of people. When others might give up on someone, the I sees potential (see table 12). They will express encouragement and hope when other people are ready to "throw in the towel." The continuum below contrasts the High I's capacity to trust with the other DISC styles:

Table 12

Projecting Trust Continuum

greater trust --- lesser trust

I	S	D	C

I   Believes in others unconditionally

S   Makes assessment of others balanced by objectivity

D   Tends to distrust others and puts limits on personal
     contact

C   Suspicious of others unless past performance indicates
     trust is warranted

SOURCE: Adapted from Life Associates, Inc., The *DISC Model: Trainer and Consultant's Reference Encyclopedia.*

Within the High I family of Representative Patterns, those who possess the Encourager Profile show the greatest capacity for accepting someone perceived as an outcast. The best example of an Encourager style in the Bible is Barnabas. Even though he did not pen a word of Scripture that we are aware of, we owe much of the New Testament to him. Without his belief in and encouragement of Paul and John Mark, the Acts of the Apostles might have been much different, and we would not have the Pauline letters and the gospel according to Mark.

Nine years after Paul had been run out of Jerusalem (following his conversion), Barnabas, whose very name means "son of encouragement," traveled from his church in Antioch to Paul's hometown of Tarsus. There he found the tentmaker Paul and encouraged him to embark on the mission for which God had called him. Barnabas brought him back to Antioch to give testimony before the leaders of the church in Jerusalem. Following this, Paul entered into active service for the Lord. (Acts 11).

Later, in Acts 15, Barnabas demonstrates the same capacity for acceptance by trusting John Mark even though he had deserted Paul and Barnabas on the first missionary journey. You may recall that Paul (the High D) refused to allow Mark to accompany them on the second journey because of his abandoning them during the first trip. He would not give John Mark a second chance. But Barnabas extended the hand of encouragement to John Mark just as he had done years earlier to Paul himself. The disagreement over this matter was the primary reason Paul and Barnabas went their separate ways on the sec-

Table 13

Tendency to be Affectionate, Approachable, and Understanding Continuum

greater -- lesser

I	S	C	D

I   Accepts, appreciates, and is affectionate toward others

S   Approachable, but tends to use caution before accepting others

C   Tactful and diplomatic, but reserves affection for those close to them

D   Will approach others when they have a need for help on a task (generally not viewed as approachable)

SOURCE: Adapted from Life Associates, Inc., The *DISC Model: Trainer and Consultant's Reference Encyclopedia.*

ond missionary journey. Barnabas took John Mark with him on a different mission venture (Acts 15).

IS AFFECTIONATE, APPROACHABLE, AND UNDERSTANDING

As you can see, High I's are most comfortable when they are relating to and interacting with people in a positive, friendly environment. They have excellent verbal skills and send out nonverbal signals indicating that they can be easily approached (table 13).

IS SOCIALLY ORIENTED

"Dad," the excited daughter began, "I've figured out a way to talk to two of my friends on the phone at the same time! Thanks for adding that new service from the phone company!" she added. That was probably the most important discovery of the year for this fifteen-year-old. As a High I, she possessed a natural drive for relating to others socially. "Oh, by the way," she continued, "on Friday I'm going to the overnight lock-in party at the church, and on Saturday night Anna is coming over to spend the night." A person can get tired just listening to a High I's social calendar.

POTENTIAL BLIND SPOTS OF THE HIGH I

NEED FOR PERSONAL RECOGNITION

Tensions can occur when a High I must share attention with another, for the need for recognition is a strong force in his life. This is illustrated in an incident in 1 Samuel 18. Saul and David had fought as a team against the Philistines and were so successful that a song was written in their honor.

As [the women] danced, they sang:

"Saul has slain his thousands,
    and David his tens of thousands."

Saul was very angry; this refrain galled him. "They have credited David with tens of thousands," he thought, "but me with only thousands. What more can he get but the kingdom?" And from that time on Saul kept a jealous eye on David. (vv. 7-9)

Sharing the stage with David was extremely difficult for Saul. His inability to control this weakness produced jealousy and distrust. David was mature enough to always honor Saul as king. However, Saul had difficulty handling David's popularity. Saul's inability to deal with this problem ultimately destroyed him.

NEED FOR SOCIAL ACCEPTANCE

The need for recognition is one of the most important measurements of a High I's' self-acceptance. Without it a High I feels empty. An important lesson for High I's to learn, as well as us all, is that a need for lasting acceptance can only be fulfilled in a personal relationship with Jesus Christ. Looking to others to fulfill this need will lead to compromise and failure.

Mylon LeFevre is a prominent Christian recording artist who leads Broken Heart Ministries. Through his concert ministry across the country he has been used of God to lead thousands of people to Christ. But Christ was not always the source of acceptance for Mylon.

For over a decade he sought acceptance and recognition within the secular world of rock and roll music. And to some extent he achieved that acceptance and recognition. He acquired fame and fortune through the sales of his albums and through having the songs he wrote recorded by such stars as Elvis Presley. He traveled around the world with famous bands and had whatever he wanted in terms of popularity and material possessions. But he also had a drug and drinking problem that nearly destroyed his life.

Mylon warns, "For many years the driving force behind my success within rock music was wanting to be recognized and accepted by others. Only by my performance was I considered someone special. Along with this recognition came the opportunity and pressure to get involved with drugs. At first I had control of myself and what I could handle. Eventually, my ability to choose was gone and I became a slave to drugs and its destructive forces. My need was never satisfied. I did not experience personal peace and freedom until I was willing to allow Jesus' love and acceptance to take control me. That is when I realized true acceptance and meaningful success."

FEAR OF SOCIAL REJECTION

If nothing stimulates the High I more than being publicly accepted, nothing is more likely to create intense fear than is the prospect of social rejection. Social rejection can destroy the confidence of a High I. Just facing the *possibility* of being rejected is enough to cause major tension in his life. If this fear is not controlled, it can lead to failure.

In 1 Samuel 15, the Lord instructs Saul to destroy the nation of Amalek and afterward take no spoils. However, Saul succumbed to the pressure of the people and saved some of the choicest spoils for himself and others. Because of this failure of obedience, Samuel, God's spokesman, reported to Saul that his leadership would be given to another.

Saul attempted to offer explanations for his actions but was unsuccessful in defending himself. Samuel did allow the king to achieve a temporary reprieve by agreeing to walk with him in front of his people so that it would *appear* that Saul was still in good standing with God, but this moment of reprieve was short-lived. Eventually irrational fears and emotional instability took control of Saul. When it became obvious to him that David had become the Lord's replacement as king, he became emotionally unstable and obsessed with killing David. His compromise in the incident in 1 Samuel 15 and his inability to control his pathological fear of David's prominence led to Saul's destruction.

The High I can be helped to control fears of this nature if he is willing to admit his need and seek counsel from others.

TENDENCY TOWARD DISORGANIZATION

Nothing gets in the way of a High I's drive to socialize —not even the simple chores and organizational duties of daily living. Remember the socially oriented teenager above? Listen to her as she tries to get out of doing the dishes. " Mom, I can't load the dishwasher. I have to go do my homework." It sounded admirable, so Mom proceeded to handle the dish chores for the evening.

Later, when Mom looked in on her daughter, a telephone —and not a book—was in her hand. Since High I's tend to rely upon their verbal skills and quick thinking, the teenage daughter responded, "Well, I've just had a terrible day, and I had to talk to Cheryl because she needed to know about . . ." And so on, and so on.

Excuses and good intentions often keep the High I from being productive and achieving his potential. It is not unusual for a High I to have several major projects lying around the house or in the office waiting to be completed. High I's never have sufficient time to finish the projects—and if they are challenged about their reasons, they are likely to react defensively. They are quick to offer what they believe are justifiable reasons for their not completing tasks.

This difficulty with organization causes many High I's to lose or misplace items. In *Personality Plus* Florence Littauer describes taking a survey of the things one High I group reported missing. The list included over four hundred articles lost within a week. Numbered among them were car keys, car, wife, husband, children, and grandmother. Ooops!

Overview of the High I Family
of Representative Patterns

The four Representative Patterns that make up the I Family include *Affiliators, Persuaders, Encouragers,* and *Negotiators.* Although these four patterns all project High I tendencies, they are different from one another. The Affiliator Pattern exhibits the most pure tendencies of the influencing style. The Persuader, although verbally expressive, has the added dimension of

Table 14
Primary High I Pattern

I. Distinctive tendencies of this pattern:

Primary drive	Creating a favorable, friendly environment
Personal giftedness	Quick of tongue, special ability to affirm and encourage others
Group giftedness	Relieving tension, articulating information
Potential spiritual gifts	Helps, Hospitality, Mercy
Internal fear	Public or social rejection
Strength out of control	Speaking without thinking
Under stress becomes	Careless and disorganized
Blind spots	Remembering past commitments
Needs to work on	Remaining objective when encountering social pressure
Best team members	Pure C, C/S, C/S/D, S/C

II. Biblical characters who represent this pattern:

1. Aaron
2. King Saul

III. Further Bible study:

Strengths	Ex. 4:14, 27-31; 6:28–7:2
Weaknesses	Ex. 20:1-2; 24:1-24; 32:1-6, 21-24; 1 Sam. 15:1-3, 7-9, 13-30

dominance and is gifted in the salesmanship skills of the seller and the closer. The Encourager is the most rational of the group and seeks to build harmony. The Negotiator is the most emotionally intense of the group and has a bent toward creative style and flair. These subtle difference are crucial to understanding the uniqueness of the four High I Patterns.

THE AFFILIATOR (PRIMARY I)

POSITIVE TRAITS

Of the sixteen Representative Patterns, the Affiliator (table 14) possesses the greatest natural ability to express verbal approval and acceptance. Affiliator Profiles truly have a gift for verbal communication. This skill is extremely important to High C's, who have difficulty expressing themselves. Moses, the High C, used his inability to speak as a reason for not accepting the Lord's calling. But God had already solved the problem by preparing his brother to meet him. Listen to the Lord's words describing Aaron's behavior: "I know he can speak well. He is already on his way to meet you, and his heart will be glad when he sees you" (Exodus 4:14b).

Affiliators are second to none in conveying encouragement and acceptance. What a positive influence Aaron must have been to Moses, who had to endure forty years in a desert with a people who would seldom express appreciation.

PERSONAL GIFTEDNESS

Individuals with the Affiliator Pattern are extremely skilled in getting others to support a project or cause. When the Ammonites challenged the unorganized tribes of Israel, Saul used a symbol of a broken oxen yoke to unite the nation and form an army. He formed three companies and was successful in defeating the Ammonites. When they receive their credit, Affiliators will use praise of others as a way of expressing their appreciation for any successes. Following the Ammonite campaign, the people gave sole credit to Saul. Saul corrected them and gave thanks to the Lord for the victory.

Table 15
High I/D Pattern

I. Distinctive tendencies of this pattern:

Primary drive	Independence, uninhibited risk taker
Personal giftedness	Friendly manner, verbal and nonverbal adeptness
Group giftedness	Reading people's needs and persuading them to action
Potential spiritual gifts	Evangelism, Hospitality, Exhortation
Internal fear	Being rejected by friends
Strength out of control	Overconfident in self, verbalizes without direction
Under stress becomes	Stubborn, argumentative, and verbally reckless
Blind spots	Connecting past events and commitments with present actions
Needs to work on	Attending to details, follow-through
Best team members	S, S/C, S/D, SCI

II. Biblical characters who represent this pattern:

1. Peter
2. Rebekah

III. Further Bible study:

Strengths	Acts 2:11-47; 3:1-26; 4:1-22
Weaknesses	Matt. 26:31-35, 69-75

STRENGTH OUT OF CONTROL

When they make mistakes, Affiliators will frequently use the praise of others in an effort to cover up their errors. In 1 Samuel 15:13, Saul uses this tactic on Samuel by complimenting him for no apparent reason but flattery. The Lord enabled Samuel to discern the truth and respond accordingly. Another reaction of Affiliators is to shift to others the blame for their own mistakes. In 15:15-20 Saul also tries this tactic by trying to blame the people for being disobedient, rather than taking the responsibility on himself where it belonged. Once again, Samuel saw through Saul's attempt to make an excuse. The stories of a Promoter can be so convincing they often get away with acting irresponsibly.

THE PERSUADER (I/D)

POSITIVE TRAITS

Persuaders (table 15) have the special ability to reach out to strangers with openness and a friendly spirit. They naturally speak to anyone, can quickly discern needs, and warmly extend a helping hand to others. In Genesis 24:12-20, Rebekah's initial encounter with Abraham's servant is a classic example of a Persuader reaching out to a stranger. She responded to the servant's need for water and also satisfied the thirst of his camels. Little did she know that God was working through her actions. Physical contact is also a natural trait of the Persuader style. They are quick to shake hands, give hugs, pat shoulders, and kiss cheeks. In Acts 3, the action of Peter grasping the hand of a lame man and raising him up as he was being healed is an example of the Persuader's natural tendency for reaching out through touch.

PERSONAL GIFTEDNESS

Persuaders are gifted communicators and are particularly comfortable in making impromptu speeches that are personalized to the needs of any group. They have an additional gift in knowing when to capitalize on the momentum generated by their verbal persuasion. In Acts 2 Peter takes an opportunity to preach and his message causes three thousand people to make a decision for Jesus. This ability is known as possessing a closer skill in getting others to make a favorable decision. As mentioned previously, Peter used the healing of a lame man to present the gospel of Christ to a gathering of Jews (Acts 3). So persuasive was his message on this occasion that five thousand men made a decision to follow Christ (Acts 4:4).

STRENGTH OUT OF CONTROL

Persuaders tend to listen selectively. They often react to the first few words of a speaker and then inappropriately offer comments out of context. In Matthew 16 Jesus asks the disciples to respond to the question explaining the nature of His identity. Peter boldly answered, "You are the Christ, the Son of the living God." He was right; Jesus commended him and foretold of a leadership role Peter would have in the church. Jesus then proceeded to explain how He would die on the cross and later be raised from the dead. Because Peter wasn't patient enough to hear the whole message, he reacted by trying to assert that he could prevent Christ's going to the cross. It was a good intention, but completely out of context. The Lord publicly rebuked Peter. Persuaders need to monitor this tendency to get carried away with their own momentum.

THE ENCOURAGER (I/S)

POSITIVE TRAITS

Encouragers (table 16) are approachable, affectionate, and understanding. A person with problems usually feels comfortable talking to them since counselors generally have good listening skills and are sensitive to feelings. Encouragers are also gifted with the ability to see the good in others, rather than just look for their faults. Barnabas was used by God to encourage two significant writers of the New Testament, the apostle Paul and John Mark. Barnabas listened, evaluated, and made a con-

Table 16
High I/S Pattern

I. Distinctive tendencies of this pattern:

Primary drive	Maintaining peace and harmony
Personal giftedness	Seeing the potential in people in spite of their flaws
Group giftedness	Constantly affirming and encouraging others
Potential spiritual gifts	Giving, Helps, Pastor-Teacher
Internal fear	Disappointing friends, Experiencing disharmony
Strength out of control	Being too tolerant and trusting
Under stress becomes	Overly accommodating to maintaining relationships
Blind spots	Determining when a situation is too abusive
Needs to work on	Being more objective about people and situations
Best team members	D/C, C/D, S/C/D

II. Biblical characters who represent this pattern:

1. Barnabas
2. Abigail

III. Further Bible study:

Strengths	Acts 9:26-29, 1 Sam. 25:3-35
Weaknesses	Acts 15:36-40, 1 Sam. 25:19-36

scious decision to support both of these men when they needed a friend. Paul went on to write thirteen of the twenty-seven books of the New Testament. John Mark would write what many believe to be the first gospel. What is significant to note is that Barnabas saw the potential and encouraged them when no one else would.

PERSONAL GIFTEDNESS

Encouragers possess excellent interpersonal skills along with being stable and dependable. They are often key participants in an informal communication system and generally exert positive influence because of their optimistic attitudes. The Jerusalem church was so impressed with Joseph's positive attitude that they changed his name to Barnabas, which means "son of encouragement," and later sent him to encourage the new church at Antioch.

Because Encouragers are naturally warm, friendly, and approachable, they make excellent peacemakers. They will seek to resolve conflicts between disagreeing groups by focusing on objective facts and personal insights. Their goal is to maintain friendships and keep everybody happy and satisfied. In Acts 15, Barnabas is a major influence in helping the Jerusalem council work through the problem of accepting Gentiles in the church.

STRENGTH OUT OF CONTROL

Encouragers have a tendency to use an indirect approach and tolerance in dealing with problems. In 1 Samuel 25, Abigail goes around her foolish, drunk husband to protect him from David and his men. She waited until the next day before she told her husband of her actions. This caring nature of an Encourager can become a weakness if overused in situations where establishing firm boundaries would lead to responsible behavior in others.

Table 17
High I/C Pattern

I. Distinctive tendencies of this pattern:

Primary drive	Being innovative with flair and committed to excellence
Personal giftedness	Working through people and having fun
Group giftedness	Inspiring people to be excited about working together and enjoying it
Potential spiritual gifts	Faith, Leadership, Mercy
Internal fear	Coming under public criticism, made to look bad before peers
Strength out of control	Becomes emotionally assertive, competitive, and sometimes reckless
Under stress becomes	Impatient, critical, and emotionally intense
Blind spots	Being rational when under emotional stress
Needs to work on	Controlling mood swings, being more tolerant of the "shoulds" and "should nots"
Best team members	S/C, S/C/D, C/S, I/S

II. Biblical characters who represent this pattern:

1. David
2. Mary Magdalene (*)

III. Further Bible study:

Strengths	1 Sam. 16:18; 18:5-8, 20-30
Weaknesses	2 Sam. 11:1-27; 12:1-24

*Not enough information to be absolutely certain of the specific style.

THE NEGOTIATOR PATTERN (I/C)

POSITIVE TRAITS

Negotiators (table 17) are highly driven to win but prefer to achieve their victories by working with and through people. They usually have the charisma to persuade team members to join them in achieving their personal goals and objectives. However, Negotiators are committed to the "win-win" philosophy. They strive to succeed with flair and style, but truly desire that others be a part of any success achieved. David typified this behavior in getting his men to help him complete the dowry required for him to marry Saul's daughter. The requirement was the foreskins of one hundred Philistines. In typical I/C style, David and his men brought in two hundred. The presentation was made by David and his men while King Saul was officiating over his full court (1 Samuel 18). This is an example of winning with style!

PERSONAL GIFTEDNESS

Negotiators have the gift of making others feel like important and valued members of the team. They are committed to communicating the point that the efforts of others really count toward achieving a team's goals. This can result in increased morale and productivity. David had a reputation among his peers for being an extremely wise, charismatic leader, and his soldiers considered it a privilege to serve under him. Whatever David attempted, victory was expected and usually assured. So popular was his style that the women wrote a song about him. Scripture records that David's name became highly esteemed throughout the nation of Israel.

UNDER STRESS

I/C's must contend with two emotions, one positive and one negative, that continually pull at them. They are driven by both a need for close relationships and a need to accomplish tasks. Under pressure, these two drives produce a person who acts like a coiled, quivering spring. They can become restless, impatient, and aggressive. It is common for them to walk or jog to release stress. In 2 Samuel 11, David was in Jerusalem awaiting word from Joab, his general, about the campaign against Ammon. He became restless and decided to walk on the roof of his house to relieve his tension. He saw Bathsheba taking a bath, and his emotional need got away from him. His later actions led to adultery, deception, and the murder of an innocent man—all of that because David was unable to control his response to pressure. Negotiators need to learn the art of relaxation in order to guard against being driven to burn out.

A LOOK AHEAD

Now that we have examined the High I family of Representative Patterns, we can appreciate the uniqueness of this personality style. Further understanding of the ways in which people with Influencing patterns can be misunderstood will help to improve the quality of our interactions with them.

EIGHT

RESPONDING TO THE NEEDS OF THE INFLUENCING PERSONALITY

As a marriage therapist, I (Ron) frequently see couples whose difficulty with communication is influenced by the degree of difference in their behavioral styles. Bill and Carolyn had experienced one struggle after another in their twelve years of marriage. As a High C Perfectionist, Bill preferred stability and order. He also expected orderliness from his wife. Carolyn, a High I Persuader, enjoyed being spontaneous and preferred involvement with a variety of people and activities.

Early in their marriage, Bill could not understand why Carolyn acted the way she did. He experienced conflict when Carolyn did not plan and complete her tasks in a timely fashion. He expected her to be home during the daytime accomplishing household responsibilities so that she could be at his side in the evenings while he watched television or read the newspaper. In the beginning, Carolyn really tried to be the wife Bill wanted her to be. She kept the house as clean as she could, had dinner ready on time, and spent many evenings together with him. Carolyn made attempts to involve Bill in some of her interests but was not very successful in getting him away from the house.

As the years passed, Carolyn's suppressed need to be with people and to enjoy activities outside the home began to surface. Gradually she took on responsibilities and projects that required her to be gone in the evenings. People at church or in the community began to seek out Carolyn's participation because she would always add life to their programs. As she became more involved, she found the recognition she received from others very rewarding, whereas at home she felt taken for granted and unappreciated.

As Carolyn became more involved in activities outside the home, Bill became more and more frustrated. He began to think Carolyn cared more about others' needs than those of the family's. He was unsure how to address the problem and developed a passive resistance to Carolyn. He found himself criticizing her and voicing complaints about a messy house. When this did not do any good, Bill gradually closed himself off from his wife. Finally, he decided to make a point and express his angry feelings in one demonstrative act. What he did led Carolyn to demand that they either seek counseling or seek a divorce.

In our first counseling session, Carolyn described what took place.

> One of the responsibilities I had taken on was being president of the PTA at my children's school. If I were totally honest, I enjoyed the recognition more than the work. However, I was committed to do my best. It was nice hearing that the principal and teachers liked my ideas and were willing to help me try some new things to get other parents involved. Bill never said that he didn't want me to take this position, but I knew he felt it was too big a commitment for me to undertake.
>
> Everything was going great until the day of our first PTA meeting. I had been so busy that week that somehow I had forgotten to plan for the meeting. I thought that would not be a problem—I would just spend the day working on the program and give it my best effort! I was so caught up in getting ready for the meeting that I did not have time to straighten up our home.
>
> That night I put on my new outfit and went to my meeting. Bill stayed home with the children. I was anxious about the program, but it turned out great! I could hardly wait to get home to tell Bill how great everything had worked out and how many new people I had met. I felt so good!
>
> When I got home, Bill was in our den reading the paper. I went upstairs to change before coming down to tell him how good everything had gone. When I entered our bed-

room, I looked around and could not believe my eyes! Piled on the floor were our clothes. In addition, every item that was not in its usual place was now stacked in the middle of the room. This same scene met me in every single room of our house. I was furious!

After talking to Bill, I found out that he had reached his own emotional limit and decided to make a point. He thought this action would demonstrate to Carolyn how he felt when her outside activities seemed to be more important than home responsibilities. When asked if the point he had made was worth risking his marriage, he replied, "No, not really."

Bill later admitted that he should have used a different method to deal with his anger, but he didn't know what to do. He expressed an interest in learning more about his wife's needs and what he could do to restore his marriage.

The first step I had to take was to help Bill understand himself and then to learn how to respond to Carolyn and her Influencing personality style. Successful efforts to respond to the High I come from understanding how they tend to think, act, and react.

Core Need Issues of the High I

As I was making copies of handouts for a class, Jeff asked me about a situation he was having with one of his children. He had been in the class long enough to have determined that Judy, his daughter, was a High I.

With an uncertain tone in his voice he said, "I don't know what to do with her. She's a High I and is driving me up the wall. She's a good kid but doesn't follow instructions. She says she understands but somehow gets sidetracked. When I confront her, she always has an excuse and blames someone else. I must admit some of her stories are creative. I know what happens—she gets with her friends and tries to please them. She ought to be pleasing me. I'm her father. What do you think?"

What commonly happens in relationships is miscommunication of needs. We frequently impose our need system on others and expect them to react accordingly. When they don't, we push harder, only to become more frustrated. The result is added stress and often the severing of a relationship.

High I's are first, relational creatures. They desire a positive social environment and are particularly sensitive to maintaining a positive social relationship with their peers. The fear of rejection is a real and dynamic force in the life of a High I. We are being unrealistic in expecting them to not let social pressure affect them. Instead, they need our support in dealing with the issue—not our criticism. If this factor does not affect their decision-making process, real maturity has occurred. The following Stress model shows what typically happens to the High I.

COMMON RESPONSES OF THE HIGH I UNDER STRESS

The High I follows a typical pattern when he is under stress (table 18). The following biblical case study will show Aaron, a High I, and Moses in a stress situation with frustrating results. Later in the chapter we will look at Jesus' handling of Peter in a similar stress model but with a positive result.

Table 18

When a High I Encounters Stress

- Clear instructions

- Agreement and commitment by the High I

- Peer pressure to disagree with commitment

- Cave-in to peer pressure

- Confrontation in the form of questions that ask him to explain his actions

- Creative shift-blame

CLEAR INSTRUCTIONS

In Exodus 20:1-17, Moses communicated the Ten Commandments to the nation of Israel. Here is the initial portion of that passage (vv. 1-3):

> And God spoke all these words:
> "I am the Lord your God, who brought you out of Egypt, out of the land of slavery.
> "You shall have no other gods before me.
> "You shall not make for yourself an idol in the form of anything in heaven above or on the earth beneath or in the waters below."

It was completely clear that Israel was to worship only the Lord.

THE AGREEMENT

In Exodus 24 the covenant is publicly ratified, written down, and ratified again with various rituals, including a blood covenant. The Lord revealed Himself to the people and requested that Moses come up the mountain to receive tablets of stone with the commandments written on them. In the meantime, Aaron was instructed to handle any issues involving the application of the law and the people.

SOCIAL PRESSURE

In Exodus 32 Moses is delayed in coming down from the mountain, and the people become restless. They gathered together and suggested to Aaron that they build a god they could worship. Aaron had two choices: (1) apply the first commandment and face rejection or (2) agree to the people's request and have a party.

CAVE-IN TO SOCIAL PRESSURE

Exodus 32:2-6 sadly records that Aaron chose option number 2. Not only did he take part in building the idol, but he suggested the idea of having a feast to commemorate the event. The party turned into a drunken orgy.

THE CONFRONTATIVE QUESTION

God skillfully got Moses to go down the mountain and attempt to correct the problem. Moses did so, but not without a confusing dialogue with Aaron. Moses, the High C, could not understand how this could happen, particularly after the events of Exodus 20 and 24.

Moses handled the situation with the worst possible strategy for dealing with a High I: a direct, confrontational question. In 32:21 he asks, "What did these people do to you, that you led them into such great sin?"

THE SHIFT-BLAME SYNDROME

Aaron did what any High I would do: he gave a highly creative "Who me?" answer.

> Do not be angry, my Lord. . . . You know how prone these people are to evil. They said to me, "Make us gods who will go before us. As for this fellow Moses who brought us up out of Egypt, we don't know what has happened to him." So I told them, "Whoever has any gold jewelry, take it off." Then they gave me the gold, and I threw it into the fire, and out came this calf! (vv. 22-24)

Scripture does not record Moses' response. I am not sure he had one. Who would? You must admit Aaron's response was unique. As I share this story in the various classes, I always get volunteers who are ready to top Aaron. It never ceases to amaze me how verbally creative and convincing a High I can be in shifting the blame to someone else. What you must understand is that they first convince themselves and then work on you. The key is to know how to prevent the exercise from happening in the first place before it gets out of hand.

The 3 R's in Loving the High I

In order to relate to a High I effectively, we need to understand how their needs influence their behavior. Overall, they seem to function best in an environment that is positive and encouraging rather than negative and demanding. Remember the things a High I often wants: social acceptance, freedom of expression, freedom from control, freedom from details, freedom from formal chain-of-command structure, and opportunities for social interaction.

Below are nine principles in knowing how to respond to, relate to, and reinforce the High I.

HOW TO RESPOND TO A HIGH I
- Be friendly and positive
- Allow for informal dialogue
- Allow time for stimulating and fun activities

HOW TO RELATE TO A HIGH I
- Use friendly voice tones
- Allow time for them to verbalize their feelings
- You transfer talk to an action plan

HOW TO REINFORCE THE HIGH I
- Offer positive encouragement and incentives for taking on tasks
- You organize the action plan
- Communicate positive recognition

Jesus followed these principles in His dealings with Peter and his failure to withstand the stress model distinctive for his personality type.

RECOGNIZE THEIR NEED TO BE LEADERS IN GROUPS
AND TO EXPRESS THEMSELVES VERBALLY

High I's enjoy being given leadership roles and have a need to express themselves verbally. When they are in a group discussion, these influencing personalities are generally the first to respond.

Simon Peter is a classic example of a High I leader who took opportunities to speak out. Matthew 16 describes an occasion where Peter made a significant contribution by his insightful response. The opportunity came when Jesus asked His disciples to report on the kind of reactions He was generating as a result of His teaching and miracles.

> When Jesus came to the region of Caesarea Philippi, he asked his disciples, "Who do people say the Son of Man is?"
>
> They replied, "Some say John the Baptist; others say Elijah; and still others, Jeremiah or one of the prophets."
>
> "But what about you?" he asked. "Who do you say I am?"
>
> Simon Peter answered, "You are the Christ, the Son of the living God."
>
> Jesus replied, "Blessed are you, Simon son of Jonah, for this was not revealed to you by man, but by my Father in heaven. And I tell you that you are Peter, and on this rock I will build my church, and the gates of Hades will not overcome it. I will give you the keys of the kingdom of heaven; whatever you bind on earth will be bound in heaven, and whatever you loose on earth will be loosed in heaven." (vv. 13-19)

Jesus blessed Peter for his insightful assessment. He also took this opportunity to declare in front of the other disciples that He would entrust to Peter a leadership position in establishing the church. This must have been a wonderful moment in Peter's life. God had spoken through him and he was commissioned as a leader among his companions. For a High I, receiving such recognition was a personal victory.

RECOGNIZE THEIR TENDENCY TO TEST
BOUNDARIES TO THEIR LIMITS

Along with their need to speak out and gain positions of influence comes a tendency to test and, at times, overstep their boundaries. One way a High I can get "out of bounds" is in offering his opinion when it is not asked for. In Peter's case, after wonderfully expressing the messianic insight, he proceeded to go too far in what he said. The passage occurs in Matthew 16:21-24.

> From that time on Jesus began to explain to his disciples that he must go to Jerusalem and suffer many things at the hands of the elders, chief priests and teachers of the law, and that he must be killed and on the third day be raised to life.
>
> Peter took him aside and began to rebuke him. "Never Lord!" he said. "This shall never happen to you."
>
> Jesus turned and said to Peter, "Get behind me, Satan. You are a stumbling block to me; you do not have in mind the things of God, but the things of men."

Hearing how Jesus would be persecuted by the priests and ultimately killed must have been hard for the disciples to accept. It was at that point that Peter began to get out of line and speak inappropriately. "'Never, Lord!' he said. 'This shall never happen to you'" (16:22).

Peter's first act as leader of the church was to rebuke Jesus! He asserted that he could prevent Jesus from suffering and death. Surely, Peter's motives were right, but he was out of line. Look at the way Jesus responded to him. "Jesus turned and said to Peter, 'Get behind me, Satan! You are a stumbling block to me; you do not have in mind the things of God, but the things of men'" (16:23).

Peter must have gone from feeling on top of the world to being in shock. It was a hard lesson to learn, but he needed to be shown that the human viewpoint is different from the divine viewpoint. At times, it is good to shock a High I back into bounds in order to point out the necessity of recognizing limits.

Jesus closed His discussion with the disciples by describing the true nature of following Him.

> Then Jesus said to His disciples, "If anyone would come after me, he must deny himself and take up his cross and follow Me. For whoever wants to save his life will lose it, but whoever loses his life for me will find it. What good will it be for a man if he gains the whole world, yet forfeits his soul?" (16:24-26)

A commitment to Jesus meant taking up a cross rather than reigning with an earthly crown. Peter needed to heed that message, as do each one of us. Sometimes we want so much to have a good time that we lose sight of the hard work and intense sacrifice necessary to complete a task. On other occasions, we achieve our monetary goals only to find out that we have lost sight of eternal goals.

RECOGNIZE THEIR TENDENCY TO HAVE HIGH LEVELS OF CONFIDENCE IN THEMSELVES AND OTHERS

High I's, particularly I/D's, have a great deal of confidence in their ability to influence others. Therefore, they can accept people as they are and encourage them to move forward, no matter what the obstacles. Environments created by High I's are generally upbeat and can produce great results, especially in business pursuits.

I (Ron) have been associated with several people who have an amazing ability to influence others and to encourage and inspire action.

Duane had such an ability to motivate others. At first he started out in business by selling life insurance. He could take just about any person and in a little time convince him of his need for a policy. His next venture was in setting up residential and commercial real estate partnerships. From there he went into oil and precious metals speculation. Duane became a multimillionaire. It seemed there was no end to his level of confidence in himself and his ability to inspire others. Family and friends wanted to be associated with Duane and share in his good fortune.

It is possible, however, to become overconfident. Persuaders are likely to have too much faith in their abilities and the abilities of others. Too often they believe their personal energy can positively affect the outcome of any situation. Out of control, this optimism can have disastrous consequences.

One morning, a friend called and suggested I get a copy of the morning paper. On the front page was Duane's picture along with a detailed description of how he had gotten involved with a business deal that ended up losing several million dollars. There was nothing unethical about the venture, only a case of Duane's being overconfident in a venture in which he had little experience. It was an expensive lesson, but if you were to talk to Duane today he would probably tell you that he was ready to try again—and he would end up convincing you to try it with him.

At the Last Supper, when Jesus predicted that the disciples would all fall away following His arrest and crucifixion, Peter expressed confidence in his ability to be faithful to Jesus regardless of the outcome: "Even if I have to die with you, I will never disown you" (Mark 14:31). Peter likely believed with all his heart that he would remain faithful no matter what the circumstances might be. Peter was so confident that he inspired the other disciples to say the same thing.

Desiring a positive environment, High I's often will respond to negative events with optimism. Although this can be a good quality, it becomes a problem when the High I's confidence in himself extends beyond his ability to keep his promises. There can be too much talk and not enough action. It is difficult for a High I to ask himself questions like, "Can I really follow through on what I am saying?" "Am I really being helpful?" "Should I just be quiet?"

Even though Peter desired with all his heart to support Jesus, the emotional chaos following Christ's arrest overwhelmed Peter, and he could not follow through on his verbal commitment. Such is often the case in a Persuader's life—and it leads to the third principle in dealing with them.

RECOGNIZE THE DIFFICULTY THEY HAVE
IN FOLLOWING THROUGH ON COMMITMENTS

When a High I gets under stress, he tends to protect and defend himself. If push comes to shove, he will usually deny his responsibility and fail to follow through on the commitments he has made.

Note Peter's response to questions in the courtyard of the high priest's home when he was identified as a follower of Jesus (Matthew 26:69-75).

To a servant girl he stated: "I don't know what you're talking about."

To another servant girl he denied with an oath: "I don't know the man."

To a bystander he cursed: "I don't know the man!"

Peter relied on his own ability to persuade others, and it failed him. His strength of confidence became his greatest weakness. Jesus tried to warn him, but Peter refused to acknowledge he had any weaknesses. After this painful experience, Peter was willing to admit that he needed help in controlling his impulsive tendencies. Jesus used a special method of restoring confidence in Peter, as we shall see.

But before we present that episode, one piece of advice: when you suspect that a High I will be unable to follow through on a promise he has made to you, try talking with him in a nonconfrontational manner and attempt to work out an agreeable solution.

PROVIDE A FRIENDLY AND POSITIVE ENVIRONMENT

High I's enjoy having fun and respond best in an environment that is friendly and bustling with activity. They resist situations that require waiting with little or nothing to do. So it is useful in dealing with them to seek to create a fun and friendly environment for them.

Following His resurrection, Jesus had instructed His disciples to go to Galilee and wait for Him. There He would give them further information regarding the next steps in their ministry. In John 21 is a record of the events surrounding their meeting at the Sea of Galilee.

Peter had found it difficult to do nothing while they waited for Jesus and had decided to go fishing. Some might suggest that because of his failure the evening of Christ's arrest, he lost confidence in his ability to be a leader for Christ and was considering leaving the ministry to return to his old profession as a fisherman. However, since a High I rarely wants to be left with no activity, restlessness probably also contributed to Peter's need to go fishing.

A High I usually prefers companionship to being alone. Notice that seven of the other disciples had joined Peter on his all-night fishing trip, but they caught nothing. By morning, the disciples must have been cold, wet, miserable, and hungry. No doubt the environment was less than favorable, particularly for Peter, who had come up with the idea in the first place!

As dawn approached, Jesus arrived at the shore. The disciples didn't recognize Him there, but they heard His advice.

> "Friends, haven't you any fish?"
> "No," they answered.
> He said, "Throw your net on the right side of the boat and you will find some." When they did, they were unable to haul the net in because of the large number of fish. (vv. 5-6)

You can be sure that Peter was willing to offer some excuse as to why they had not caught any fish, but he was too tired to do so. Probably to prove the man on the shore to be wrong they followed his suggestion. Immediately they caught a net full of fish (later counted to be 153). Obviously, the climate in the boat changed from doom and gloom to joy in one short moment.

John realized the man on the beach was Jesus and told Peter, "It is the Lord!" In typical High I fashion, Peter impulsively jumped overboard and swam ashore to greet the Lord. Peter left to the other disciples the work of pulling in the net full of fish.

When they got to shore, Jesus had already prepared a fire to cook the breakfast. He suggested that they bring some of the catch and place it on the fire. I am sure the smell of fresh fish cooking on an open fire with biscuits qualified as a great time together. Jesus wanted to make sure they had a positive experience and waited until Peter's hunger had been satisfied before He spoke with him regarding His plans for Peter's future ministry. We can all learn a lesson from Jesus about creating the proper environment before getting into a serious discussion with a High I profile.

GIVE THEM THE OPPORTUNITY
TO VERBALIZE THEIR FEELINGS

People with the Influencing profile need to have the opportunity to express their ideas and opinions. This makes them feel important and gives them the sense of having a say in their future.

Having now created a positive environment, Jesus asked Peter three direct questions, giving him an opportunity to express himself. Twice the Lord asked Peter if he loved Him. The Greek word He used for love is the term *agapao*. The word is used in Scripture to define God's type of self-sacrificial love. Each time Peter replied that he *did* love Jesus—but in his responses he used a different word for love, *phileo*. The word implies a commitment for someone out of fondness or friendship. The third time Jesus asked the question He used Peter's word *phileo* in asking for his commitment (John 21:17).

Peter was saying, "Lord, you know my heart, You know it is my desire to love you." In order for Peter to have his dependence on the Lord renewed, Jesus allowed him to get his doubts out into the open. Each time Jesus responded to Peter, He carried the discussion deeper. Finally, all of Peter's doubts were out in the open, and they could move forward.

When talking with a person who is a High I, give him time to talk through his ideas. Usually it will take him several minutes to get to the point. Don't take everything he says literally.

The High I differs from the other styles on this matter. The High D individual usually gets right to the point, even if what he says comes out sounding blunt. A High C person won't speak unless he has thoroughly considered the meaning of his words. Then he will say what he wants to say—cautiously. The High S person may not speak at all and just be quiet.

GIVE THEM IDEAS FOR TRANSFERRING TALK TO ACTION

High I's can benefit from ideas that help them transfer talk into action. After Peter answered each question concerning his love for Christ, Jesus offered three challenges for Peter to respond to:

1. "Feed [pasture] my lambs" (v. 15).
2. "Take care of [shepherd] my sheep" (v. 16).
3. "Feed [pasture] my sheep" (v. 17).

The Lord was giving Peter a simple job description for his future ministry. The first directive emphasized teaching God's Word (spiritual nourishment) to those who are young in the faith. The second directive had to do with ministry to mature believers. The third directive was to teach the principles of Scripture to the mature believers. Jesus was providing Peter with a plan of action for ministry—and it is a model any disciple desiring a ministry can use, regardless of his DISC Pattern.

GIVE THEM POSITIVE SOCIAL RECOGNITION

Positive recognition helps a High I choose to motivate himself to succeed. This recognition can come in the form of titles, commendations, or acknowledgments before his peers.

Throughout the exchange between Jesus and Peter in John 21, the Lord centers His discussion primarily on reaching people rather than on details for accomplishing the task. His final message to Peter was, "Follow Me!"

It was a simple message, but the implications were dynamic. Because Peter had denied the Lord three times, he thought he had forfeited his role as a leader. Jesus used the breakfast meeting as a stage to give Peter the opportunity to undo his three denials. In front of his peers, Peter was commissioned again as the leader. This act of grace reestablished Peter in good social and spiritual standing before Christ. Not only did Jesus give Peter his job back, but He did so in the presence of his friends—an act of kindness that fulfilled Peter's need for recognition. You will have better success in working with High I's when you give them the opportunity to be recognized for their efforts.

USE CONFRONTATION ONLY WHEN NECESSARY

In general, a High I does not respond favorably to confrontation. It tends to demoralize and demotivate him. However, there are times when it is necessary to use confrontation with High I's in order to get their attention. This is because High I's have a tendency to lose their concentration, and confrontation is a way to get it back quickly.

Confrontation has a more positive impact if it centers on future actions rather than past events. When asked to explain their past actions, High I's usually respond with an array of excuses. For the best results, challenge them to do better in the future.

In His message to Peter in John 21, Jesus predicted Peter would be restored to faithful service but in the end would face a violent death because of his faith. However, instead of concerning himself with his own future, Peter became intent on knowing what was going to happen to John. Jesus' response to Peter's question was strong and direct: "If I want him to remain alive until I return, what is that to you? You must follow me."

Jesus was saying that it was none of Peter's business what would happen to John. Peter's focus was to be on Christ and on Christ alone! The message was confrontational but necessary if Peter was to carry out the mission that was intended for him. Peter got the message.

A WOMAN'S PERSPECTIVE ON THE INFLUENCING PROFILE

When Jesus restores Peter in John 21, He encourages him as well as confronts him. Both were necessary to get Peter back on target to accomplish his mission. We asked Patricia, who is also a Persuader Profile, to comment on how Jesus dealt with Peter in this passage.

> While reading the passage in John 21, I speculated on how Peter might have felt when Jesus spoke to him following their breakfast together on the shore. He must have been encouraged to know that Jesus had forgiven him for his denials, but I also think he still felt some emotional pain. In addition to our achievements, there are many times in the life of a Persuader when we "blow it." When we do, we feel "in the pits"! We hope for another chance to prove ourselves. Jesus did give Peter another chance to lead, but only after He questioned him three times about his love and willingness to serve. Peter confirmed his love, but I would have felt some grief as well. I am glad Jesus let Peter express his feelings without criticizing him.
>
> Also, the emotion of the moment could have precluded me from being able to listen completely to Jesus' instructions. Usually when I am excited, I don't get all the details I should. Finally, when Jesus told Peter that it was "none of his business" what was going to happen to John, I would have been upset for the moment by being confronted. However, that would have gotten my attention! You would not have to worry about me doing that again.

WHAT THE DISC PERSONALITIES
HAD TO SAY ABOUT THE HIGH I

What do you consider the most difficult parts of relating to the High I?

High D: "It is difficult for us to listen to a problem knowing that the High I's are not necessarily interested in hearing about a solution. We have a tendency to want to get to the bottom line."

High I: "To allow another I to share the stage with me."

High S: "It is difficult for us to keep up with their need to change plans while they're speaking. We need time to process changes, whereas they can come up with new ideas in mid-sentence."

High C: "To be less inhibited, to loosen up."

What can you do in order to build a better relationship with the High I Profiles?

High D: "Be willing to accept the fact that High I's desire to build relationships first and that goals may be of secondary importance. Their bottom line is not the same as ours."

High I: "We need to be willing to share the stage with others and not be threatened by it."

High S: "We need to be willing to take risks allowing them to participate in activities that don't make sense to us. Be willing to break our routine and try something different with them."

High C: "Be willing to lower our expectations and modify our demand for perfection. We have a tendency to try to build a rigid structure around the High I and it doesn't work."

Where do you most need the talents of the High I?

High D: "We need their skills in modeling how to build close relationships; in having fun and keeping relaxed."

High I: "Other I's enjoy having a positive influence; our relational skills help to encourage others nicely."

High S: "We need their gift for expression, reassurance, and acceptance."

High C: "We need their gift for modeling how to enjoy life; their ability to encourage in the face of discouragement."

WHAT THE HIGH I'S HAD TO SAY ABOUT THEMSELVES

High I's have special gifts that model ways of relating to others with sensitivity and grace. Hopefully, the preceding information has illustrated how these gifts can be properly used to improve relationships. As with any strengths, they can get overextended. The model of Jesus dealing with Peter shows how to love the High I even when he makes mistakes. The following responses give insight into what other High I's consider important for creating a loving environment for them.

High I: "Accept me when I fail and encourage me to keep trying."
"You can be straight with me, but I have to know you accept me."
"I know I need structure and order, but I also need to know that whatever you want me to do will be enjoyable."

High I/D: "Let's have time for fun. Let me dream without being criticized."
"Give me an opportunity to express my own ideas."
"I need opportunities to interact and influence other people."

High I/C: "Understand that part of me wants to be with people and have a good time, while the other part wants some quiet moments."

High I/S: "I need a friendly environment to operate at my best; it helps to know that others appreciate my efforts."

"If I make a mistake, take me aside and correct me, but please don't do it in front of people."

When you are under stress, the most helpful thing we can do for you is . . .

High I: "Listen to me, feel with me, mirror my feelings, help me to see and focus my thoughts."

High I/D: "If I'm dealing with people problems, listen to my emotions, but don't judge me for them."

High I/C: "Listen to me, but don't try to solve my problem until I'm ready."

"Sometimes I need time to be alone, but don't interpret that to mean that I'm rejecting you."

"Be willing to laugh and cry with me."

High I/S: "I need reassurance that I'm OK and sometimes it can be nonverbal like a smile, wink, or hug. I prefer a hug."

"Do not criticize the things I do wrong in front of others, but reaffirm my value and capabilities. Later, I can better handle my errors in private conversations."

The High I Profiles continually convey their need to have others hear them out when they are under stress; however, they do not necessarily want the problem to be fixed. The wise partner is one who listens first and waits for the High I to tell him if he wants objective feedback. In dealing with a High I under stress, never ask a confrontational question that requires an answer, unless you are doing a research project on creative excuses or are writing a script for a television sit-com.

A LOOK AHEAD

The next two chapters will focus on how we can understand and effectively respond to the needs of Steadiness (High S) behavioral styles. You should now begin to integrate an understanding of one family of profiles with that of the other DISC Profiles. This is an important step for learning how to improve our relations with people who are different from ourselves.

NINE

UNDERSTANDING THE STEADINESS STYLE

Did you ever stop to think about the axles of an automobile? Certainly the engine gives the car its power, and the wheels move it down the road. Engines can be big and powerful, and wheels can be sporty. However, the car is not going to move safely without the strong support of the axles. Every automobile needs axles.

Or consider, if you will, the anchor of a ship. No matter how magnificent the ship, in a stormy sea it is destined for destruction upon the rocks unless the anchor holds firm beneath the surface, keeping it connected to the solid ground far below.

The world needs anchors and axles. The Dominance personality is a hard charger who seizes authority and gets the job done no matter what it takes. The Influencer, on the other hand, is a motivator, an encourager, and a spokesperson who is often the center of attention. In their ways they both shape the environment around them. But the world also needs people who have the ability to keep both feet on the ground—people with a Steadiness (High S) personality style.

High S people are team players with a desire to please and maintain peace and stability in a group, even if it means sacrificing their own personal goals. Like the anchor and the axle, they usually do not stand out in a crowd, but they are noticed over time because of their consistent, steady work habits.

Some have concluded that people who possess the Dominance style are born to lead, whereas people with the Steadiness style are born to follow, but this is not true. Both can make excellent leaders. It is true that the High D's are naturally assertive in seeking leadership roles, whereas S's may be more reluctant to aggressively step forward. The High D or High I leaders seem to be more suited for situations that warrant fast-paced change and growth. A High S leader usually brings consistency, support, and stability to the position and can be just as productive as leaders with other personality styles.

Along with profiling biblical characters, I (Ken) have a keen interest in studying the differing styles of military and political leaders. None has been more fascinating than the American leadership team in the European theater of operation in World War II. Below is a listing and profiles of the president of the United States at the time, Franklin Delano Roosevelt, and the four highest-ranking generals in the chain of command.

Franklin D. Roosevelt, President	I = D
General Marshall, Chief of Staff	S/C/D
General Eisenhower, Supreme Commander	S/I
General Bradley, Command, 12th Army Group	C/S
General Patton, Commanding General, 3d Army	D/I

President Roosevelt gave George Marshall complete freedom to select each team. General Marshall was a master of understanding men and their particular strengths and limitations. As one British historian stated, "He picked magnificently!" He would typically put individuals together based on diversity of skills and place them in the chain of command where their strengths could best complement and balance each team. Marshall's selection of Eisenhower, Bradley, and Patton *in that order* was among his most brilliant moves. I found it interesting that the High S style was so prominent.

The four Representative Patterns that make up the family of High S personality styles are listed on page 167. Included are the primary and secondary styles and the biblical character that represents each pattern.

Steadiness Representative Pattern	Biblical Character
Persister (Primary S)	Isaac, Dorcas
Investigator (S/D)	Nehemiah, Martha
Advisor (S/I)	Abraham, Hannah
Strategist (S/C/D)	Jacob, Anna

As in the case of the other DISC styles, there are general characteristics common to the High S family. Five tendencies are somewhat unique to the Steadiness group.

GENERAL TENDENCIES OF THE STEADINESS STYLE

IS A PRAGMATIC TEAM PLAYER

Pragmatism has been defined as "an orientation toward practical action or thought; a system that stresses practical consequences as the essential criterion for determining truth or value" (*Random House College Dictionary*). This well describes how a High S evaluates choices. Their opinions usually consist of practical advice.

"Doc, it hurts when I do this!" cried the patient.

"Well, don't do it," responded Dr. S.

Although we may want a High D to lead the way over the mountain that seems too high to climb, and the High I to rally the people for the trip, it is the High S who might very well be thinking, "Do we really need to go over the mountain? We are doing fine right here on this side." If you ask him for his advice, get ready for something practical. "The road up the mountain is hard and dangerous," he might say. "And we have everything we need here where we are." Sound and practical. Steady.

On the other hand, should you ask him to make the decision whether or not the group should make the journey, you will likely hear something like, "Oh, don't ask me! Whatever everybody else wants is fine." Initially, a High S will not want to make a decision, preferring to defer to the wishes of the group. They are driven by harmony, agreement, and support.

The time to ask a person with the High S personality style for a solution to a problem is after everyone else involved has spoken and he has had an opportunity to process his thoughts. You will be amazed at his insights if he is allowed time (twenty-four hours is generally a minimum!) to review the alternatives. In some circumstances, however, there may not be the luxury of time for a decision, and the High S will defer to others to keep peace.

Abraham is a marvelous example from Scripture of a Steadiness personality style. His life illustrates practical choices, teamwork, and always striving to be a peacemaker.

For example, in Genesis 13 we read how Abraham had settled with his wife, Sarai (later called Sarah), and nephew, Lot, in a place called Bethel. In time, their livestock began to crowd the land, and Abraham's herdsmen and Lot's herdsmen began to feud. Before the situation could get out of hand, Abraham, the steady peacemaker, responded. Fully realizing that in one direction lay the green pastures and choice land toward Sodom and Gomorrah and in the other direction lay the less fertile land of Canaan, he said to Lot, "Let's not have any quarreling between you and me, or between your herdsmen and mine, for we are brothers. Is not the whole land before you? Let's part company. If you go to the left, I'll go to the right; if you go to the right, I'll go to the left" (Genesis 13:8-9).

To resolve the conflict, Abraham was willing to allow Lot to choose where he wished to settle and then go in the opposite direction. Would you care to speculate how a High D might have responded in the same situation?

Lot, of course, chose the preferred land in the direction of Sodom and Gomorrah. We learn in Genesis 14, however, that war had broken out between the kings of Sodom and Elam. Once Sodom and Gomorrah went down in defeat, all of Lot's possessions were seized and he was taken prisoner.

Meanwhile, steady and supportive Abraham was still abiding in the less preferred land of Canaan. When word came to him of his nephew's capture, Abraham immediately organized his men and mounted a brilliant rescue operation. In the end, because of his loyal commitment to the Lord, he even refused a reward offered him by the grateful king of Sodom. We can only speculate how a High I might have responded to such attention.

HE VALUES STABILITY IN THE HOME

Their need for security, peace, and support influences most High S people to place a tremendous importance on stability within their family. Should conflict exist among family members, they tend to become distressed and prone to worry and anxiety. This often leads to avoiding the conflict and letting others take the lead in creating solutions.

In the life of Abraham, when strife entered his family unit he became extremely uncomfortable. Consider how he responded when he was confronted with a conflict between his sons Isaac, born to his wife, Sarah, and Ishmael, born to his wife's slave Hagar (Genesis 21:8-11).

> The child grew and was weaned, and on the day Isaac was weaned Abraham held a great feast. But Sarah saw that the son whom Hagar the Egyptian had borne to Abraham was mocking, and she said to Abraham, "Get rid of that slave woman and her son, for that slave woman's son will never share in the inheritance with my son Isaac."
>
> The matter distressed Abraham greatly because it concerned his son.

Both Isaac and Ishmael were Abraham's children, but Sarah asked him to send Hagar away along with his son. The thought was extremely painful for Abraham, and only after God confirmed that it was indeed the right thing to do, did Abraham's discomfort subside. God assured Abraham that He would watch over Hagar and Ishmael, and He confirmed that Ishmael would be a father of a separate nation of people.

When the time came for them to depart, Abraham personally gave Hagar provisions and put them on her shoulder. He gave her the boy and made sure he was safe for the journey.

Although this action was very difficult for Abraham, his need to keep peace, support the wishes of Sarah, and obey God took precedence.

Whereas the High D attends to his own agenda regardless of circumstances, and the High I enjoys attention and opportunities for recognition, the High S individual is committed to loyalty and support. For example, a High S may remain faithful for years while a spouse or other family member sits in a prison or hospital, or serves with the military in a foreign country. When others become impatient and consider moving on, the anchor holds fast—unmoved by the storm.

IS CONSISTENT

The Steadiness personality style tends to prefer the status quo and honors traditions. In a work environment, the High S provides a stabilizing influence by the consistent manner with which he carries out his duties.

In my (Ron's) counseling organization, the routine handling of bills and records is entrusted to Shirley. Her consistent performance takes away any worry about whether these important tasks will be carried out. Her commitment and dedication provides stability for the whole staff—especially when the end of the month arrives and the therapists want to be paid.

High S leaders will hold off entrusting people with more difficult assignments until they have proved themselves to be consistent in lesser tasks. Then greater opportunities will usually follow.

Eliezer, a Steadiness person, was Abraham's oldest servant, and had proved to be so loyal that he was entrusted with the important job of finding a wife for Abraham's son Isaac. Abraham knew he could give Eliezer the assignment and that it would be carried out exactly as he wished. Eliezer was led by God to pick the girl Rebekah. You might want to read how the events of this story unfolded in Genesis 24. It is a beautiful example of how two High S styles supported each other and worked together to accomplish God's will.

Steadiness styles tend toward consistency of performance (table 19).

Table 19

Consistency of Performance Continuum

greater -- lesser

| S | C | D | I |

S   Steady and predictable

C   Marked by attention to details
     Frequently checks for accuracy

D   Distinguished by intense effort, frequently early on in a project when the work is challenging

I   Tends to talk about taking action rather than doing it

SOURCE: Adapted from Life Associates, Inc., The *DISC Model: Trainer and Consultant's Reference Encyclopedia.*

DESIRES ORDER AND TRANQUILITY

Since a steady, consistent environment without change or disorganization is preferred by this personality style, High S's do well at handling routine matters and will usually make sure everything is in its proper place.

Change, therefore, is unwelcome. They will cling to the present and battle the forces of change. On the job, even superior conditions or wages will not shake their aversion to change. One manager observed, "When change is forced on them, a High S will go from working extremely deliberately to slow, slower, stop!" This manager had tried his hand at creating change in a department heavily populated with High S personnel without too much success. Rather than judge this trait as being dysfunctional, however, we need to understand that it is normal, and a strategy does exist for dealing with High S's facing change.

In Genesis 12 when Abraham is called by God he is asked to leave his family and travel to Canaan. Abraham's home was originally in Ur, which was an extremely comfortable place to live. He might have been tempted to remain in that secure environment had God not used Abraham's father to prepare him for change.

If you recall, Abraham and his family were living with his father, Terah. In all probability, Abraham was not excited about leaving Ur but was supportive of God's calling to move. Terah chose to move his family close to Canaan and settled in the land of Haran. Years later, when Abraham was seventy-five years old, God called him again to resettle his family in the land of Canaan. The Lord's plan was to form a new nation that would bless others. God had prepared Abraham years before by getting him conditioned to the idea of moving.

When initiating change with a High S, recognize first that a slowed-down performance is a normal response to change for a High S. Then allow the High S time to process and respond rather than react to the idea of change. Finally, allow him the opportunity to communicate with others who will also be affected by the change. And remember, family stability is a critical consideration for the High S.

Steadiness personalities can benefit from looking for shortcuts in procedures and by being willing to acknowledge their important contributions to others.

POTENTIAL BLIND SPOTS OF THE HIGH S

IS FEARFUL OF CONFLICT, LOSS
OF STABILITY, AND CHANGE

The steady, supportive, traditional aspects of this personality style create a need for acceptance and assurance. As a result, the High S often struggles with the fear of conflict and/or loss of a stable environment.

One way to avoid this fear is by recognizing that any prospective changes in their lives (whether at home or work) should be preceded by some clear explanations along with practical reasons. Once a change is announced, allow for some time to get used to the idea. Don't look for immediate acceptance.

Discomfort associated with this fear is especially strong when a situation arises that is competitive and only one person can win. Imagine a High S in competition with an aggressive High D for a promotion at work. The Steadiness person desires to support his family with the increased income and support his company with a good, steady performance, yet the prospect of conflict with the High D co-worker may paralyze him with fear. He may even yield to his associate to prevent conflict, thus affecting his chance for the promotion.

OVERVIEW OF THE HIGH S FAMILY OF PATTERNS

The following pages cover the four Representative Patterns that make up the S Profiles. They include the *Persister, Investigator, Advisor,* and *Strategist.* The *Persister* represents the most pure of the Steadiness Profiles, being gifted in maintaining a steady pace. The Investigator has the added dimension of being goal-oriented and focusing on tasks. The Advisor is different in that the emphasis is on relationships and more like the High I, Encourager Profile. The Strategist has three dimensions: steadiness, goals, and compliance to standards. These subtle differences are critical in understanding the uniqueness of the High S Patterns.

THE PERSISTER PATTERN

POSITIVE TRAITS

The Persister Profile (table 20) is the purest form of the Steadiness Patterns (signified in the abbreviation "Primary S"). They tend to operate in a methodical, routine process, always knowing the amount of time they need to complete a task. They tend to be very consistent and perform excellent work day in and day out. They tend to be pictured as the classic marathon runner. As a consequence, they turn in a remarkably consistent work performance day in and day out. They generally prefer

Table 20
Primary High S Pattern

I. Distinctive tendencies of this pattern:

Primary drive	Controlled, secure, stable environment
Personal giftedness	Maintaining traditions, constancy, steadiness
Group giftedness	Team player, commitment to follow through
Potential spiritual gifts	Helps, Service, Mercy
Internal fear	Disharmony, confronting others
Strength out of control	Procrastinates, waits for things to happen
Under stress becomes	Seeks a compromise or avoids making a decision
Blind spots	Taking ownership of their individual significance
Needs to work on	Being more proactive, responding rather than reacting
Best team members	I/D, D/I, I/C, I, S, C

II. Biblical characters who represent this pattern:

1. Isaac
2. Dorcas (*)

III. Further Bible study:

Strengths	Gen. 24:62-67; Gen. 26:1-6
Weaknesses	Gen. 26:7-31

*Not enough information to be absolutely certain of the specific style.

quietly working behind the scenes. Too often, they are not fully appreciated until after they leave a job or relationship.

In Acts 9 a woman named Dorcas is mentioned who characterizes many of the traits of the Persister. She is described as a woman "always doing good and helping the poor" (9:36). She was gifted in making tunics and garments, and freely gave them to the widows of Joppa. After a sudden sickness she died, and the entire community was grieved over the news of her passing. It is common for Persisters to receive this kind of response because of the positive service they have shown to others. After Dorcas's death, two men summoned Peter to her side in demonstration of belief in prayer and God's power. She was raised from the dead. As a result of this event, many people came to know the Lord.

PERSONAL GIFTEDNESS

Persisters have the ability to maintain the pace that others have started. They show a remarkable consistency of performance over long periods of times without fanfare. Abraham's son Isaac was entrusted with the responsibility of passing on the promise of God. He was one of the critical links leading to the birth of the Messiah, and Genesis 24-26 indicates that he lived a full and fruitful life. He was married to Rebekah at the age of 40. They had two sons, Jacob and Esau, and many grandchildren. He lived to be 180 years old and was honored in death by his sons.

UNDER PRESSURE

When pressured, Persisters tend to adapt to those in authority. When forced to make changes, they usually become accommodating rather than fight for their rights. In Genesis 26, God tells Isaac not to travel to Egypt, although there is a famine in the land where he lives and Isaac believes the trip needs to be made to obtain food. God advised him that he would be blessed if he withstood the pressure and obeyed Him. The Philistines harassed Isaac by filling up his wells with sand to dry them up, and Abimelech, the king of the Philistines, suggested that he move his family. Isaac was obedient through it all, and God later caused Abimelech to recognize that he was wrong in the way he and his people had treated Isaac. Abimelech sought out Isaac, made peace, and invited him to return to their land. Isaac's patience under pressure paid off.

THE INVESTIGATOR PATTERN

POSITIVE TRAITS

Terms like *industrious* and *diligent* accurately describe the behavior of the Investigator Pattern (table 21). Investigator personalities have a tendency always to be busy accomplishing something while displaying an intensity during their involvement. Possessing High S relational skills, they can stop and chat for a brief time, but they tend to become impatient as they quickly refocus on the task at hand. Luke records the account of Jesus' stay at Martha's home for a meal. After the initial welcome, Martha immediately went to the kitchen to complete the meal. In typical Investigator fashion, she was concerned with the goal of serving a special meal, whereas her sister, Mary, was more interested in being with Jesus and hearing what He had to say. Martha even became impatient with Mary for not helping (Luke 10:38-42). Investigators would be happier if they allowed themselves to relax and not be so absorbed in a task.

PERSONAL GIFTEDNESS

Investigators tend to possess outstanding organizational skills and can balance the process and the product equally in order to get the job done. They can make excellent administrators with a company, having the ability to look at a goal and devise a logistical plan to achieve it in a realistic time frame. Investigators also have a special talent for setting up procedures and schedules with an accountability structure so that everyone knows what he is to do. When planning the next church social, look for an Investigator to organize the event.

It is recorded in Nehemiah 2-4 that the Lord gave Nehemiah, a cupbearer to King Artaxerxes, the responsibility of re-

Table 21
High S/D Pattern

I. Distinctive tendencies of this pattern:

Primary drive	Diligence in taking ownership of tasks, industrious
Personal giftedness	Follow-through in completing tasks
Group giftedness	Strong administrative skills
Potential spiritual gifts	Administration, Service, Leadership
Internal fear	Noncompliance to their standards
Strength out of control	Tends to be too direct, blunt, and demanding
Under stress becomes	Frustrated and intense, impatiently takes charge
Blind spots	Not seemingly aware that relationships are as important as tasks
Needs to work on	Being sensitive to people issues over tasks
Best team members	I/D, D equal I, I, I/C, I/S

II. Biblical characters who represent this pattern:

1. Nehemiah
2. Joseph
3. Martha (*)

III. Further Bible study:

Strengths	Neh. 2:1-7; 6:15
Weaknesses	Neh. 13:1-31; Luke 10:38-42

*Not enough information to be absolutely certain of the specific style.

building the walls of Jerusalem. Before agreeing to let Nehemiah return to Jerusalem, the king requested that he devise a plan to accomplish the task. Nehemiah carefully made plans including having the king sign letters addressed to governors of the regions authorizing the project and allowing him safe passage. As an additional precaution, he arranged for an armed escort. A letter was sent to Asaph, the keeper of the king's forest, instructing him to get the materials needed for the project. After he arrived in Jerusalem, Nehemiah organized the work force and completed the project in just fifty-two days—an amazing accomplishment.

UNDER PRESSURE

Because of their intensity for accomplishing personal goals and objectives, Investigators can, under pressure, become frustrated and impatient with others. When their instructions are not carried out, they become quite demanding, which is somewhat uncharacteristic for a High S personality and comes from the D traits that they also possess.

In Nehemiah 13, Nehemiah reacts in a confrontational manner when the high priest fails to care for the needs of the Levites. He also dealt harshly with those Jews who intermarried with the women of Ashdod, Ammon, and Moab. As Investigators mature they need to develop the ability to negotiate and work through circumstances with which they are in conflict.

THE ADVISOR PATTERN

POSITIVE TRAITS

Advisors (table 22) have a special gift for caring. They are willing to be extremely transparent in personal relationships. Advisors reach out to meet the needs of people in distress. They often use their friendly, supportive style to persuade others to be forgiving in difficult situations.

God told Abraham that He was going to bring destruction on Sodom and Gomorrah because of their sin. Abraham became burdened for the lives of the many people of Sodom, in-

Table 22
High S/I Pattern

I. Distinctive tendencies of this pattern:

Primary drive	Maintaining peace and harmony, security
Personal giftedness	Expressing gentleness and kindness
Group giftedness	Projecting hospitality, being loyal to friends
Potential spiritual gifts	Faith, Hospitality, Mercy
Internal fear	Having to face dissension and conflict
Strength out of control	Overuses kindness, compromises self to maintain harmony
Under stress becomes	Gentle, accommodating, internalizes conflict
Blind spots	Being able to free oneself of security blankets
Needs to work on	Being firm and following through with actions
Best team members	D, D-I, D/I, I/D

II. Biblical characters who represent this pattern:

1. Abraham
2. Hannah

III. Further Bible study:

Strengths	Gen. 18:1-33; 1 Sam. 1
Weaknesses	Gen. 16:1-6

cluding his own nephew, Lot. In verses 22-33 of Genesis 18, we read of an interesting negotiation between God and Abraham that illustrates these caring influencing traits in action. Abraham began by requesting a promise from God to spare Sodom if fifty righteous men could be found in the city. As the dialogue proceeded Abraham ultimately got the number down to only ten.

PERSONAL GIFTEDNESS

The caring nature of Advisors leads them to create environments in which people feel comfortable sharing their concerns and problems. Unconditional acceptance seems to come quite natural for them, even toward someone who has failed them in some way. Advisors model what it means to be a true friend.

The Advisor employer is typically an open door manager. Rarely would you feel intimidated by such a person, and he would likely give you your instructions in a caring, supportive manner. Your business discussion would probably be intermingled with talk about your family and his. When you leave his office, you will usually feel warm, accepted, and grateful to have such a good boss.

FEARS

That warm fuzzy feeling you have about your Advisor boss might change a little when you see him under fire! Probably the greatest fear these caring, harmonious people have is the fear of aggression. They will run from it, dodge it, go around it, under it, or over it to avoid facing it head on. If they cannot avoid confrontation, they will do everything possible to terminate a negative conversation, including verbally agreeing with their aggressors. Running from conflict seldom produces any desired results, and most Advisors will admit that they would greatly benefit from the ability to withstand aggression and say no when it is appropriate.

THE STRATEGIST PATTERN

POSITIVE TRAITS

Strategists (table 23) are tenacious and determined profiles. Once they set their sights on a goal, they never waver until the task is complete. For example, Jacob, a Strategist, showed incredible determination in working fourteen years in his quest to marry Rachel, the daughter of his uncle Laban. After falling in love with her, Jacob agreed to work seven years for Laban in exchange for Rachel's hand in marriage. His willingness to work even for seven years reveals a tenacity well beyond anyone but a Strategist, but Laban tricked Jacob into marrying Leah first and requiring Jacob to work an additional seven years for Rachel (Genesis 29). He did.

PERSONAL GIFTEDNESS

Their value to a team is their excellent follow-through skills. Preferring to work alone, they will, year after year, quietly go about getting things done. Luke recalls the story of Anna, a prophetess, who spent over fifty years quietly working in the Temple serving God. She had been married for seven years when her husband died. After becoming a widow, she dedicated herself to the task of serving the Lord night and day, never leaving the Temple. At the age of eighty-four, her devotion was rewarded when she received the special privilege of seeing the Christ child when Mary and Joseph brought Jesus to the Temple for dedication (Luke 2).

UNDER PRESSURE

Because of their tendency to quietly work alone, if Strategists are in a disagreement with others, they tend to internalize their feelings. In addition, they will remember for some time wrongs that have been done to them. Instead of expressing their anger and forgetting about it, they store up a list of grievances, which in turn leads them to be suspicious of others. One by-product of this suspicion is their questioning of the mo-

Table 23
High S/C/D Pattern

I. Distinctive tendencies of this pattern:

Primary drive	Tenacity, determination, never gives up
Personal giftedness	Investigates, explores, and determines options on complex problems
Group giftedness	Demonstrates unwavering loyalty to close friends
Potential spiritual gifts	Service, Helps, Wisdom
Internal fear	Having to match wits with strong personalities in selling ideas
Strength out of control	Unbending, stubborn determination
Under stress becomes	Quiet, worrisome, and introspective
Blind spots	Being unaware of people issues when preoccupied in solving a complex task
Needs to work on	Confronting difficult people issues, expressing feelings
Best team members	I/D, D/I, I/C, I/S, I/S/C

II. Biblical characters who represent this pattern:

1. Jacob
2. Anna (*)

III. Further Bible study:

Strengths	Gen. 30:25-43
Weaknesses	Gen. 31:1-55

*Not enough information to be absolutely certain of the specific style.

tives of others. Learning to communicate their conflict with the person they distrust can help clarify if their concerns are correct.

Laban tricked Jacob into working for him for twenty years and changed Jacob's wages ten times. Jacob worked long hours and never complained, but internally he became increasingly angry at his father-in-law. When Laban accused Jacob of stealing his idols, Jacob released his built-up anger against Laban. After this confrontation, they settled their differences but never saw each other again (Genesis 29-31).

A Look Ahead

Now that we have examined the four Representative Patterns that make up the Steadiness style, we will take a deeper look into the uniqueness of this personality. Further descriptions will make it easier to understand how the High S Profiles contrast with the High D and High I styles.

TEN

RESPONDING TO THE NEEDS OF THE STEADINESS PERSONALITY

Not so long ago, Layton, the parent of a high school student, asked me (Ken) what he could do to encourage his son Daniel to return to his high school football team. Daniel was a good athlete, having led the team in rushing during his junior year. At the time, he was a senior and predicted to be the team's star tailback. However, he had developed a personality conflict with the head coach and had decided not to continue playing for the team.

Layton described the chain of events that had developed over the past several months. The head coach at the high school had an I/D Profile. He was enthusiastic and very authoritarian. According to his coaching philosophy, football was an aggressive sport that had to be played with a great deal of emotion. Any athlete who didn't fit this mold didn't belong on the team.

During his junior year, Daniel played out the I/D style expected by the coach although he was a High S, Persister Profile. When spring practice began in preparation for his senior year, something changed. Instead of altering his behavior to suit the coach's expectations, he began to act more like his true self. That style involved being more laid back and unemotional. Daniel's consistency on the playing field didn't change, but his emotional response off the field did. However, the coach viewed Daniel's change of emotional intensity as unacceptable.

His reasoning was that Daniel's "bad attitude" was a problem that could affect the team. Daniel became his special project. He attempted to change him back into a highly emotional player, which he believed to be the "right attitude." The coach's attempt failed and led to putting the young athlete under a lot of stress.

In their book *Kids in Sports,* Bill Perkins and Dr. Rod Cooper offer practical suggestions of ways a coach can change his style of relating to players in order to meet their individual needs. They describe several key elements to consider when working with the High S athlete. "Specialists fear confrontation and avoid conflict. Whenever they are being taught something, be supportive of their efforts, not confrontive."[1] In Daniel's case, the coach was locked into his own program and considered differing views as detrimental to the team's success. The intensity grew so bad for Daniel that he refused to continue football in the fall. At this point, Layton asked for my counsel.

I told him that unless the coach was willing to change his style of handling Daniel, there probably was not much of a chance he would decide to play. If Daniel did play and was pressured into conforming to the coach's expectations, he would not only be miserable, he might even become physically ill. My concern was whether Daniel would be allowed to play as himself or be forced to play as someone else.

My mentioning the possibility of Daniel's becoming sick was a shock for Layton. He remembered that Daniel had become seriously ill seven weeks into the season of his junior year. He was unable to attend classes until late in the semester and never really physically recovered until the spring of the following year. Maybe this illness was a coincidence, but we have found that emotional stress wears down a person's immune system, making him vulnerable to sickness.

Layton asked if I would be willing to talk with the coach for the purpose of helping him understand Daniel. The opportunity never took place. The coach maintained his strong posi-

---

1. Bill Perkins and Rod Cooper, *Kids in Sports* (Portland, Oreg.: Multnomah, 1989), p. 123.

tion, and Daniel didn't play. For the record, the team had a dismal season. It was a scenario that did not have to happen, but did.

One of the most difficult concepts to comprehend is that individuals are motivated by their own reasons and not ours. If we are to have success in coaching, parenting, business, or even in marriage, we must understand how others think and respond. Understanding the many different needs of others and then seeking to create an environment where they can choose to motivate themselves is much more effective than imposing our needs and expectations on them. Forcing our style on others will create stress for them and for ourselves. Daniel's case was a no-win situation. He saw that in light of his coach's attitude, his only alternative was not playing football and staying healthy.

The High S style has the greatest struggle where a continuous confrontational environment exists. That does not cancel out the fact that confrontation may be necessary with other personality profiles. However, the wise supervisor, parent, or spouse understands that confrontation is not a useful strategy to follow in motivating a High S. There are other approaches that will create a loving environment and get much better results.

A CONTEMPORARY CASE STUDY OF A HIGH S UNDER STRESS

Under stress, the High I has a tendency to talk, the High D becomes intense and physical, the High C escapes, and the High S sleeps. In our seminars when we describe the High S's typical reaction to stress we always pause and watch the partners of the Steadiness Patterns—because we can see on their faces that we have given them an instant breakthrough in understanding.

After I (Ken) had described the stress patterns of the four personality styles at one of our seminars, Kathy raised her hand. She had some very strong D tendencies and recognized that her response and that of her High S spouse were just like the ones we had described. She said that when she and her husband had a disagreement he would respond by walking away in silence. The major problems in their marriage centered on his response to facing changes in his routine. He would avoid her—and go to bed. Sometimes it would be two or three days before he would give her feedback on how he felt. The pattern was always the same. It would make her furious. In the earlier years of their marriage, she thought his style was a weakness in his character. Her need system was to respond immediately to a change or crisis and get it over as soon as possible. His wasn't. She kept hoping to find some sort of pill that would cure him of his disease. Fortunately, she had come to realize that his actions were normal for him. She still did not understand why he behaved the way he did, but she had learned to accept his behavior rather than try to change him.

I asked Kathy if she and her husband had fewer disagreements. Her response was his silent periods were not as long, but he still worked in the yard or went to bed when they had a disagreement. She had learned not to fight late at night—their conversations then were the least productive.

Kathy's insights were excellent, but it was clear that she did not understand the root causes of her husband's reactions. The High S's goal is to maintain the status quo through maintaining an agreeable environment. Sometimes the need to maintain the status quo is energized because of the fear of change and disorganization. When Kathy made a change in their routine without giving her husband a chance to think through the new way of doing things, she was directly threatening a deeply held goal in her High S husband. Her insights into her husband's behavior were good as far as they went, but her method of communication with her husband was still incongruent with his need system. Her style would naturally cause him to become fearful, to resist change through adopting conservatism, and to dig in his heels and stubbornly refuse to move.

When I shared this information with Kathy, her response was, "Bingo! Now what do I do about it?" My reply was that she needed to adopt a strategy that would enable her to overcome her husband's fear of change and allow him to be more open to her ideas.

As I described the strategy, Kathy saw what I was proposing, and she exclaimed, "That takes too much time. I can't do that. Isn't there another way?"

"Sure," I said, "you can always go back to three days of silence and the turtle syndrome."

"No, thank you. I guess I need to know more about how to build this communication bridge."

COMMON RESPONSES OF THE HIGH S UNDER STRESS

The first step Kathy needed to take in developing that strategy was to understand the High S stress model—the sequence of events that will naturally lead the High S to feel stress combined with the typical reaction the High S will have to this stress.

The High S needs a stable, predictable environment if he is to feel comfortable. Of particular importance is a home life free of conflict. If the home is in constant disarray, it is not unusual for the High S to begin to experience various physical problems. As we saw in 1 Samuel 1, Hannah experienced extreme mental anguish over not being able to have children. In attempting to deal with this issue, Hannah developed stomach problems. This is a High S response to stress. Another core

Table 24

When a High S Encounters Stress

- Routine action without apparent results

- Aggressive "take control" strategy by partner

- Confrontation by partner—"more is better" strategy

- Passive-aggressive retreat, i.e., noninvolvement, silence, or turtle syndrome need of the High S is time to adjust to change. Without this buffer, the natural High S defenses—silence, slow-down, and stubbornness—will raise their ugly heads. The typical elements of the High S stress model are given in table 24.

ROUTINE ACTION WITHOUT APPARENT RESULTS

High S's can develop a sense of security within routine. They may resist change for the better even though it may not appear that progress is presently being made. This behavior can be extremely frustrating to the High D or the High I. In Genesis 15 God promises Abraham a son after he has suggested that Eliezer be his heir. In verse 6, we see Abraham's response to God's prophecy: "Abraham believed the Lord, and he credited it to him as righteousness." God responded to Abraham's request to show him various signs and gave him the Abrahamic covenant. Abraham continued on with the faith that God would do what He said and patiently waited for it to happen. Sarah, the High D, had a different time schedule.

AGGRESSIVE, "TAKE CONTROL" STRATEGY BY PARTNER

One of the common responses of High D's and I's in relating to High S's involves decision making. Kathy's comments were, "If I don't make the decisions, nothing will get done!" What Kathy did not understand is that so long as confrontation is in her body language and voice tone, the High S will generally not make decisions. High S's prefer keeping the peace to debating issues. They have found it is easier and safer to go along with someone else's plan than to defend their own.

Sarah took stock of her age and concluded that her giving birth to a child was out of the question. She reasoned that God had prevented her from having children and that having a child through her Egyptian maid, Hagar, was a creative alternative. Obtaining a child in this way was a common practice in their culture.

HIGH S COMPLIANCE WITH PASSIVE RESULTS

High S's often react to change with compliance to keep the peace but will not aggressively support the new direction. This can become an additional irritation to the more aggressive profiles.

Abraham agreed to Sarah's plan. He did have relations with Hagar. Hagar did conceive, but became rebellious toward Sarah. Abraham did not get involved in settling this problem, nor did he show any support for Sarah.

CONFRONTATION BY PARTNER—THE "MORE IS BETTER" STRATEGY

As was previously stated, a common mistake the aggressive partner makes in a crisis involving a High S is in thinking that if a little confrontation moves a High S to a little action, more confrontation will move him further. In reality, the opposite is true. More confrontation will generally cause a regression.

Sarah became extremely displeased with Hagar and gave Abraham an ultimatum:

> You are responsible for the wrong I am suffering. I put my servant in your arms, and now that she knows she is pregnant, she despises me. May the Lord judge between you and me. (Genesis 16:5)

Abraham had no choice but to react.

PASSIVE-AGGRESSIVE RETREAT—
NONINVOLVEMENT, OR TURTLE SYNDROME

Depending on how strong the confrontation is, the normal High S reaction is to not get involved, or to retreat into a shell of silence.

Abraham reacted to Sarah by choosing not to get involved and letting Sarah deal with the problem. Sarah took command of the situation and dealt very harshly with Hagar—and Hagar fled. Fortunately the angel of the Lord comforted Hagar and told her to return and submit to Sarah's authority. Hagar did so and bore Ishmael. Later, there would be continued conflict between Hagar, Ishmael, and Sarah. Abraham would grieve over the problems but attempt to remain uninvolved.

IMMEDIATE STEPS TO TAKE IN A CRISIS

The High S's fear of change and disorganization is as real as the High I's fear of loss of social recognition and the High D's fear of loss of control. To discount its significance would be insensitive to his needs. The individual who is already in a crisis with his High S partner can take three immediate steps to defuse the High S's fear reaction.

RECOGNIZE FEAR AS BEING REAL

It is important for the High S and his partner to accept his fear as *real* without seeing him as, or making him feel, abnormal or guilty.

ALLOW FOR THE DELAY REACTION

When presenting a plan that involves change, allow the High S freedom to process the information before reacting. As previously mentioned, that will throttle fear by permitting the individual to get used to the idea emotionally before having to take ownership of the new plan.

GIVE FREEDOM TO SOLICIT MORE INFORMATION

Provide the High S with information on the steps that will be required to effect a smooth and orderly transition. Reassure him as to where he fits and where you fit into the new arrangement and how the change will benefit him. And do not ask him for an immediate decision, but encourage him to talk to others and give him the opportunity to sleep on the new idea.

THE 3 R'S IN LOVING THE HIGH S

In order to respond, relate to, and reinforce a High S, we must understand his needs. High S's function best in an environment that is affirming and encouraging rather than antagonistic. Remember, the things a High S needs are: status quo, security within his environment, time to process, affirmation and appreciation, defined expectation, and structured routines.

Below are nine principles to keep in mind when dealing with a High S.

HOW TO RESPOND TO A HIGH S
- Be nonthreatening and patient
- Allow time to process and adjust to change
- Make allowances for family

HOW TO RELATE TO A HIGH S
- Use friendly tones when instructing
- Give personal, nonverbal acceptance and assurances
- Allow time to process information

HOW TO REINFORCE THE HIGH S
- Repeat any instructions
- Provide hands-on reinforcement
- Be patient in allowing time to take ownership

If you understand these nine principles, you are on your way to creating a loving environment for those who have the Steadiness Profile.

ALLOW TIME TO ADJUST TO CHANGE

Most people with the High S personality style will go to great lengths to be accepted and to maintain stability within their environment. They generally accomplish this by neglecting their personal preferences and deferring to the wishes of others. Compromise is always an option, even if it means giving up their own rights or freedom—especially when their family is involved.

In Genesis 12 God tells Abraham to leave his family and country and move to the land of Canaan. The High S Abraham must have shuddered at the prospect of abandoning the comfort of his home and family in Ur. In fact, the verse construction of the story (which begins in chapter 11 and continues in chapter 12 of Genesis) seems to indicate that Abraham's initial response was to take his entire clan with him! And they didn't even make it all the way to Canaan, but stopped and settled in a place called Haran, where Abraham's father, Terah, ultimately died. When Abraham did finally move on to Canaan, he must have found it difficult to completely remove himself from family, for he took his nephew Lot with him.

NEED TO KEEP THE STATUS QUO UNLESS GIVEN SPECIFIC REASONS FOR CHANGE

Not only do the High S's desire to maintain stability, they also prefer to maintain the status quo, even though their situation may seem not desirable to anyone else. They rationalize that though their present situation may be uncomfortable, it is something they understand and to which they have adapted. Their fear of the unknown generally breeds feelings of insecurity, and they will usually avoid new ventures if at all possible.

There may be times when this model member of the family needs to venture out. The tranquillity of stability can turn into rigor mortis of the spirit. Sometimes the status quo isn't acceptable, especially when God says, "Go." That's what the Lord told Abraham to do. He went on to give Abraham a reason for the change to take place (Genesis 12:2):

> I will make you into a great nation
> and I will bless you;
> I will make your name great,
> and you will be a blessing.

MAKE ALLOWANCES FOR FAMILY

Although the security of the family is critical to the High S, the fear of dissension and conflict can have an even greater impact. To most people with this style, conflict is an unsettling emotion that threatens the very core of the environment and is generally viewed as something to be avoided at all costs.

Remember the episode between Abraham and Lot when strife broke out between their herdsmen? To avoid a conflict with Lot over land rights, Abraham parted company with his nephew. It wasn't until then that Abraham was totally free of the influences of his family—which is what God had desired all along.

Strengths will become weaknesses if they cause us to depend on ourselves. On the other hand, weaknesses can become strengths when they help to get us out of our comfort zones and depend upon God. In order to develop his relationship with God, Abraham had to give up his need to maintain the status quo. The Lord was patiently committed to creating the specific environment that allowed Abraham to make the decision to follow Him.

DEMONSTRATE LOYALTY TO AND SUPPORT OF THOSE THEY RESPECT

High S's are loyal friends with staying power that lasts through thick and thin. This is truly one of the outstanding qualities of persons with this style. While so many other people come and go like shadows, these are the friends who seem never to fade from our lives.

They are also supportive, making deliberate efforts to meet the needs of their friends and family. And if they make a promise, you can usually count on them to keep it.

STRIVE FOR SECURITY WITHIN THEIR FAMILIES

A natural complement to the High S's need for family stability is his need for family security. When it comes to his family, the High S doesn't want anything or anybody to rock the boat, and he surely doesn't want to take the boat into any storms. Let's just row peacefully around a quiet pond, thank you. No big outboard motors allowed on this family boat either —that's just a little too fast and dangerous for his liking. You can really improve your relationship with a High S by understanding his need for calm in the family port.

NEED TO BE GIVEN TIME TO ADJUST AND THE OPPORTUNITY TO VISUALIZE REQUESTS MADE OF THEM

When changes have to take place, a High S person needs a sufficient amount of time to adjust to the change and the opportunity to visually process information concerning the change.

God patiently allowed Abraham time to get accustomed to the idea of leaving Ur before moving to Canaan, and He allowed Abraham to visualize his future. Note the picture God provided in Genesis 13:14-18:

> The Lord said to Abram after Lot had parted from him, "Lift up your eyes from where you are and look north and south, east and west. All the land that you see I will give to you and your offspring forever. I will make your offspring like the dust of the earth, so that if anyone could count the dust, then your offspring could be counted. Go, walk through the length and breadth of the land, for I am giving it to you."
>
> So Abram moved his tents and went to live near the great trees of Mamre at Hebron, where he built an altar to the Lord.

It was not until Abraham took the time to walk through the land and experience it firsthand that he began to understand the plans of the Lord and became more at ease.

NEED PERSONAL ASSURANCES OF SUPPORT

Since High S's prefer a peaceful, agreeable environment, they feel insecure before and after an emotional confrontation. You can help a High S during pressure-packed times by giving him your personal assurance of support. Simply being with him spiritually and emotionally will mean much and will help reduce his anxiety. Most everyone appreciates the support of a friend in fearful times, but a High S will be especially grateful.

SEEK OUT CLOSE PERSONAL FRIENDSHIPS

People with the High S personality style are not only grateful for good friends, they seek them. As you cross the paths of such people, be aware that even as an acquaintance, they see you primarily as a potential friend. Whereas a High D may initially ignore you before he assesses your production ability, the High S will most often immediately assess your "friend-ability."

It is easy to become close friends with a High S. When you do, their loyalty and support will carry through a lifetime. James, the brother of Jesus, comments on the special relationship Abraham had with God: "And the scripture was fulfilled that says, 'Abraham believed God, and it was credited to him as righteousness,' and he was called God's friend" (James 2:23).

Isaiah also speaks of God's friendship with Abraham (Isaiah 41:8):

> "But you, O Israel, my servant,
>   Jacob, whom I have chosen,
>   you descendants of Abraham my friend."

Abraham became God's friend, but the Lord was first Abraham's friend. God consistently projected a personal, agreeable, and friendly environment that gave Abraham the opportunity to respond as a loyal partner. It is important to understand that God never used confrontation in His relationship with Abraham. He was always supportive, patient, and relational. S/I Patterns respond to fond feelings but will reject acts of aggression. The Lord's supportive environment was extended to him even when he was out of God's will. For Abraham, the High S, restoration was offered in an accepting, nonconfrontational environment. God's patience resulted in gaining a loyal companion.

GREATEST STRUGGLES ARE IN
HANDLING CHANGE AND SAYING NO

Probably the greatest hindrance to the High S is handling change with confidence and a positive attitude. Biblical examples seem to indicate that God continued to encourage and support the High S's through difficult change experiences, giving them permission to grow by inches first rather than miles. Initially, progress was slow, but gradually they became more independent and responded positively to change.

In addition, the High S typically has difficulty being firm and assertive, preferring that others take action and make decisions.

The High S is not the one you want to answer the door when the widget salesman comes calling. Because of a desire to always support and please others, they have difficulty saying no. "What?" the High S may say to the crafty peddler. "You say your mother is ill and you can't go to college unless you sell a thousand widgets by Friday?" Families with a High S and a checkbook are likely to have a closet full of widgets.

One last thing helpful to know in understanding the High S personality better is that he often has difficulty realizing his own strengths and what he can accomplish. This is certainly not a problem for the High D person, but it is a very real obstacle for the Steadiness ones. However, once they begin to develop confidence in their skills, they can become very effective leaders. Abraham showed dynamic effectiveness as a leader when he launched out with confidence and successfully rescued Lot, who had been captured by enemy forces (Genesis 14:1-16).

A WOMAN'S PERSPECTIVE ON THE HIGH S

Kayle is the mother of three young children, and she has Abraham's and Hannah's Advisor Profile. She identified with how God created a loving environment for Abraham. She shares some of her impressions:

> In the case study of God and Abraham, I saw for the first time how threatening it must have been for Abraham when the Lord asked him to leave the security of his family and homeland. For me, this would be next to impossible, except as it related to the two things that mean the most to me (two things I will fight for), my faith and my family.
>
> God would have ministered to me, as He did with Abraham, when He allowed him to take along his family members, even though it was against God's initial directions. Loyalty to family is very important to me, though I can be

loyal to a fault. If God would have rebuked or confronted me in this situation, I would have been crushed, considered myself to be a failure, and, I am sure, not have been able to proceed. Instead, God patiently waited and seemed to understand the reasons for Abraham's actions in taking along his nephew Lot.

Personally, it is important for me to feel understood, even if you don't agree with me. I need the kind of encouragement God gave Abraham. I wonder "Is the job I'm doing OK?" "Is this the right direction?" It's not a constant flatterer that motivates me, but an occasional "That's a good job," or "Now go in this direction" that keeps me on track.

I need my space, rather than someone looking over my shoulder. I also need the kind of freedom God allowed Abraham in their relationship. To be close to a warm, accepting, trusting, understanding, patient-with-my-faults God appeals to me. Having the freedom to be who I am and nothing else is ideal. Knowing the Lord was committed to being Abraham's friend and my friend is very comforting to me.

God's best to you,
Kayle

WHAT THE VARIOUS PERSONALITY STYLES HAD TO SAY ABOUT THE HIGH S

What is the most difficult part about relating to a High S?

High D: "Without a doubt, patiently giving them time to process information before making a decision."

High I: "Accepting the status quo and allowing them time before accepting change."

High S: "Having to carry a conversation so that a meaningful interchange takes place. I'd rather just listen, but they are usually not talking."

High C: "Knowing what to say in order to draw them out."

What can you do to build a better relationship with the High S Profiles?

High D: "Backing off from our need to have immediate answers and working within their pace."

High I: "By being more patient in drawing them out."

High S: "By patiently listening as they try to give their insights."

High C: "We need to be more patient in knowing we won't get a lot of feedback from them. We have a tendency to desire a great deal of information, and High S's are not in the habit of sharing that much."

Where do you most need the talents of the High S?

High D: "Their follow-through and consistency; being a peacemaker; their dry humor."

High I: "Their gift in seeing the big picture and commitment to seeing work completed no matter how long it takes."

High S: "Their consistent commitment to a friendship."

High C: "Their ability to handle adversity without a great deal of emotion. They just keep plugging along."

REACTIONS FROM HIGH S'S

High S's have a special interest in creating harmony in their relationships. They make good team players and work well in a stable environment. As with any of the other profiles, over-extensions can and do occur. The following comments come from High S Representative Patterns who were willing to give us their insights concerning how to respond better to them.

High S: "Allow me time to process information before asking me to make a decision, and give me reassurances when I do."

"Never use confrontation in correcting me. I cannot handle that. I prefer a nonconfrontational approach. I need to know we are friends!"

High S/D: "Let me work out issues in my mind. I cannot always put into words what I desire you to do. Be patient with me as I try to explain my plan."

"I know I can be blunt at times, particularly under stress. Use humor to relax me, but do not attack me. If you do, I will generally give you feedback you don't want to hear."

High S/I: "I need reassurances that I am accepted as a person. If I make a mistake, explain my error in a gentle way. Give me time to think about how I am going to correct the problem."

"Give me broad time frames, outline your expectations, step back and let me meet them. Show genuine interest in my feelings and views. Accept the fact that perfection is not important to me."

High S/C/D: "I'm not always sure what my feelings are in a given situation, so be patient with me as you draw me out."

"Use humor to relax me before asking tough questions. Afterward give me verbal or nonverbal reassurances—just being there with me means a lot."

What is the most responsive thing we can do for you when you are under stress?

High S: "Provide me with time and space in which I can enjoy peace and quiet. I need time to think and assimilate."

               "When I'm under stress, I don't always know how to put in words what is happening to me. It's OK to use reassuring, supportive humor to relax me so that I have a better opportunity to express to you what I am feeling."

High S/D: "I can be fairly blunt when I'm under stress. Give me time and an opportunity to work out my internal difficulties and then let's talk."

High S/I: "Come alongside me and offer understanding and empathy, but don't take over and try to fix my problem. In extreme stress allow me 'down time' to escape for a while."

               "Sometimes I just need a hug from my husband without any words being spoken."

High S/C/D: "Allow me process time, which may appear to you to be mindless activities. I need to break my mind away from the stressful activities to reflect and recharge."

"I have difficulty expressing my feelings. Allow me to give you random thoughts without judging or analyzing them."

CONCLUSION

Each profile has its own set of defenses to handle stress. As members of the Body of Christ, our response must be to recognize and accept the behavior for what it is. Then we can create an environment for the person so that he has the best opportunity to work through his internal struggles and grow. In the case of High S's, giving them assurances of support, providing them with concrete information, and allowing them time to ponder are key elements in helping them work through their personal stress.

A LOOK AHEAD

The last family of Representative Patterns is the High C style. We will now explore the unique characteristics of this group. Comparing this family to the D, I, and S Patterns will complete the picture of the four major personality styles.

ELEVEN

UNDERSTANDING THE COMPLIANCE STYLE

There are times in life when we need not just results but quality results, when the job not only needs to be done but to be done with sterling precision. Long before any man put his hands to a task, the world was divinely created with accuracy, order, and quality. Fortunately, some people still strive for achievements that manifest those characteristics.

When we want every *t* crossed and every *i* dotted, just as God did when the time had come to set His law in stone, we look to a person with the Compliance (High C) personality style. Indeed, God chose a High C, Moses, to accurately proclaim His law to the Hebrew people. Just getting the job done would not have been sufficient.

We have seen that a Dominance personality sets his sights on the objective and vigorously pursues it, generally preferring to live by his own rules along the way. The Influencing personality arouses the people, always motivating and encouraging them to give their best. The Steadiness personality is a rock of support, a team player, and someone we can count on to be loyal.

A person with the Compliance personality style prefers to set the standard for a group—and expects everyone to comply, always with the objective of insuring quality, accuracy, and order. A High D will get us over the mountain, to be sure, but the High C will get us over with everyone and everything in its place, at the proper time and destination, and within budget.

Much like people with the High S personality, High C people prefer the status quo. Sudden change can produce an unsettling response in them. In fact, when they are approached with new ideas, they will usually ask numerous clarification questions. Those who prefer less structure and environments more filled with adventure (High D and I people) might view such inquiries are unnecessary and distracting. However, the cautious approach toward change that the High C's possess can uncover errors in a planning process before it is too late. In a church or business environment it is not uncommon for new programs utilizing enormous energy and financial resources to be introduced only to discover that something important has been overlooked in the planning stages. Momentum is lost and the programs are either delayed or fail. As they fulfill their need for quality control and accuracy, High C people can save organizations much time and money.

On the other hand, the cautious need to heed a caution: too much attention to detail can become a weakness. Constant checking and rechecking the accuracy of data can damage a relationship. Consider the wife who refused to go on an outing simply because she was unable to balance the family checkbook. She spent an hour trying to find a five-cent error and rejected her husband's suggestion to make an ESP entry (Error Some Place) and forget about it. Finally, her frustrated husband left without her. Her compulsion for complete accuracy ruined plans for a date with her husband. A drive for perfection can have its negative side.

Below is the list of the four High C Representative Patterns and the parallel positive biblical characters who represent those patterns.

Compliance Representative Patterns	Biblical Character
Perfectionist (primary C)	Luke, Esther
Analyst (C/S/D)	Moses, Thomas, Naomi (*)

Compliance Representative Patterns   Biblical Character

Cooperator (C/I/S)   Elijah, Deborah (*),
                                      Ruth

Adaptor (C/S)   John, Mary (*)

*Not enough information to be absolutely certain of the specific style.

GENERAL TENDENCIES OF THE COMPLIANCE STYLE

TENDS TOWARD PRODUCT AS OPPOSED TO PROCESS

Both High D and High C people are task rather than people oriented (as opposed to the High I and High S styles). However, the High D personality seems to be driven by the process
of achieving a goal, whereas the High C personality tends to
concentrate on producing a quality product.

Consider the publishing of this book, or any book. Someone of the High D persuasion would likely concern himself with
the step-by-step process involved in getting the manuscript
written, edited, to press, and ultimately delivered to you, the
reader. He would be interested in controlling the process of
getting the job done. But a typical High C would concentrate
his efforts on insuring that the manuscript was accurate, gram-
matically correct, printed on quality paper in a timely manner
—all, of course, within budget. His attention would be on the
quality of the product. High C's are more interested in the
product, and high D's more interested in the process (table 25).

As we often stress, no style is better than any other and all
are needed to get the job done. In fact, it takes the efforts of
both High D and High C styles to get a good book published.
And don't forget that it was probably the High I who developed
the marketing plan and attractive display in order to distribute
the book to your bookstore and ultimately into your hands.

PREFERS STRUCTURE AS OPPOSED TO SPONTANEITY

Part of the High C's drive for quality, accuracy, and order
is derived from his strong desire for a structured environment.

Table 25

Tendency Toward Product versus Process Orientation

product -- process

C   S   I   D

C   Emphasizes the "correct" or "right" way to carry out a
     task.
     Sees the quality of the product as most important.

S   Focuses on how and when to carry out a responsibility.
     Provides support in standardizing how a product is
     produced

I   Actively voices opinions as to how a project should pro-
     ceed and be distributed.
     Will stimulate the decision-making process and influence
     others to act.

D   Wants control of the process for carrying out tasks.
     Will stimulate action that produces the best results.

SOURCE: Adapted from Life Associates, Inc., The *DISC Model: Trainer and Consultant's Reference Encyclopedia.*

High C's prefer an inch-by-inch, step-by-step approach to a task. For them, even life itself should proceed along a predictable path. Their motto might be "I can't move on until I get it right!"

    The High I and D personalities, in opposite fashion, seek spontaneity and freedom of expression (table 26). "Let's get on with it or move on to something else!" might be their motto.

    The Johnson family illustrates the way the four styles approach spontaneity. Jack (High D) had been studying for his semester exams for several days. The night before the tests were to begin, he was on the phone making arrangements to meet with his friends for breakfast the next morning before school. He asked his Dad (High C) for the OK to proceed with the plans.

Table 26

Tendency Toward Structure Continuum

greater -- lesser

| C | S | D | I |

C   Firmly in control of emotions.
     Attends to detail and doing things right.
     Prefers organization.

S   Moderately in control of emotions.
     Has steady work habits and is well organized.

D   Not restrained with expression of emotions.
     Enjoys responding to challenges.
     Bored with routine.

I   Freely expresses emotions and ideas.
     Is difficult to keep on schedule.
     Relates work to strong social interest.

SOURCE: Adapted from Life Associates, Inc., The *DISC Model: Trainer and Consultant's Reference Encyclopedia.*

Dad could not understand why Jack would even consider going out right before an exam. To him the right thing would be for Jack to keep his mind focused on the information he had been studying and go right to school without any distractions. As you can imagine, that was just the opposite of what Jack wanted. He felt the best way to perform well on his tests would be to have a good breakfast with friends and go in refreshed, relaxed, and ready for the challenge.

Being the good counselor, Mom (High I) resolved the potential conflict by helping Jack and his dad see that they both were right, considering their individual needs. Dad preferred structure, whereas Jack preferred freedom from routine. Father and son were able to clear up the misunderstanding and negotiate an agreeable solution.

DESIRES ACCURACY AND PRECISION

As we noted earlier, God used the High C Moses to record His law. Where could accuracy and precision possibly be more important? Scripture reveals other instances of how the Lord used High C's to give us details. Luke, for example, did not actually walk the dusty roads of Galilee with Jesus, but he must have spent many hours interviewing people who had. As a physician, he was someone concerned with accuracy. Consider what you understand about the High C personality style as you read the opening of his account (Luke 1:1-4):

> Many have undertaken to draw up an account of the things that have been fulfilled among us, just as they were handed down to us by those who from the first were eyewitnesses and servants of the word. Therefore, since I myself have carefully investigated everything from the beginning, it seemed good also to me to write an orderly account for you, most excellent Theophilus, so that you may know the certainty of the things you have been taught.

Luke recorded much material not found in the other gospels. He was fascinated by the uncommon or unusual people that came into contact with Jesus—Zacchaeus, for example, or the penitent thief. He recorded Mary's most intimate thoughts concerning the events surrounding the birth of Jesus. There is much we would miss about the life and ministry of Jesus had it not been for Luke's attention to detail.

The High C person's preoccupation with detail leads him to prefer an environment where everything has a name, label, and place. Ever visit a High C uncle and found yourself needing a tool from his garage? Remember his instructions? Find the right tool, use it properly, clean it when you're done, oil it if necessary, and then put it back exactly where he has labeled it to go.

TENDS TO BE CAUTIOUS ABOUT CHANGE AND IS
LIKELY TO ASK QUESTIONS FOR CLARIFICATION

Before a person with the High C personality style is at all comfortable with change, he must process information—all the information—that might pertain to the impending change.

The company president stood before his employees and announced, "We are moving our offices downtown!"

"That's great!" shouted one person. "Think of all the restaurants and places to go!"

"Fantastic!" shouted another. "We will be closer to most of our clients and we'll meet our objectives by mid-year!"

"I have my reservations about this," said yet another, "but if that is what everyone wants to do . . ."

A fourth spoke up. "And just how will we get all of our equipment down there without having to stop production? How many square feet of space will we have downtown? What is the difference in rent? Are you sure we will have the resources we need to deliver our goods on schedule? How will this move affect the quality of our products?" And so on. You can probably guess the various personality styles portrayed.

In spite of facing pressure and obstacles, the High C person will generally comply with those in authority. And as we mentioned earlier in this chapter, his questions just might yield some improvements to the plan. Just how *will* that company get all of their equipment downtown without stopping production?

Although part of the High C person's needs are met through asking questions, he will usually remain cautious for a long time before completely accepting the change. Moreover, he will constantly test new procedures to determine whether or not the change has been for the good. However, once satisfied that the change is an improvement, he will be quite faithful in his assignments.

The processing of information is critical to a Compliance person if he is to feel comfortable with a change. In Luke 1:26-28 the angel Gabriel announced to Mary that she would conceive and bear a son. The Scriptures indicate that Mary was "greatly troubled at his words and wondered what kind of greeting this might be" (v. 29). You can imagine how confused she must have been. Finally, she asked a question. "How will this be," she asked, "since I am a virgin?" (v. 34).

The angel answered her question by explaining that God was involved and the child would be His Son. This was a start, but we may be sure there were dozens of other questions she wanted a response to. As a means of trying to comfort Mary, Gabriel gave her the news that her barren relative, Elizabeth, had also conceived and would bear a son. Elizabeth would later be instrumental in comforting this young virgin.

In spite of facing pressure and many obstacles, the High C will generally comply with those in authority. Mary quickly told Gabriel that as the Lord's servant, she would be a willing participant in God's plan. But you will notice also that she went immediately to the home of Elizabeth for support. It appears that she stayed with Elizabeth until John "the Baptist" was born before she returned home to face the completion of her own divine mission.

BLIND SPOTS OF THE HIGH C

USUALLY FEARS CRITICISM

Because of their high standards of performance, people with this personality style can be extremely critical of their own work and have a tendency to internalize criticism from others.

Whereas a person with the High I or S personality style might be sensitive to criticism because he perceives it as a sign of his not being accepted (a relational issue), the person with a High C personality has difficulty with criticism because he sees the criticism as dissatisfaction with his standard of performance.

Remember the woman we mentioned earlier who missed the family outing because she could not find a five-cent error in her checkbook? You can imagine the impact on her if someone criticized her ability to keep accurate records!

Since High C's can be extremely harsh in evaluating their own work, their tendency to internalize criticism usually leads them to experience feelings of insecurity and depression—and in the most extremes cases, even thoughts of suicide. Quite often their greatest vulnerability to criticism comes after an emotional high combined with a lack of food and rest.

That pattern can be seen in the story of Elijah in 1 Kings 19. Following Elijah's victory over the prophets of Baal, Jezebel sent a message to Elijah declaring that she was going to have him killed. Elijah became afraid and fled. When he finally stopped to rest, Elijah's fear had become so intense he prayed to the Lord to take his life. Even after the prophet had rested and eaten food, he continued to lament over his problem. He saw himself as being totally alone. Criticism had taken a heavy toll. Finally, when Elijah was willing to express his true fears to God, the Lord provided him with an action strategy that changed his focus and renewed his hope. Being patient and encouraging to a High C can be valuable to his recovery from fearful events.

TENDS TO BE CRITICAL AND DEMANDING UNDER PRESSURE

The High C person does not intend to stand alone in his quest for quality and order. On the contrary, not only is he critical of himself, he can be quite demanding of others as well. If we make a commitment to someone with this personality style, he will expect us to follow through, and if the agreed upon plan is changed, we can expect ongoing reminders. Like any other strength overextended, a commitment to excellence can produce negative reactions.

Jonah was given the opportunity to represent God's plan to the people of Nineveh. Jonah was commissioned by God to enter the city and proclaim the wickedness of the people. God announced that He would overthrow the city unless the people repented. Typical of the High C, Jonah did not feel qualified for the position and fled to Tarshish (Spain). After a detour in the belly of a fish, Jonah finally agreed to become the Lord's messenger. He preached to the people in such a manner that most of the city repented and turned to God.

When God saw how the people's hearts changed, He held back His judgment on Nineveh and did not bring about the disaster that He had mentioned to Jonah. Jonah's message had helped the people to believe and repent. But Jonah was not pleased with the Lord's sparing of Nineveh.

Instead of being joyful about God's grace, Jonah was angry and depressed! He was actually mad at God for not following through on the plan He had outlined. That seems absurd, but it goes to show how a High C feels about completing a planned course of action.

It did not matter to Jonah that the change had a positive result and that 120,000 lives were spared. Negative feelings overcame this High C prophet. To help Jonah, God allowed him the freedom to express his feelings out loud without fear of being punished. Then He answered Jonah's questions and neutralized his negative thinking process by providing him with a different perspective.

OVERVIEW OF THE HIGH C REPRESENTATIVE PATTERNS

Four styles characterize the High C: *the Perfectionist, the Analyst, the Cooperator,* and *the Adaptor.* The following pages list the ten categories of each pattern and amplify the High C behavioral style by giving biblical parallels for each pattern. There are distinct differences between the four Compliance patterns. The Perfectionist represents the classic High C, whereas the other styles incorporate a blend. For example, the Analyst tends to be more assertive and outspoken in his criticism. The Cooperator possess greater verbal skills than either the Perfectionist or the Analyst. The Adaptor tends to be more amiable and supportive. Recognizing these general differences is helpful in relating effectively to the four styles.

PERFECTIONIST PATTERN

POSITIVE TRAITS

Perfectionists (table 27) tend to be low-key, factual, and painfully accurate. This style is reliable, precise, conscientious, and tactful. They tend to prefer a predictable environment free

Table 27
Primary High C Pattern

I. Distinctive tendencies of this pattern:

Primary drive	Being cautious, desires to follows instructions
Personal giftedness	Attention to details, validation of data, diplomatic, loyalty
Group giftedness	Dependable, the conscience for any group
Potential spiritual gifts	Pastor-Teaching, Helps, Service
Internal fear	The unknown and undefined
Strength out of control	Overanalyzes the importance of issues and data
Under stress becomes	Cautious and indecisive
Blind spots	Loses sight of the big picture by continued focus on details
Needs to work on	Letting unimportant details and issues take care of themselves
Best team members	I, I/C, I/D, I/S, S/C

II. Biblical characters who represent this pattern:

1. Luke
2. Esther

III. Further Bible study:

Strengths	Luke 1:1-4; Esth. 4:1-17, 5:1-6
Weaknesses	Esth. 5:7-8, Esth. 7:1-10

of surprises. If change and/or antagonism occurs, they tend to become cautious and avoid conflict. It is not unusual for them to solicit the advice of several counselors to clarify issues, mentally cross-check and process the information, and then make a decision. They prefer being a part of a team and are uneasy about public recognition.

Luke, the "beloved physician" and companion of Paul, best represents this style. Luke was among the most scholarly men of the New Testament writers. His gospel is among the most poetic and personal of the four gospels. Luke takes great care to accurately and systematically present his version of who Jesus was. He had personal interviews with those who had intimate knowledge of the specifics of Christ's life, and he recorded those events after cross-checking each story. His historical accounts are held in the highest regard to their accuracy, beauty, sensitivity, and poetic style. True to his profile, Luke never mentions his name as the author either of the Gospel of Luke or the Acts of the Apostles. We only know of his authorship through the pronoun "we" in the book of Acts and Paul's writings.

VALUE TO A TEAM

Once committed, Perfectionists are extremely thorough and loyal to completing the task at hand. Luke's mission was to proclaim the humanity of Christ. His recording of Jesus' life is characterized as the gospel to the gentiles. As Paul's companion, Luke faithfully recorded the apostle's activities during his three missionary journeys. Luke's detailed accounts give us an accurate record of the historical workings of the first-century church.

RESPONSE TO PRESSURE

When threatened, Perfectionists tend to become cautious and indecisive. However, if supported and given time, they can offer a diplomatic and tactful response. God chose Esther to be His representative in a very difficult situation when the Jewish people were in danger of being destroyed. She responded to the pressure by devising a plan in order to save her people.

When Queen Esther heard that an edict had been given to kill the Jews, she sent inquiries to her Uncle Mordecai in order to find out who was behind the order. She learned that the king's assistant, Haman, was responsible. Mordecai asked Esther to go before the king and speak to him herself. In her cautious manner, Esther gave Mordecai all the reasons why his directive was unwise. She knew that anyone going to the king uninvited was in danger of being killed. Mordecai countered by reminding her that she had nothing to lose, for as a Jew she would naturally be included in the death decree. After three days of fasting, Esther committed herself to approaching the king. Realizing this was a pressure situation, she was careful in developing a plan to address the problem.

Esther's strategy was classic High C. She planned an elaborate banquet for the king and Haman in order to prepare the king's heart for her inquiry to save her people. Esther pioneered the idea that the way to a man's heart is through his stomach!

After the meal, the king asked Esther the nature of her petition and ended up offering her up to half of the kingdom. Esther remained cautious, did not respond, and asked that the king and Haman return the following evening for another celebration. One thing a High C will do is to make sure his plan of action is perfectly positioned before he proceeds to carry it out.

During the second banquet, Esther finally petitioned the king to save her life and the lives of her people, the Jews. The king asked who was responsible for such a decree and who would dare to touch the queen. Esther pointed to Haman. Haman realized the danger and pleaded for his life. It didn't work, and he was hanged. Because of her cautious nature, Esther worked through her plan in systematic fashion and faithfully carried out Mordecai's instructions. The result of her actions was that she saved the Jewish nation from being slaughtered at the hand of the Persians. Esther was the perfect person to carry out this pressure-packed plan.

THE ANALYST PATTERN

POSITIVE TRAITS

Analyst Profiles (table 28) are models of quality control. In addition, they respond well to those in authority and follow written and verbal instructions in a methodical, orderly manner. If they are required to communicate instructions to others, Perfectionists are extremely diligent in giving the exact message with the same intent and spirit of the author.

In Exodus 19-23, it is Moses, the Perfectionist, through whom God chooses to communicate His laws to His people. Moses faithfully and accurately recorded each of the commandments given to him by God. In Exodus 24, the covenant is written down and publicly ratified. On each occasion Moses remained true to God's instructions and consistently represented His intent to the people.

VALUE TO A TEAM

Analyst Profiles are critical to a team when high standards and specific procedures need to be implemented and maintained. This style tends to be extremely reliable, factual, steady, and a stickler for system and order. Once committed to a plan, Analyst Profiles can be counted on to complete the assigned task without regard to time.

Thirty-nine years after Moses communicated God's laws to the generation that departed Egypt, he would communicate the same message to the next generation. The record detailing his instructions is the book of Deuteronomy, which Jesus quoted when He summarized the law of God (Matthew 22:37-38). Of the twenty-seven books that make up the New Testament, seventeen quote from Deuteronomy.[1] By any standard of measurement, this is a valuable contribution.

1. Charles Caldwell Ryrie, ed., *The Ryrie Study Bible, New International Version* (Chicago: Moody, 1985), p. 240.

Table 28
High C/S/D Pattern

I. Distinctive tendencies of this pattern:

Primary drive	Validating the accuracy of data, doing things right
Personal giftedness	Steadiness in completing the assigned task
Group giftedness	Unwavering dependability, commitment to quality
Potential spiritual gifts	Pastor-Teacher, Helps, Service
Internal fear	Criticism directed toward them
Strength out of control	Legalistic in interpreting rules and regulations
Under stress becomes	Diplomatic with others and/or introspective, self-critical
Blind spots	Focusing on the optimistic side of new ideas, plans, thoughts
Needs to work on	Being critical of self and others, lowering expectations
Best team members	I/D, D/I, S/I, I/S

II. Biblical characters who represent this pattern:

1. Moses
2. Thomas (*)
3. Naomi (*)

III. Further Bible study:

Strengths	Ex. 19, 24, 32; Deut. 4
Weaknesses	Ex. 3:1-22; 4:1-17

*Not enough information to be absolutely certain of the specific style.

STRENGTH OUT OF CONTROL

Analyst Profiles tend to put a great deal of emphasis on seeing the hard facts with their own eyes. They lives by observing, validating, studying, and touching the evidence before drawing any sound conclusions. When stories of a resurrected Christ were shared by Thomas's fellow apostles, he publicly discounted faith in these testimonies until he could see the nail wounds in His hands and put his fingers into them and place his hand into Jesus' side. Jesus provided him with that opportunity, and then he believed.

The Cooperator Pattern

Cooperators (table 29) have the distinction of having three of the DISC styles in the makeup of their personality. They combine high levels of the Compliance and Influencing styles along with a lesser Steadiness drive. They are people who are motivated by a preference for Compliance to the standards they have established for themselves and others. To understand their actions is to realize that they are driven by the interaction of these separate needs: to control, to influence, to cooperate.

POSITIVE TRAITS

People with Cooperator qualities are skilled at breaking down complex ideas into practical steps and systematic procedures. They are also able to persuade people that what they have developed will be useful. The progression of their thoughts as they work on a project goes from *I'm sure we can find a way to do it* to *This is the* right *way to do it!*

Cooperators can be practical in devising a plan to prove a point. In 1 Kings 18:22-39, Elijah outlines a method for proving who was the true God of Israel: Jehovah or Baal. The test he proposed was a big challenge, and much was at stake. What he proposed was this: the people of Israel and all 450 priests of Baal were to meet him at Mount Carmel for a contest (cooperators love competition). Two bulls were to be placed upon two different stacks of wood. The prophets of Baal were to call upon

Table 29
High C/I/S Pattern

I. Distinctive tendencies of this pattern:

Primary drive	Intense desire to maintain quality; cooperation
Personal giftedness	Conscientious in communicating standards and traditions
Group giftedness	Being able to assume a variety of functions
Potential spiritual gifts	Exhortation, Helps, Knowledge
Internal fear	Criticism of personal effort or work
Strength out of control	Being confused by the mix of internal messages
Under stress becomes	Self-critical and paralyzed by emotions
Blind spots	Incongruent feelings making logical "bottom-line thinking" difficult
Needs to work on	Letting others help, being more open to sharing negative feelings
Best team members	D, D/I, D equal I, S/D

II. Biblical characters who represent this pattern:

1. Elijah
2. Deborah (*)
3. Ruth (*)

III. Further Bible study:

Strengths	1 Kings 18:1-46
Weaknesses	1 Kings 19:1-18

*Not enough information to be absolutely certain of the specific style.

their god to intervene by setting fire to the bull on their stack of wood. Elijah would then call upon Jehovah to set fire to the other stack of wood. Whoever answered by fire was the true God. The people accepted this procedure as a true test. Scripture records that the prophets of Baal called upon their god for hours without any response. God, on the other hand, responded quickly, and the victory was won! Victory can be sweet to a Cooperator. His satisfaction comes in accomplishing something that others might not have succeeded in doing.

VALUE TO THE TEAM

It is common for Cooperators to have knowledge about many subjects and to network well within differing groups. If in leadership, the combination of interpersonal *and* problem-solving skills are critical when technical and people-problems collide. Cooperators have high ambitions for themselves and others. This causes them to stand out from others in a group. Innovation and being unconventional is what they strive for in accomplishing personal or professional goals. A Cooperator works hard at becoming a key person in a specialized field. It is not uncommon for a Cooperator to strike out on his own, even though it might involve giving up a measure of the security that also drives him.

Cooperators need to be careful to expect others to take the same initiative they feel is important in order to complete a project. It is not uncommon for an employer to evaluate the commitment of his staff by how much initiative and innovation they exercise when they fulfill their responsibilities for the company. Getting employee expectations into the open will help resolve the Cooperator's tendency to suppress feelings of disappointment in the performance of others.

RESPONSE UNDER PRESSURE

Unlike other High C's, Cooperators possess good verbal skills and can respond to most opposition with great proficiency. In 1 Kings 18:27, Elijah mocks the priests of Baal as they try to call on their gods to rain down fire upon their offering. Obviously, Elijah knew his position was the superior one and seized the moment to make his point. He was not only confident but a little arrogant in how he taunted the prophets. As we have seen, his overconfidence came back later to haunt him when Jezebel threatened to have him killed.

THE ADAPTOR PATTERN

POSITIVE TRAITS

Adaptors (table 30) tend to be critical thinkers but are also cooperative with those in authority. Typical of any High C, Adaptors will ask clarification questions if they are instructed to do something new. However, once given logical, affirming reasons for a particular course of action, Adaptors will generally *adapt*. They desire to fit in quietly with a team and will tend to reject interpersonal aggression. As long as a peaceful environment exists, Adaptors will faithfully carry out the instructions given to them. However, if conflict arises, they will tend to avoid conflicts.

The Old Testament records a positive example of how a High C demonstrates extreme loyalty. Ruth had developed a special relationship with her mother-in-law, Naomi. After Ruth's husband died, she chose to remain close to Naomi and return with her to Bethlehem instead of remaining in her native land of Moab. In order to support them, Ruth asked Naomi for permission to work in the fields to gather grain for food. While there, she met Boaz, Naomi's relative, who took the responsibility of watching over her. When Ruth told Naomi of her encounter with Boaz, Naomi affirmed that Boaz was a good man. In other words, he might be the kind of man you could have a future with. Naomi gave Ruth counsel and explicit instructions as to how to meet and be responsive to Boaz. Ruth carefully followed Naomi's instructions. Boaz responded favorably to Ruth's actions and ultimately took her to be his wife. Her loyalty and willingness to follow instructions resulted in events that had eternal consequences. Ruth is one of only four women to be named in the genealogy of Christ.

Table 30
High C/S Pattern

I. Distinctive tendencies of this pattern:

Primary drive	Critical thinking, being cooperative, validating data
Personal giftedness	Team player, good at follow-through, commitment to quality and order
Group giftedness	Maintains traditions, adapting to those in authority
Potential spiritual gifts	Knowledge, Teaching, Service
Internal fear	Surprises and illogical thinking
Strength out of control	Questions all data for accuracy and flaws
Under stress becomes	Introspective and overly concerned with "what ifs"
Blind spots	Being preoccupied with having to resolve every experience logically
Needs to work on	Talking about negative thoughts and feelings
Best team members	I, I/C, I/S, I/S/C, S

II. Biblical characters who represent this pattern:

1. John
2. Mary (*)

III. Further Bible study:

Strengths	John 19:26-27; Luke 1:26-56
Weaknesses	Luke 2:15-19; 2:41-51

*Not enough information to be absolutely certain of the specific style.

VALUE TO THE TEAM

Adaptors are loyal team players and are good at follow-through. This style is stable, accommodating, and faithful. Once an Adaptor takes ownership of specific instructions, it will be done. Others may talk about being available and supportive, but the Adaptors *are the models*. Peter, the High I, boldly stated that if Jesus were ever threatened, he would give up his life in order to protect Him. John said nothing. At the cross, only one disciple was present, John. From the cross, Jesus asked him to take care of Mary. From that day Mary became part of John's household.

INTERNAL FEAR

Although extremely cooperative, Adaptors do not like surprises of illogical thinking. They prefer to follow traditional rules, regulations, and procedures. The latter defines their level of security. When the former happens, they tend to ask questions in order to validate information and reestablish order and stability.

When the angel Gabriel announced that Mary would have a child, she asked a technical question as to how this was possible. The angel's declaration certainly qualified as an illogical surprise, since Mary had never had relations with a man. Her question was certainly in order. Gabriel answered her question and gave her additional information about her aunt, Elizabeth, 'the barren one." In her old age, Elizabeth, too, was pregnant. This additional information seemed to satisfy Mary because of her compliant response: "I am the Lord's servant, and I am willing to do whatever He wants. May everything you said come true."

What is intriguing is Mary's response to the announcement of Elizabeth's pregnancy. After the angel left, Mary hurried to see Elizabeth. When she arrived, Elizabeth's baby jumped in her womb, and Elizabeth confirmed that Mary's child would be the Messiah. Still, Mary stayed until Elizabeth gave birth to John the Baptist. To feel secure, Adaptors need to check and recheck data to confirm that their information is accurate and correct. Even after the birth of Jesus, Mary continued to ponder in her heart the meaning of what had happened.

A LOOK AHEAD

We have now completed an overview of the sixteen Representative Patterns. Each Representative Pattern is different from the others, but there are characteristics in each style that can be correlated with other styles.

- The High D's are motivated by getting results.
- The High C's are motivated by maintaining consistency.
- The High I's strive for flexibility and place much importance on the quality of relationships as they influence others.
- The High S's seek to maintain a favorable, supportive, and loyal position as they respond to others.

By now you can see that there is a sense of order and harmony in these four personality styles—we need all of them to be whole. The Dominance person has the capacity for vision—he can get us over the mountain that seems too high to climb. Indeed, he will get us over one way or another! The Steadiness and Influencing personalities remind us that people are more important than the climb itself. And the Compliance personality recognizes that the real reason for getting over the mountain is to board a ship that is to sail for a promised land. If we don't make it over the mountain and arrive at the right destination at the right time, we will all miss the boat altogether.

TWELVE

RESPONDING TO THE NEEDS OF THE COMPLIANCE PERSONALITY

Randy was a model child and, as a young man, was always polite, actually using words such as "please" and "thank you" at the appropriate times. He made straight A's throughout high school and was valedictorian of his class. Having become a Christian at an early age, he was conscientious about living up to a high moral standard. He was disciplined enough to maintain a consistent commitment to Christ throughout his teen years.

When Randy was fifteen, at the suggestion of his youth director, he committed himself to a discipleship program that called for one hour of daily Bible study. Randy, who also happened to have a High C Analyst Pattern, saw this commitment as a minimum standard in growing spiritually. He began to experience guilt feelings if he missed even one day of hourly study. Fortunately, he had a good enough relationship with his parents to tell them of his struggle. His dad was concerned about the intensity of Randy's involvement in the Bible study and recognized that his son's commitment had become a spiritual duty—a "have to" rather than a "want to." He suggested to his son that he give himself the freedom not to read his Bible until his motivation changed. Even though it was a struggle, Randy followed his father's advice. It took several weeks before Randy discovered that the amount of time he spent studying the Bible was not a measure of God's acceptance. Fortunately, he was able to continue his personal Bible study without feeling obligated. Struggles along these lines are common for High C personalities.

High C's have a special talent for organizing and following instructions correctly. An important part of life is obeying laws, following the rules, and fulfilling commitments. In short, they believe that if they are compliant, good things will happen and, conversely, that if they resist, bad things will happen. Much like the High S's, they fear antagonism and confrontation and tend to avoid situations and people that produce conflict. This fear-based thinking develops into a life-style where pleasing others and conforming to authority become the criteria for measuring success. Their behavior takes on an "acceptance by performance" theme.

Even in church, a High C can find undue stress. Without intentionally doing so, many churches reinforce "you must be perfect" thinking by keeping certain rules. The do list—attend worship services, study the Bible, have a quiet time, pray, and witness—sounds good but often becomes the criterion for measuring spirituality. The don't list—don't drink, don't smoke, don't go to any movies, and don't think bad thoughts—is to be strictly avoided. The High C often sees the path to God's acceptance as compliance with the dos and don'ts. They can have a difficult time accepting the idea that God's love is not conditional. As Christians, our acceptance is based upon the grace of God and Christ's finished work on the cross.

Christian psychologist Don Sloat states in *The Dangers of Growing Up in a Christian Home* that "when a person is serving God out of fear, the Christian life becomes a series of duties to perform in order to avoid punishment and it is difficult to have a joyful, thankful heart under these circumstances."[1] High C Profiles have the strongest tendency to being fear-prone and frequently fall into this trap. Life becomes a process of conforming to the "do" lists, which often leads to basing our acceptance upon our ability to live up to prescribed standards of

1. Don E. Sloat, *The Dangers of Growing Up in a Christian Home* (Nashville, Tenn.: Thomas Nelson, 1986), p. 112.

holiness. Submission to Christ is the only way a God-honoring life can be achieved.

Christian parents need to be careful of three points, Sloat says:

1. *The personality type of their children*. Of particular concern are children with a High C or High S Profile who also have extremely low D and I traits. These children have a tendency to have very sensitive personalities.

2. *The nature of one's family*. Parents who use fear and guilt to control children are in danger of damaging their personal security.

3. *Emphasis of church training*. A legalistic church can overemphasize the fear of God as a means of motivating its people.

"Persons who are on the receiving end of all three areas simultaneously will definitely have deeper struggles than others who have experienced only one or two of the danger points," Sloat says.[2] Sloat concludes by stressing that the most important element in countering these danger points is to have parents who are warm, accepting, and encouraging. Modeling unconditional love does wonders.

A CONTEMPORARY CASE STUDY OF A HIGH C UNDER STRESS

The High I perceives life in general to be wonderful and upbeat, whereas the High D goes about the process of changing the world to conform to his wishes. The High S typically prefers to maintain the status quo and generally does not see where he can impact society one way or the other. However, the High C will look at society and see the flaws. The C can look at the same data the I sees and conclude that society is self-destructing. The High C is labeled the pessimist and the High I the op-

2. Ibid.

timist. But all four views are normal, God given, and create a necessary balance.

To create this balance, *initial* perceptions must be respected and at the same time be controlled by the Holy Spirit. If such an environment exists, healthy disagreement can take place, so that issues can be more clearly defined. Frequently, the High C holds the key to making sure no element is left unnoticed. Unfortunately, the common perception of the High C is to view him as always being negative and against any new idea. What is particularly disturbing to High I's is the High C's apparent mistrust of their inputs. The High I's offer their ideas, and C's typically disagree or recheck their story before even thinking about making a decision.

During one of my (Ken's) High C presentations, George, High I, Affiliator Pattern, had a breakthrough in understanding his wife's behavior. She was a High C, Perfectionist Profile.

George had difficulty understanding why Sherry would seek his counsel about assuming a new responsibility within the church and then ask someone else the same questions. Most of the time she would seek the counsel of the senior pastor. She would outline her plan, note George's inputs, and ask for his opinions. Typically her ideas were conservative but well thought out and solid. The senior pastor would wisely repeat George's reassurances and give her permission to make a decision—and she would. George wrongly concluded Sherry did not trust his judgment, when the opposite was actually true. It frustrated George until he understood her need-system—to check and recheck.

High C's need *reassurances of support*. By nature they will gather information and then check and recheck the data until they are sure it is accurate. Part of the process is asking different sources in order to confirm their initial conclusions. High C's typically choose *independent* resources to assimilate information into a quality-control check. Sherry honestly valued George's judgment, but part of her mental processing included talking with another trustworthy resource, the senior pastor.

Once Sherry got the reassurances she needed from both individuals, she was ready to deal with her second important need, the need for order and defined responsibility.

High C's need *order* and *defined responsibility*. After Sherry gathered her information she would meticulously write down the information and develop a plan of action. Each plan had a point-by-point objective with answers written down.

Occasionally, I have couples share their differences in the class. For one session I asked Sherry and George to be the guest High I and High C couple. They agreed. Normally I provide the couples with the interview questions so that each will have time to prepare. I try to meet with them about a week ahead of time to answer any questions they might have. I knew Sherry would want to talk with me—but George would be a different story.

I started with George and offered to review seven questions I wanted to ask him. I prefaced my opening statement by allowing him veto power over any of the questions.

George responded with, "I don't want to look at them. I'll just wing it, anyway."

Sherry was different. She carefully looked over each question and asked for the following clarifications: Was an outline for the class available? When would their interview begin? Where would they stand? Would a podium be available on which she could put her notes? Would George be able to stand next to her? Who would be asked the first question? What was my phone number in case she needed to call me during the week? Could I give her the notes for the High C's so that she would know what had been covered? Those were *some* of the questions she asked.

Preceding the sessions, I generally review some of the profile characteristics of the people being interviewed. In this particular case, I didn't. I wanted to see if the class could discern differences on their own. It was a classic experience.

Sherry came prepared with a copy of my questions and had outlined her answers. George stood next to her, gently putting his right hand about her waist. She neatly placed her notes on the podium I had prepared for her, and we went down the list of questions. She answered each one concisely, speaking directly to the class. When she was through with a question, she would turn and look at me, indicating she was ready for the next question. She was wonderful. George was impressed!

I asked George one question, and he rambled for five minutes. He closed by asking what the question was. The class exploded into a sea of laughter.

George was on a roll, so he offered, "I may not know what I'm talking about, but at least I'm a lot of fun."

The class erupted again. My experiment was a howling success, to say the least.

COMMON RESPONSES OF THE HIGH C UNDER STRESS

George and I had provided Sherry with the elements she needed if she were ever to attempt being in front of a group of strangers talking about her inner feelings. We *reassured* her of our support, *defined* her responsibility, and placed a high priority on creating an *orderly process* by which she would be asked to respond. Also, I gave her time to prepare and process the information. Without those elements, Sherry told me later, she would not have have agreed to be interviewed.

Sherry confirmed the reality of the High C need system. Too often we discount their feelings and put them under unnecessary stress. Like any profile, High C's have developed a defense system to cope with internal conflict. Unfortunately, because of our lack of understanding, we can complicate the process by driving them further into a negative scenario. On the following page are the common elements of the High C stress model that places them into a negative downward spiral (table 31).

Moses, Elijah, Luke, and John experienced all of the trauma of the High C stress model. God helped all four biblical characters work through the pain of a stressful situation and toward a positive conclusion.

Table 31

When a High C Encounters Stress

• Change in plans causes the High C to ask many "what about" and "what if" questions

• Criticism causes feelings of hopelessness and of being totally alone in the problem

• Partner(s) becomes impatient with the continual reservoir of questions

• Total self-image breakdown, "poor me" attitude

CHANGE IN PLANS OR CRITICISM OR WORK

It is important to understand when a High C begins to feel insecure. High C's feel secure when they have identified and categorized their territory. Internally, they work toward making sure everything is done correctly and is in its place. But when "change" is the option, the normal behavior for a High C is to resist. In addition, they possess extremely high expectations and are sensitive to criticism that exposes errors in their work. Even if the comments are not directly aimed at them, the High C's have a tendency to take the remarks personally. If both change and criticism are present, it is normal for a High C to feel extremely uncomfortable and to experience internal stress.

After the Lord gave Moses the law, He led the people toward the Promised Land. Moses was unfamiliar with the land and asked his brother-in-law to help him explore the new territory. We don't know whether Hobab agreed, but it obviously was stressful for Moses to travel into unknown territory.

In Numbers 11, the people begin to criticize the provisions and the manna and complain that they long for the foods of Egypt: fish, cucumbers, melons, leeks, onions, and garlic.

They went so far as to weep, causing the Lord to become angry. Moses was displeased, also, and took their complaints personally.

STRESS CAUSES QUESTIONS TO BE ASKED

The major tip-off that a High C is moving into the stress model is to listen to the kinds of questions he asks. If his inquiries take on a personal tone, it is a strong indication that he senses a problem. Observe Moses' comments in Numbers 11:11-13:

> He asked the Lord, "Why have you brought this trouble on your servant? What have I done to displease you that you put the burden of all these people on me? Did I conceive all these people? Did I give them birth? Why do you tell me to carry them in my arms, as a nurse carries an infant, to the land you promised on oath to their forefathers? Where can I get meat for all these people? They keep wailing to me, 'Give us meat to eat!'"

It is obvious Moses is having difficulty with his assignment. This is not the time to become impatient or even try to reason with him. The proper strategy is to listen and offer support.

CRITICISM CAUSES FEELINGS OF HOPELESSNESS,
INADEQUACY, AND OF BEING TOTALLY ALONE

Under stress, it is common for High C's to feel that they are the only people in the history of the world to face the problems they are experiencing. High C's have told me they feel a personal, lonely ownership of their pain. Although they may have memorized 1 Peter 5:8-9,

> Be self-controlled and alert. Your enemy the devil prowls around like a roaring lion looking for someone to devour. Resist him, standing firm in the faith, because you know that your brothers throughout the world are undergoing the same kind of sufferings,

they cannot claim the reality of the verses. They experience feelings of total isolation—and the perception is real, although obviously untrue. Observe Moses' words in Numbers 11:14:

I cannot carry all these people by myself; the burden is too heavy for me.

In 1 Kings 19:10, 14, Elijah expresses similar feelings.

PARTNER(S) BECOME IMPATIENT WITH THEIR QUESTIONS

At this stage, no answers will satisfy the High C. The normal response of the partner(s) is to become frustrated and respond in a tone of voice that further complicates the conversation. The wiser response is to reject any "poor me" statements, offer support, and end the conversation. At this point, High C's need time to process and reflect. They don't need more information; they need a show of support.

SELF-IMAGE BREAKDOWN, "POOR ME" ATTITUDE

If the High C is allowed to remain locked in his thoughts, he has the tendency to continue playing negative tapes in his mind until he has a complete self-image breakdown. Statements that discredit personal worth or value are immediate indicators that that is about to occur. More severe responses may include thoughts of killing himself. Any time a person talks about suicide, it should be taken seriously. When a High C mentions it, you can be certain he has thought about it before and that it is not something to be discounted or overlooked. It is time to offer action and support!

Moses had had it with the people and wanted out. He graphically told God what he wanted to do (11:15).

> If this is how you are going to treat me, put me to death right now—if I have found favor in your eyes—and do not let me face my own ruin.

In 1 Kings 19:4 and Jonah 4:3, Elijah and Jonah have the same request. The Lord responded to the two prophets by refocusing their thinking and getting them moving.

High C's comment that refocusing their thinking and creating action for them are the keys to helping them out of their stress model.

THE 3 R'S IN LOVING THE HIGH C

In order to respond to, relate to, and reinforce a High C, we need to understand their unique needs. High C's function best in an environment that is a structured and clearly defined setting. They become overly cautious in an antagonistic environment. Remember, the things a High C needs are: no quick changes, security within their workplace, time to validate information, specific affirmation regarding work done, and a safe environment.

At first glance, the motivating environments for the High C appear similar to that of the High S. Both types prefer the status quo, security, and identification with a group. But the High C is task oriented, whereas the High S is relationship oriented. High S's are most comfortable working cooperatively within groups, whereas High C's prefer working alone.

Below are nine principles to keep in mind when responding to, relating to, and reinforcing the High C.

HOW TO RESPOND TO A HIGH C
- Be specific and accurate
- Make allowance for initial responses to be cautious and/ or negative
- Allow freedom to ask questions

HOW TO RELATE TO A HIGH C
- Answer questions in a patient and persistent manner
- Mix accurate information with assurances
- Allow time to validate information

HOW TO REINFORCE THE HIGH C
- Provide a step-by-step approach to a goal
- Provide reassurances of support
- Give permission to validate data with third parties

THEY HAVE A PREFERENCE FOR INTELLECTUAL PURSUITS

High C's enjoy exercising their reasoning abilities. The pleasure of intellectual pursuit can bring them a sense of satisfaction much like running a race brings enjoyment to an athlete. To the High C, the life of the mind is of prime importance and takes precedence over emotions. Spending hours alone developing new thoughts can be fun and pleasurable for them.

If anyone would find an instruction manual intellectually stimulating, it would be a High C. When Johnny's bicycle must be assembled on Christmas Eve, the High D Santa struggles to figure out where each part goes because the instruction booklet is still in the bottom of the box. "No problem!" are often the famous last words heard from High D's. In all likelihood, the High I Santa paid to have someone else assemble the bike because he did not want to take the time necessary to get the bike put together. The High C Santa, on the other hand, goes straight for the instruction book and methodically reads it through. Then he likely will lay out the parts and count them before proceeding. By the way, instead of doing this on Christmas Eve, he probably had the bicycle assembled and stored away before Thanksgiving.

WHEN REQUESTING THEIR PARTICIPATION IN A PROJECT, BE PREPARED TO GIVE SPECIFIC AND ACCURATE DETAILS

The instinct to go for the instruction book is present in all areas of a High C's life. Just as he read the directions before attempting to put together Johnny's bicycle, so he needs specific details, up front, concerning how you want him to participate in a project.

Notice how thoroughly God explained to Moses the details of His plans for the Exodus (Exodus 3):

1. *He identified the one making the request:* "I am the God of your father, the God of Abraham, the God of Isaac, and the God of Jacob" (v. 6).

2. *He stated the purpose of His visit:* "I have indeed seen the misery of my people in Egypt. I have heard them crying out because of their slave drivers, and I am concerned about their suffering" (v. 7).

3. *He gave Moses a description of His plan:* "So I have come down to rescue them from the hand of the Egyptians and to bring them up out of that land into a good and spacious land, a land flowing with milk and honey" (v. 8*a*).

4. *He told Moses the part he would play in the plan:* "So now, go. I am sending you to Pharaoh to bring my people the Israelites out of Egypt" (v. 10).

To sum it up: after the Lord identified Himself to Moses, He offered specific details and answered the "who, what, and why" questions regarding His plan.

MAKE AALOWANCES FOR INITIAL RESPONSE TO BE CAUTIOUS

Moses did not accept the call immediately. This is commonly the initial response of a High C when he is asked to make a change. Before agreeing to participate in a project, he usually exercises caution and restraint.

Moses remembered what had happened many years before when he had tried to help his people. His attempts to confront the problem then had failed and resulted in his fleeing the land to save his own life. But God assured him that there was a difference in the present plan. God was indeed offering Moses the opportunity to become involved with delivering his people, but this time God would play the confrontational role and Moses the role of the messenger—a job well-suited for the High C.

Some individuals would have found it an easy decision to elect to turn in their shepherding license and answer the Lord's call. But not the High C's. The Lord's plan involved change, and that can be difficult for a High C to handle. Look at Moses' initial response to the Lord: "Who am I, that I should go to Pharaoh and bring the Israelites out of Egypt?" (v. 11). Moses was cautious and restrained and responded in classic High C fashion: "I'm not the person for the job!"

OFFER ASSURANCES OF SUPPORT

Let us return for a moment to the story in the previous chapter about the company planning to move its offices downtown. The High C in the group reacted to the change with a multitude of questions: Do we have the resources we need? How will the move affect the quality of our product? What about down time?

The High C needed assurance and support—assurance that everything was going to be all right and support for his position and significance in the company and its plans. Failure to give them this assurance and support may make them feel as though they were out of place for asking questions and will make them vulnerable to internal conflict.

BE PREPARED TO ANSWER QUESTIONS
IN A PATIENT AND PERSISTENT MANNER

The clarification needs of a High C can be annoying to High D's and High I's. Persons with those action-oriented styles usually do not require as much information before taking on a new project, and they expect others to operate in the same way. The High D in the group immediately saw how the move downtown would help him reach his goals, and the High I was excited about being closer to downtown restaurants and activities— what else do we need to know? The High C, however, needed each of his concerns patiently addressed.

Moses had many questions about the task before him (vv. 13-24):

> Moses said to God, "Suppose I go to the Israelites and say to them, 'The God of your fathers has sent me to you,' and they ask me, 'What is his name?' Then what shall I tell them?"
>
> God said to Moses, "I AM WHO I AM. This is what you are to say to the Israelites: 'I AM' has sent me to you."

God's answer, "I AM WHO I AM," is understood in Hebrew as YAHWEH—"I am the One who is." The Lord assured Moses that the elders of Israel would understand this definition and heed his voice.

In true Compliance fashion, Moses responded to God with another question, "What if they do not believe me?" (4:1).

BE WILLING TO PROVIDE REASSURANCE
THAT NO SURPRISES WILL OCCUR

As you address a High C's concerns, it is also helpful to reassure him that all the homework has been done and that he can expect no surprises. "Bill," the company president says to the High C, "you have my word that you will have the same kind of office in our new location as you do now. And besides, the expressway from your area will be complete by then, and you can get to work almost as quickly as you do now." That kind of reassurance will help a High C adapt to change.

Moses certainly needed much reassurance to face the mission God had for him (Exodus 4:1-2):

> Moses answered, "What if they do not believe me or listen to me and say, 'The Lord did not appear to you'?"
> Then the Lord said to him, "What is that in your hand?"
> "A staff," he replied.

Instead of just saying to Moses, "Trust Me," God showed him in a tangible way His power to deliver.

SUPPORT YOUR PLANS WITH ACCURATE
DATA AND SPECIFIC INFORMATION

High C's usually seek out specific ways to validate information. This has been described as the "Trust, but Verify" attitude. The best way to confirm the accuracy of your message to a High C is to involve as many of the five senses (sight, touch, taste, hearing, and smell) as possible.

God verified His plan for Moses by giving him an impressive demonstration of how the staff would be a useful instrument to confirm His power (4:3-10):

The Lord said, "Throw it on the ground."

Moses threw it on the ground and it became a snake, and he ran from it. Then the Lord said to him, "Reach out your hand and take it by the tail." So Moses reached out and took hold of the snake and it turned back into a staff in his hand. "This," said the Lord, "is so that they may believe that the Lord, the God of their fathers—the God of Abraham, the God of Isaac and the God of Jacob—has appeared to you."

Then the Lord said, "Put your hand inside your cloak." So Moses put his hand into his cloak, and when he took it out, it was leprous, like snow.

"Now put it back into your cloak," he said. So Moses put his hand back into his cloak, and when he took it out, it was restored, like the rest of his flesh.

Then the Lord said, "If they do not believe you or pay attention to the first miraculous sign, they may believe the second. But if they do not believe these two signs or listen to you, take some water from the Nile and pour it on the dry ground. The water you take from the river will become blood on the ground."

God used three illustrations, involving most of the five senses, to verify His message to Moses.

1. God took the staff and turned it into a serpent.
2. God had him place his hand in his bosom and turned it white and leprous. When he returned it to his bosom it became normal again.
3. Finally, the water from the Nile was poured on the ground and turned into blood.

Moses was running out of objections, so he tried another strategy to get the Lord to choose someone else.

STRONGLY REJECT ANY "POOR ME" STATEMENTS

Always answer High C clarification questions, but do not accept statements that discount his value as a person. High C's have a tendency to give "poor me" statements highlighting what they perceive to be their inadequacies.

"Moses said to the Lord, 'O Lord, I have never been eloquent, neither in the past nor since you have spoken to your servant. I am slow of speech and tongue'" (Exodus 4:10).

Moses was saying that he did not have the ability to give quick responses. The ability to react quickly with verbal messages is usually found among the High I Profiles, i.e., among the Affiliator (Aaron), Persuader (Peter), and Motivator Patterns (Apollos). Those who traditionally lack this skill are the High C and High S Profiles; i.e., the Perfectionist (Esther), Strategist (Jacob), and Pioneer Patterns (Paul). Moses, as a Perfectionist Profile, needed time to process information.

Even though it was self-effacing, Moses was providing God with accurate information about himself. However, the job the Lord wanted him to do did not require someone with quick responses. God was more interested in someone who could communicate His commands accurately and diplomatically. Moses had the skill God wanted. Moses' fears prevented him from realizing what skills God needed for the job. As we will soon see, God dealt wisely with the "poor me" statement.

DISAGREE WITH THE FACTS AND NOT THE PERSON

Remember, High C's are sensitive people. If it is necessary, disagree with the facts, but avoid personal attacks. God did not agree that Moses' inability to speak was a valid excuse.

> The Lord said to him, "Who gave man his mouth? Who makes him deaf or mute? Who gives him sight or makes him blind? Is it not I, the Lord? Now go; I will help you speak and will teach you what to say." (4:11-12)

The Lord assured Moses He would be with him and teach him what to say.

At this point Moses had depleted his reservoir of questions and offered one more "poor me" statement: "But Moses said, 'O Lord, please send someone else to do it'" (4:13). In essence Moses was saying, "Lord, send someone else. I can't do this!"

BE WILLING TO OFFER ASSISTANCE
AND SUPPORT IF THEIR FEARS PERSIST

Even after presenting all the facts to a High C, his fears might persist. If you still want him to be a part of the project, be willing to consider providing him assistance. "OK, Bill," the company president might say, "I realize that transportation is a real problem for you in this move we are planning. I can't make the drive for you each day, but I will arrange to pay for your parking."

Normally, confrontation is unproductive with High C's, but it becomes appropriate when their fear turns into stubbornness. It is easy to become frustrated and angry at the High C for his unwillingness to change his mind.

Notice how God became angry at Moses and confronted his stubbornness but at the same time provided additional support.

In the Lord's closing comments, see if you can discern how in rejecting Moses' "poor me" attitude the Lord also offered assistance to cope with Moses' fears (4:14-17):

> Then the Lord's anger burned against Moses and he said, "What about your brother, Aaron the Levite? I know he can speak well. He is already on his way to meet you, and his heart will be glad when he sees you. You shall speak to him and put words in his mouth; I will help both of you speak and will teach you what to do. He will speak to the people for you, and it will be as if he were your mouth and as if you were God to him. But take this staff in your hand so you can perform miraculous signs with it."

Moses felt he needed a spokesman, so God gave him Aaron, Moses' High I brother. The Lord again confirmed to Moses that he was His choice and would get His full support. God then cut off the conversation and let Moses process the information. Given time, Moses would follow God's instructions.

REMEMBER THAT THEY ARE CONSCIENTIOUS, MAINTAIN HIGH STANDARDS, AND COMPLETE ASSIGNMENTS GIVEN TO THEM

Once a High C becomes committed to a project, he has the ability to maintain his focus through extreme difficulties. Assigned responsibilities are taken seriously, and he meticulously goes about the process of working until the job is done right. Extremely conscientious, High C's typically follow instructions carefully and maintain high standards with a genuine commitment to quality.

Moses had the necessary talents, and God intended to use them to carry out His plan. The Lord knew that once Moses was committed to the task, the children of Israel would be in good hands for the exodus from Egypt.

UNDERSTAND THEIR GREATEST STRUGGLES

Compliant people are driven by a commitment to excellence. However, one of their greatest struggles is with unrealistic expectations. Their self-imposed minimum standards are frequently next to perfection, which is impossible to achieve. Therefore, they will at times put themselves down unnecessarily, because they perceive that they have failed to meet their own standards.

Since High C's also struggle with the fear of criticism, they may keep good ideas to themselves. The tragedy of this is that others fail to benefit from a potentially outstanding contribution. One mark of High C maturity is a willingness to take the risk of expressing his own opinions. True confidence in himself can only be gained as a High C assumes sole accountability for his actions. Two factors important to High C's in developing independence are these:

1. To learn how to lower their own expectations to a reasonable level by getting personal feedback from discerning friends.
2. To clarify their role in a project so that they know what is expected and can avoid setting unrealistic and unachievable standards.

A MAN'S PERSPECTIVE ON THE HIGH C

Tom is a High C, Adaptor Profile. He was willing to express his impressions concerning how God related to Moses and other High C biblical characters. The following are his insights:

> I am so thankful that the Living God knows just how to deal with someone like me . . .
>
> > A God who knows my hands are good with detailed things but my heart burns to accomplish eternal good, and He uses both.
> >
> > A God who is willing to sensitively shock me out of the safe, comfortable, secure haven in which I'd like to live so that I can be useful for Him.
> >
> > A God who believes in me even though I do not believe in myself, who trusts me with a big assignment even though I feel inadequate.
> >
> > A God who is willing to deal visually and concretely with me so as to overcome my innate fears and doubts.
> >
> > A God who is patient with me as I try to decide if I dare walk by faith and not by sight.
> >
> > A God who refuses to allow me to replace Him (how foolish to think I could) but insists that I follow Him.
> >
> > A God who answers my numerous questions with potent and patient replies.

As you can see, the comments are different from the other styles, but they relate to the same God who lovingly responds to each of the profiles.

WHAT THE DIFFERENT PROFILES HAD TO SAY ABOUT THE HIGH C

What is the most difficult part of relating to the High C?

High D: "It is difficult providing the kind of detail they need in order to satisfy their questions."

High I: "To patiently deal with all their questions without getting defensive. Sometimes we just respond without intending to be taken seriously, but High C's take everything to be a concrete commitment."

High S: "Consistency in understanding their sensitivity levels."

High C: "Being able to forgive ourselves and lower our expectations."

What can you do to build better relationships with the High C Profiles ?

High D: "If our plan to include them involves change, we shouldn't expect them to make a decision right away. The loving thing is to allow them time to think about it."

High I: "Submit to the fact that a little structure in our life won't hurt us."

High S: "Understand their sensitivity levels and being more patient with their questions."

High C: "Being able to state my position, whether it's popular or not."

What High C skills do you most appreciate?

High D: "High C's provide us with a commitment to quality control that we need but don't want to take the time to do ourselves."

High I: "High C's are our heavenly sandpaper who remind us when we've missed the mark."

High S: "High C's have the skill and commitment to
check and recheck data until it is right."

High C: "Critical thinking and commitment to accuracy; having a sensitivity level on a par with each
other."

REACTIONS FROM HIGH C FAMILY MEMBERS

High C's have been referred to as the conscience of society. They naturally see the flaws within the system and are
committed to maintaining quality control. Knowing their commitment to high standards, the Lord continually raised up
High C prophets to speak out when Israel strayed from God.
Many times, they would be beaten or killed when their messages filled with warnings of judgment were rejected. As with
the other profiles, under pressure High C's can develop negative aspects to their natural tendencies. The following are
thoughts from High C Representative Patterns who were willing to share their insights on how to create a loving environment for them.

High C: "Focused attention, i.e., I need to know you
are willing to listen to me, but I am not asking that you always understand my logic."

High C/S: "Be patient with my questions and understand I need time to process your responses.
Also, if I cross-check your answers, it doesn't
mean I don't trust you—I just have to be
sure."

High C/S: "I need an environment that includes patience, understanding, encouragement, and
gentle firmness."

High C/S/D: "Allow me time to adjust to change and give me reasons why it is necessary."

"I need an environment that includes encouragement, assurance, appreciation, structure, and order."

High C/I/S: "I need an environment that exhibits acceptance, forgiveness, honesty, and logical thinking."

"I often have several messages going on in my head. I frequently am confused by my mixed emotions. Be patient with me and be willing to give me nonjudgmental feedback."

What is the most loving thing we can do for you when you are under stress?

High C: "Allow me to be alone with my thoughts until I am ready to speak. I need time to process all the information."

"Don't crowd me; allow me quiet time."

High C/S/D: "Give me the freedom to express my true feelings and understand that they are real to me. You can offer a different point of view, but don't expect or demand me to agree with you right away."

High C/S: "After I hear your input, let me get off by myself and give me the freedom to talk with someone else."

High C/S/D: "Let me verbalize my feelings, but don't judge me for them. Be patient with me."

"Help me to refocus my thoughts; give me something to do, but reassure me as to how you will support me if I need help."

Compliance persons have the potential to be extremely valuable members of the Body of Christ. However, their behavior when they are loaded down by stress is often misunderstood. Being private individuals with extremely high standards, they often have thoughts of unworthiness and feel uncomfortable sharing their inner struggles. What we typically observe is someone trying to be perfect and committed to a performance process that is impossible to achieve. It is critical that we remain available to them to assist them in processing information, respect their need for time, are available to listen to their heart pains, and are supportive when they are willing to reach out for help.

A Look Ahead

Individual and relational maturity is not an overnight process. It requires a willingness to grow beyond our personal preferences and natural strengths. When behavioral styles are carried to extremes, they become weaknesses. Transforming our personality weaknesses into strengths requires a physical, emotional, and spiritual commitment. It is to this topic we turn in the next chapter.

THIRTEEN

TRANSFORMATION WITHIN PERSONALITY STYLES

The story is told of a king whose son was deeply depressed. All attempts to cheer the prince having failed, the king summoned his wise men for their counsel in the matter. After a great deal of discussion, they agreed that the best plan would be to search the kingdom and find the happiest man in the country. Once they found him, they would remove his shirt and bring it back for the prince to wear. Putting on the shirt would cure his depression and transfer happiness to him.

The wise men searched far and wide, interviewing everyone in the kingdom. Finally, they settled on one they concluded to be the happiest man of all. Unfortunately for them, he was a servant of the king, and he didn't own a shirt. It would, of course, be impossible to take a shirt for the prince to wear if it did not exist! So, the wise men returned to the king and reported their dilemma.

What an absurd story! It is ridiculous to think that depression can be cured and happiness be transferred by wearing a shirt. Yet many of us are guilty of trying to find happiness using similar tactics. How often do we think that "buying a car," or "changing a job," or "building a home" will make us happier? It sounds almost as ludicrous as "wearing a shirt."

It is true that new possessions can give a temporary emotional lift. However, they cannot provide lasting satisfaction. As much as we try, happiness cannot be transferred by things. It must come by experiencing a transformation from within.

Once we have experienced the initial transformation that comes by a relationship to Christ, contentment is no longer dependent upon personal circumstances, people, and material possessions but upon the indwelling presence of God. It is then that He can begin to make us all that He intended for us to be. It is then that our inadequacies can become divinely transformed into strengths.

Throughout the pages of this book, we have emphasized that no one personality style is superior, and that the behavior of each style is normal when understood in terms of an expression of needs. Indeed, we can all be grateful for our God-given personality styles. Furthermore, we can choose to understand more about those around us and strive to meet their needs, or we can choose to indulge in self-serving behavior that ends up draining our relationships of life and energy.

We have also repeated that the strengths of our personality styles can become weaknesses when taken to their extremes. We have noted times when biblical personalities, such as Peter, Paul, Abraham, and Moses, responded poorly to stressful situations. Their actions were normal behavior responses consistent with their personality styles. We can understand their respective DISC Profiles and recognize that many of their reactions were predictable, though not necessarily excusable.

But as children of God, we need to go further in our spiritual and emotional growth. We need to transcend our natural tendencies and do something supernatural. When the old ways are inadequate, and something entirely different must take place, we need to shift from our usual responses into something highly unusual. This process is called transformation.

Paul said:

> Do not conform any longer to the pattern of this world, but be transformed by the renewing of your mind. Then you will be able to test and approve what God's will is—his good, pleasing and perfect will. (Romans 12:2)

Before we began a personal relationship with Christ, the only resource for behavior modification available to us was sheer willpower. Now some people have had a measure of success in changing unpleasant personality traits on their own. But in Christ we have the divine source for experiencing change within us. Transformation ceases to be our responsibility. It becomes our response to His ability.

PAUL'S AND PETER'S TRANSFORMATION

Two excellent New Testament examples of this transformation process are found in the lives of Paul and Peter. Both Paul, the fiery High D man on a mission, and Peter, the quick High I disciple and leader of the early church, needed transformation in their lives before they could be more effective for Christ.

In Paul's travels, he constantly ran into opposition. He would utilize his debating skills, academic background in the law, and D/C Profile talents to verbally overwhelm his opposition. One writer comments on Paul's style of personality: "He is an excellent debater. In fact, never take him on in a debate unless you are assured of your facts, for he will make mincemeat of you, combining verbal aggressiveness and attendance to detail. This man is extremely competitive and forceful in all that he does. His battle plan is always the same: 'Go for the jugular vein.'"[1] That accurately describes what Paul must have had to go through as he dealt with the Jews who sought to kill him as he took the gospel into Asia Minor and Eastern Europe.

In addition to facing the wrath of many of the Jews in his time, Paul faced other severe trials on his journeys: beatings, shipwrecks, stonings, hunger, sickness, and imprisonment. Paul endured each one of these physical and emotional sufferings. He was a committed man who was in control.

Through all his difficult experiences, it was possible for him to boast about his faithfulness. He records an interesting transformation that God permitted in order to remind him of where his strength came from. Paul was given a "thorn in the

1. Tim LaHaye, *Understanding the Male Temperament* (Old Tappan, N. J.: Revell, 1977), p. 103.

flesh," which became a source of physical torment for him. Three times he asked God to remove this weakness, which he believed was keeping him from maximum effectiveness. The Lord answered Paul by saying, "My grace is sufficient for you, for my power is made perfect in weakness" (2 Corinthians 12:9a).

It was a humbling answer for a High D. Is it really possible to find strength in weakness? Paul had grown in his understanding of God's intent. He wrote, "To keep me from becoming conceited because of these surpassingly great revelations, there was given me a thorn in my flesh, a messenger of Satan to torment me" (12:7).

However, more than understanding is needed for transformation. Acceptance and obedience round out the process. Paul made what has to be one of the more incredible statements of a High D: "Therefore I will boast all the more gladly about my weaknesses, so that Christ's power may rest on me. That is why, for Christ's sake, I delight in weaknesses, in insults, in hardships, in persecutions, in difficulties. For when I am weak, then I am strong" (12:9b-10).

Before maturity, Paul's natural, High D attitude would probably have caused him to write something like, "Strength is made perfect in strength, brothers! Let there never be any weakness among you!" Do you see the transformation within Paul that allowed him to transcend his natural tendency so that he might serve in the will of the Lord? The transformed Paul was able to release his need for control to the Lord—a critical crossroads for a High D to face.

Simon Peter also went through a transformation that allowed him to rise above some of the natural tendencies of his personality style. When he was under pressure, Peter, the High I, would often say things he would later regret, or make commitments that he did not follow through on. Remember, for example, how Peter buckled under pressure during the events surrounding the arrest of Jesus. He denied any association with Christ only a short time after he verbally professed his undying commitment.

In a positive environment, people like Peter can wax eloquent, but when situations are negative they often become soft and persuadable, and their verbal defense system takes over by avoiding responsibility. Peter's transformation came as he began to assume more responsibility for his commitments and grew to remain strong under social pressure.

One afternoon during the days of the early church, Peter and John were going up to the Temple to pray. Upon encountering a crippled beggar, Peter extended the power of Christ to the man, resulting in his lame condition being healed. Immediately the man followed them into the Temple courts "walking and jumping, and praising God" (Acts 3:8).

Shortly after that, the captain of the Temple guard arrested Peter and John and threw them in jail for the night. Being arrested by this man would today be comparable to being arrested and charged by the Attorney General of the United States. No doubt Peter and John realized that they were in for a difficult time.

As usual, things got worse before they got better. Acts 4 records that the following day the two were brought before the "rulers, elders, and teachers of the law" (v. 5) and the high priest and members of his family. The assembly was the Sanhedrin, the highest court in the land, the Supreme Court, so to speak. This was the same governing body that worked with the Roman government to have Christ crucified. Indeed, Peter and John were in big trouble.

There the two apostles stood in the center of seventy big shots seated around them in semicircular fashion, all eyes on them. They were asked, "By what power or what name did you do this?" (v. 7b). An intimidating moment for anyone, but especially so for Peter, the High I.

Previously, Peter would have responded defensively by denying any responsibility, shifting the blame to someone else, and talking fast in order to save his neck. We can only speculate, of course, but a typical response may have been, "Guys, I don't know how this happened! This lame man hopped up and started walking around right in front of me! You know how these Temple crowds are. They started yelling and screaming and making a big scene. I was simply an innocent party caught in the middle. Next thing I know your guards arrived, overreacted by arresting John and me, and here we are. Listen, I'm willing to forget the whole thing if you would just let us go. We promise not to do this sort of thing again. As for this lame fellow, you can do whatever you want with him, but don't let him blame me for this. He's the one you need to talk to!" If you think this couldn't have happened, review the account of Peter's denial of Jesus in Luke 22.

Instead, the transformed Peter rose above what would have been a natural response under pressure, proving what is good and acceptable and perfect:

> Rulers and elders of the people! If we are being called to account today for an act of kindness shown to a cripple and are asked how he was healed, then know this, you and all the people of Israel: It is by the name of Jesus Christ of Nazareth, whom you crucified but whom God raised from the dead, that this man stands before you healed. He is
>
> "the stone you builders rejected,
> which has become the capstone."
>
> Salvation is found in no one else, for there is no other name under heaven given to men by which we must be saved. (Acts 4:8b-12)

The Sanhedrin sat stunned and unable to reply. After some consultation, they decided to release Peter and John with just a warning.

One writer said of the address, "There was nothing of compromise or accommodation in [Peter's] preaching. As this magnificent declaration shows, he was wholly committed to the uniqueness of Jesus as the only Savior."[2]

Peter's transformation was nothing short of divine. In fact, verse 8 tells us that Peter was "filled with the Holy Spirit."

2. *The Expositor's Bible Commentary,* vol. 9, *John-Acts* (Grand Rapids, Mich.: Zondervan, 1981), p. 103.

Most likely Peter was tempted to cave in under the stress. However, he worked through the pressure of his fearful feelings, focused on the power that was available to him through the Holy Spirit, and then claimed that power before the powerful Sanhedrin.

The observation of the Sanhedrin is interesting: "When they saw the courage of Peter and John and realized that they were unschooled, ordinary men, they were astonished and they took note that these men had been with Jesus" (4:13). They perceived Peter and John's strength to be out of the ordinary and correctly assumed that it had something to do with their relationship to Jesus.

This transforming power is available to everyone who believes in Christ. It reveals how the Lord can take a weakness in our personality style and miraculously change it into a strength.

Abraham's Transformation

Throughout the life of Abraham, God requested that he leave his family because of their worship of other gods. The Lord knew he would not become His faithful servant until he was free from their influence. It was not until Abraham was into his seventies that he was able to separate himself from his family.

Following Abraham's separation from Lot in Genesis 13, God began the process of developing a friendship relationship with him. The Lord continually reinforced His covenant with Abraham, which included an heir. Constancy and unconditional support were the key ingredients of the environment God created.

Genesis 16 marks the beginning of strife within Abraham's immediate family. The conflict between Sarah, Hagar, Ishmael, and Isaac became particularly stressful to him. Two behavioral reactions are typical of High S's under stress. In Genesis 16, when Sarah asked him to settle the conflict with Hagar, Abraham used a "flight" strategy and chose not to get involved. This is a completely normal reaction for an Advisor

Pattern in a hostile environment. This style tends to reject and avoid conflict. Also, they typically find it extremely stressful when they must face separation or be the instrument of discipline to another family member. The statement "This is going to hurt me more than you" is internally and emotionally real for this style. In Genesis 21, during the celebration feast for Isaac, Abraham grieved at having to be the instrument for asking Hagar and Ishmael to leave home. In having to be the aggressor, Abraham predictably would feel uncomfortable. However, he complied with the Lord's wishes but personally provided Hagar and Ishmael with provisions as they left.

After a time of peace and harmony, God created the ultimate test for Abraham, the High S, Advisor Pattern.

> Then God said, "Take your son, your only son, Isaac, whom you love, and go to the region of Moriah. Sacrifice him there as a burnt offering on one of the mountains I will tell you about." (Genesis 22:2)

The request had the potential to short-circuit the emotional system of Abraham's profile. This style tends to deny or suppress their own aggressive thoughts. The normal reaction for Advisor Patterns in this situation would be to avoid or ignore the request. If pressured or confronted, they would be expected to become persuasive with factual data. Abraham had years of factual data regarding God's plan for Isaac. He also had the experience of negotiating with the Lord over issues that placed his family in danger. The classic example is his conversation with God over the fate of Sodom and Gomorrah. In Genesis 18:23-33, he skillfully reduced the quota of righteous men from fifty to ten in order to save Lot's life—the basic High S rescue strategy.

If the profile information is the absolute in describing all behavior, the passage realistically would be expected to read like this:

> But Abraham became distressed and pleaded with God that sacrificing Isaac should not be required since he was to be

his heir. Instead, he offered the Lord all his possessions as a means of showing his loyalty.

But in actuality it reads like this:

> Early the next morning Abraham got up and saddled his donkey. He took with him two of his servants and his son Isaac. When he had cut enough wood for the burnt offering, he set out for the place God had told him about. . . .
> When they reached the place God had told him about, Abraham built an altar there and arranged the wood on it. He bound his son Isaac and laid him on the altar, on top of the wood. Then he reached out his hand and took the knife to slay his son. (Genesis 22:3, 9-10)

Abraham's actions cannot be explained by understanding his need system—and, in fact, are in total contradiction to it. The New Testament book of Hebrews gives insight into his actions.

> By faith Abraham, when God tested him, offered Isaac as a sacrifice. He who had received the promises was about to sacrifice his one and only son, even though God had said to him, "It is through Isaac that your offspring will be reckoned." Abraham reasoned that God could raise the dead, and figuratively speaking, he did receive Isaac back from death. (Hebrews 11:17-19)

As a human being, and specifically as a human being with a High S personality, Abraham should have felt totally distraught with the assignment. Instead, he made a value judgment in placing his faith in the Lord and followed instructions. His decision obviously overrode his need system to produce harmony in the home. Was it difficult to do? From a purely behavioral perspective, it was impossible. But Abraham's actions give testimony to his having passed the ultimate test of maturity for a High S Profile.

MOSES' TRANSFORMATION

High C's prefer an environment that is controlled and structured. They feel comfortable when working as part of a group, rather than being put into a position of having to make independent decisions. It is wrong to assume that High C's cannot make decisions, because they can; however, it is their nature to remain cautious when exploring new territory. High C's are stretched when they are put into a position of being the sole authority figure. They can be effective leaders—but with a different style: leadership by example rather than force of character.

When God called Moses, He patiently offered him support. As Moses had questions, He answered them. God also assured Moses that He would be available should any surprises occur. Because Moses desired tangible encouragement, the Lord put Aaron on the team.

One reason for the ten plagues was to show the Lord's superiority over the gods of Egypt. But God could have done that much quicker. We are convinced that one of the reasons God was so deliberate was to build up Moses' confidence in leading the people. After the three plagues, Moses, not Aaron, began to carry the message. Pharaoh soon recognized the leader to be Moses.

However, throughout the exodus from Egypt, Moses' style was to closely follow the directions the Lord gave. When no message was given, he would cautiously wait. In Exodus 14, Israel is camped with its back to the Red Sea. Pharaoh perceived this as an opportunity to recapture his slaves. When the people saw Pharaoh's army, they became frightened and cried out. Moses stopped and prayed. God answered with words of exhortation (v. 15): "Then the Lord said to Moses, 'Why are you crying out to me? Tell the Israelites to move on.'" Forward, march!

We find no fault in Moses' reaction. However, to become a more effective leader, he needed to develop the ability to act independently. The events in Exodus 32 began that process.

God used a "pro" and "con" strategy to get Moses committed to confront Aaron and the people with their sin in worshiping the golden calf. Once Moses saw the seriousness of their actions, he effectively went through the process of purifying the body. He used the Levites as a means to accomplish this goal. But he did not know whether God would honor his efforts. Positionally, God was committed to destroying the people. Someone had to plead their case, and there was only one person who could do it. That person was Moses, and he had to do it alone. He did.

> The next day Moses said to the people, "You have committed a great sin. But now I will go up to the Lord; perhaps I can make atonement for your sin."
> So Moses went back to the Lord and said, "Oh, what a great sin these people have committed! They have made themselves gods of gold. But now, please forgive their sin —but if not, then blot me out of the book you have written." (vv. 30-32)

From the text, it appears that Moses was terrified to go to the Lord and ask Him to consider forgiving Israel of their great sin. Knowing the High C's need system, it is not only feasible to suggest that he had these feelings but that they were to be expected. Yet Moses did go and offered the only thing he viewed that God had previously honored—his life. The Lord declined, but was impressed. God understood how truly difficult it was for Moses to do what he did.

Following His judgment on the people, the Lord told Moses,

> Leave this place, you and the people you brought up out of Egypt, and go up to the land I promised on oath to Abraham, Isaac and Jacob, saying, "I will give it to your descendants." I will send an angel before you. . . . But I will not go with you, because you are a stiff-necked people and I might destroy you on the way. (33:1-3)

Moses diplomatically disagreed and asked that the Lord reconsider. Observe the Lord's response:

> And the Lord said to Moses, "I will do the very thing you have asked, because I am pleased with you and I know you by name." (v. 17)

Following this conversation Moses asked to see the Lord in all His glory. God gave him this privilege. Moses' leadership then took on a more independent form but remained true to his High C style.

GOD LOVES US AS WE ARE
BUT TOO MUCH TO KEEP US THAT WAY

If we take a good look into the personality mirror, we can observe, however faintly, areas where we need to grow, where we need the transforming power of Christ. We want to give several other examples of people we know who were able to catch a glimpse of themselves in that mirror.

When Jack, an Organizer Pattern, was asked to describe his greatest struggle in maturing as a High D, he replied without hesitation, "Releasing control to the Lord." He then told his story, one that illustrates the way many High D's must face the issue of control.

> In my early years, I was on a fast corporate track and experienced one success after another. My peers were giving me praise and I took the credit. I began to believe there wasn't anything I couldn't do.
>
> I finally went into business for myself and experienced failure for the first time. It was a humbling experience. Although I knew the Lord as a child, I never really submitted to His control. It seemed that I was always able to work things out on my own. I had to learn that, for this High D to mature and grow in the Lord, I needed to be broken.
>
> My lowest point came at a time I least expected, during a rain storm while in my van with my son. My business had financial problems beyond my resources or abilities. The pressures on me were enormous and I didn't know what I was going to do.
>
> I had hoped to spend a few pleasant hours escaping with my son. The road was unfamiliar, the traffic was heavy, and the storm was terrible. I was angry at God for a lot of things, but at that moment, for the storm. I asked myself, "What else could go wrong?"
>
> Then it happened. While we were sitting at a traffic light, steam started coming out from under the hood, red

warning lights flashed on the dash, and finally the engine stopped. The rain came down heavier and people behind me started honking their horns!

My emotions ran from rage to hopelessness. Then I just broke down. This High D who was always in control was crying like a baby in front of my son. Somehow my son, twelve years old, remained cool and didn't seem to mind that I had lost control. He calmly pointed out a service station across the street and suggested that I try starting the van. Sure enough, the van started right up! The honking stopped and a path through the traffic opened up to the station.

It was a minor problem, a broken radiator hose, but the lesson I learned was life changing for me. God was saying, "Jack, I want to help you, but you have to let me. I have more resources than you do. What the world rejects as too weak and simple, I can use. Even a twelve-year-old." Since that time, I have made a daily commitment to release control to Him. It's hard sometimes, but I'm getting better at it.

Jack's discovery is a common one, but is similar to what each of us faces in our own way. We, too, can get out of balance and need God's loving hand to lead us into a transformation experience with Him.

Even though a strength overused can become an individual's greatest weakness, one of the great truths we discover in Scripture is that a person's weakness can become his asset. We are given the opportunity to serve the Lord with the strengths He has given us, but we minister to others out of our limitations and failures.

Chuck Colson, for example, has become an effective spokesman for Christ as the result of time he spent in prison. As chief legal counsel during the Nixon presidency he exerted a tremendous amount of influence in the White House. Colson was a Dominant personality in a powerful position. Then his professional world came tumbling down because of his involvement with the Watergate scandal in Washington. He ended up being convicted and was sentenced to serve time in prison. This was a case where a High D was committed to a task but carried his power past legal boundaries.

Brought down by these events, Colson turned to Jesus Christ for salvation. He was transformed from a criminal to a follower of Christ. Just like the apostle Paul, God used traumatic events in his life to get this High D's attention. After his jail term he started a ministry called Prison Fellowship. It now has nationwide impact by helping thousands of prisoners and their families cope with the traumatic events of their lives.

Colson later realized that it was out of his failure rather than his accomplishments that God used him to minister to others. In *Loving God,* he recounts how he made this discovery while speaking at an Easter service in a prison:

> As I sat on the platform, waiting my turn at the pulpit, my mind began to drift back in time . . . to scholarships and honors earned, cases argued and won, great decisions made from lofty government offices. My life had been the perfect success story, the great American dream fulfilled. But all at once I realized that it was not my success God had used to enable me to help those in this prison. . . . No, the real legacy of my life was my biggest failure—that I was an ex-convict. My greatest humiliation—being sent to prison—was the beginning of God's greatest use of my life.[3]

He later concluded, "It is not what we do that matters, but what a sovereign God chooses to do through us. God doesn't want our success; He wants us. He doesn't demand our achievements; He demands our obedience. The kingdom of God is a kingdom of paradox, where through the ugly defeat of a cross, a holy God is utterly glorified. Victory comes through defeat; healing through brokenness; finding self through losing self."[4]

The apostles Paul and Peter, the Old Testament figures Abraham and Moses, and Jack, Chuck, and the authors of this book have all arrived at the same conclusion. The best way to live up to our greatest potential is to be willing for our weak-

3. Charles Colson, *Loving God* (Grand Rapids, Mich.: Zondervan, 1983), p. 24.
4. Ibid.

nesses to be transformed into strengths by God's Holy Spirit. This won't cause God to love us more, but it will allow Him to use us more. An unknown author has written:

> He loves you just the way you are today
> But much too much to let you stay that way,
> And when He's changed your life from what it was before,
> He still won't love you one bit more.

God's love is not dependent upon our performance, but He is committed to growing us beyond our natural ability and into the likeness of Christ. We can reach our greatest potential as we seek a greater understanding of ourselves and others. Truly our behavior is complex. Many factors affect how and why we do the things we do. One concept is clear, however. The Lord commands us to love one another. To seek to understand ourselves is to take a step toward extending to all the kind of acceptance God has extended to each one of us.

Remember that needs-motivated behavior (DISC) has to do with the behavior that is easiest and most natural for us. Values-motivated behavior (TICS) has to do with what we think is right, the most reasonable, the most meaningful, and what we believe others expect from us. Values behavior is an emerging process that can be learned. Moreover, it has the potential to strongly influence the needs system within each of us. Paul, for example, modified his need to always be in control after his values shifted to serving Christ.

When Jesus gave the two greatest commandments—to love God and your neighbor—He illustrated the importance of both values- and needs-based behavior. The first commandment is a value statement centered on our relationship with God. The second commandment tells us to respond to the needs of others in concert with taking care of our own needs.

Truly our behavior is complex. Many factors affect how and why we do the things we do. One concept is clear, however: The Lord commands us to love. To seek to understand ourselves and others is to take a step toward extending to all the kind of acceptance God has extended to us.

FOURTEEN

THE PERSONAL PROFILE OF JESUS

Each time I (Ken) have taught a class or seminar on behavior styles of biblical characters, someone invariably asks the question, "What was the profile of Jesus?" It's a question that needs to be addressed. Smalley and Trent believe that He had the strength of all four basic personalities held in balance.[1] This is a good starting point, but what this study will attempt to do is critically look at the three graphs of DISC behavior models and determine whether Smalley and Trent's premise is true. I believe it is.

For background, DISC is a behavior model developed by William Marston in the early 1900s and centers on four basic styles. "D" signifies Dominance, "I" signifies Influencing/Interacting, "S" signifies Steadiness, and "C" signifies Compliance/Cautious. The Dominance style desires to control the environment, whereas the Interacting/Influencer focuses on other people and having fun. The Steadiness style values loyalty and cooperating with others, whereas the Cautious/Compliance style is compelled to do things the "right" or "correct" way. This particular model has been well researched and tested for validity and is considered one of the best human resource tools in the industry today.

1. Gary Smalley and John Trent. *The Two Sides of Love* (Pomona, Calif.: Focus on the Family, 1990).

Smalley and Trent's four behavior model substitutes animals for DISC: D—Lion, I—Otter, S—Golden Retriever, and C—Beaver. What is important to understand is that no style is better in either model. Each individual style has its own set of strengths which, when left unchecked, can become imbalanced. Potential strengths can become great weaknesses. Only when all the styles choose to function in concert does balance and order have an opportunity to occur.

It may appear to some as bordering on blasphemy to speak of Jesus Christ as having a behavioral style of "temperament." However, one of the main doctrines of orthodoxy is the understanding of the true humanity of the Lord Jesus Christ. Not only was He undiminished deity in nature, but also at the same time He had full humanity, but without the sin nature. As theologian John F. Walvoord states, "It is necessary to view Him as having a complete human nature including body, soul and spirit."[2] If this doctrine is correct and Jesus was who He said He was, the evidence found in Scripture should show His personal profile with human behavior traits, but always modeling balance and order.

In theory, the most effective people are those who know themselves as well as the demands of each specific situation and take on a particular style of behavior to meet the needs of their environment. Although this is suggested as the ideal, no one is able to do it on a consistent basis. All of the profiles of the DISC model have imbalanced core styles that are prone to get out of control. As I associated biblical characters with specific patterns, the behavior of Paul, Rebekah, Abraham, Mary, and others confirmed this position. But what about Jesus' style? Did He fit into one specific pattern, or did He respond according to the needs of the situation with varying styles as the ideal suggests? That is what we intend to find out in this chapter.

The next critical question is how one can effectively research the behavior of Jesus and associate it with the DISC style. To know how this can be done requires a basic understanding of the DISC model of behavior. It is based on trait

2. John F. Walvoord, *Jesus Christ Our Lord* (Chicago: Moody, 1969), p. 111.

theory. It classifies people according to the degree to which they can be characterized in terms of a number of traits. According to trait theory, one can describe a personality by its position on a number of scales, each of which represents a trait. The DISC Trait Continuum lists a series of thirty traits on four scales from high intensity to low intensity. Below are examples of these trait words:[3]

High D Traits	Low D Traits
directing	unassuming
domineering	humble
risk-taker	dependent

High I Traits	Low I Traits
persuasive	controlled
sociable	reflective
confident	withdrawn

High S Traits	Low S Traits
patient	mobile
loyal	spontaneous
team-person	active

High C Traits	Low C Traits
accurate	"own person"
restrained	firm
high standards	defiant

By using this new paradigm (or template), we will attempt to associate Jesus' behavior with the eight High and Low style traits. If our preliminary thesis is correct, Christ's behavior will not only fit into one specific pattern, as is true for normal individuals, but will also fill the entire chart. To be more specific,

3. The DISC Trait Continuum containing all 120 trait words can be found in *Understanding How Others Misunderstand You Workbook,* rev. and enl. (Chicago: Moody, 1995), p. 23.

we are looking for situations where Jesus covers the entire behavioral range of the four styles; that is, where He is a High D,
or totally controlling and dominating in confronting specific
individuals, or a Low D, where he is a committed, submissive
team player; where He is High I, or reaching out to people, to a
Low I, choosing to be alone; where He is High S, or being patient with others' failures, or Low S, where He is being spontaneous and aggressive in confronting issues; where He is High
C, or being diplomatic in accurately communicating Scripture,
or a Low C, where He is being defiant and rebellious against
authority as it tries to impose traditions on Him.

With the use of the graphs in the DISC instrument, we
can research the Lord's style even further. As previously mentioned, the instrument measures three specific behavioral response on three different graphs. Graph I measures behavior in
a given situation, Graph II measures instinctive response when
under pressure, and Graph III is a summary graph of the first
two. In other words, we can determine what Jesus was like in a
given situation, that is, with God the Father, with the Pharisees, with common sinners, with demons, and so on. We can
also determine what His core behavior was like, or how He handled Himself under pressure. Finally, we will attempt to combine Graphs I and II into a summary graph, Graph III, to
determine who He was. As a reference point, Graph I is illustrated on the next page, Graph II on page 280, and Graph III on
page 282.[4]

Jesus is the Son of God. Therefore, the challenge for the
DISC model is to show that His profile includes all the positive
elements of all the profiles. In addition, His behavior would
have to appear perfect, without imbalances, in complete control, and He would have to be able instantly to take on whatever
style is necessary to meet the needs of the situation. Let us begin our study.

4. A more complete picture of how Graphs I, II, and III look can be found in
the *Understanding How Others Misunderstand You Workbook*, Appendix D,
pages 1093-12.

Graph I of Jesus

D   I   S   C

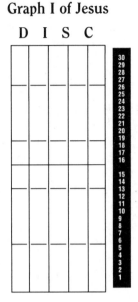

JESUS AS A HIGH D

High D traits are characteristic of an individual who imposes powerful control over the environment and the people with whom he comes in contact. Key traits: Demanding, forceful, authoritative, in control of the environment, and intimidating.

It is difficult to think of Jesus as projecting this type of behavior, but when He came in contact with demons, He did just that. Mark 1:21-28 gives a compact example.

Jesus entered the synagogue and began to instruct the people. They "were astonished at His teaching, for He taught them as one having authority, and not as the scribes" (v. 22, NKJV*), that is, the professionally trained scholars. He did not refer to the authority of others but instead gave a more personal interpretation of the Scriptures.

*New King James Version, used throughout this chapter.

A man in the synagogue who had an unclean spirit interrupted the meeting. "And he cried out, saying, 'Let us alone! What have we to do with You, Jesus of Nazareth? Did You come to destroy us? I know who You are—the Holy One of God!'" (vv. 23-24). It is obvious that the demons recognized who Jesus was and who He represented—their Creator, having total authority to judge them.

Jesus responded by saying sternly, "Be quiet, and come out of him!" (v. 25). His tone was demanding, direct, and to the point. The demon shook the man violently and came out of him with a shriek. The people were amazed and profoundly impressed: "What is this? . . . For with authority He commands even the unclean spirits, and they obey Him" (v. 27).

Conclusion: When Jesus came in contact with demons, He consistently reflected the traits of a High D—total control and authority. Although they had impressive powers, the demons never challenged Him. Instead, they were terrified in His presence. "Powerful and fearful as they are, demons are no match for the Savior, their creator and judge."[5]

JESUS AS A LOW D

Whereas the High D has a desire to be in control and operate independently, the Low D prefers to be part of a harmonious team. In addition, the Low D tends to project a nonconfrontational spirit, the opposite of the High D. Key traits: Peaceful, mild, quiet, unassuming, low key, soft-spoken, modest, kind.

Jesus tended to project this type of behavior with individuals who were society's rejects. He had several conversations with adulterous women, and one is particularly noteworthy, the encounter found in John 8:10-11. This particular woman was allegedly caught in the act and was condemned to death by the local leaders. Jesus skillfully defused the situation, dismissed her accusers, and turned his focus toward her. Observe what He said.

5. C. Fred Dickason, *Demon Possession and the Christian* (Chicago: Moody, 1987), p. 31.

"When Jesus had raised Himself up and saw no one but the woman, He said to her, 'Woman, where are those accusers of yours? Has no one condemned you?' She said, 'No one, Lord.' And Jesus said to her, 'Neither do I condemn you; go and sin no more'" (vv. 10-11).

The following is a breakdown of the message He communicated to this woman, who a moment before was facing death by stoning:

1. His address was one of respect for her as a person.
2. He did not judge her or declare her innocent.
3. He was interested in forgiving, not condemning, her.
4. He encouraged her to improve her quality of life and left no doubt He accepted her for who she was.

Conclusion: When Jesus related to repentant sinners, He consistently reflected the traits of a Low D. He had a tendency to be kind toward and understanding of people whom the religious community rejected as worthless outcasts. Though He did not condone their sins, He did accept them as persons— assuring and exhorting them, and being their resource for forgiveness through His relationship with the Father.

JESUS AS A HIGH I

High I tendencies are characterized by a desire for involvement with people. High I's typically are excellent communicators, using word pictures to express their ideas and feelings. Key traits: Interactive, enjoys socializing with others, is a master of influencing others with words of assurance and hope, senses the needs of others and sets in motion the positive energy and inputs to meet those needs.

Jesus verbally projected His High I skills in His use of parables (stories related to common experiences but with moral or spiritual meaning). Jesus used this method of teaching in every aspect of His public ministry. More than thirty parables are recorded in the gospels.

Jesus also took the time to reach out to people whenever needs were expressed. Mark 6:34-44 records one of those examples. After hearing about the beheading of John the Baptist, Jesus desired to be alone; however, the people followed Him. When He saw the great multitude, Jesus "was moved with compassion for them, because they were like sheep not having a shepherd. So He began to teach them many things" (v. 34).

As evening was approaching, His disciples came to Him and said, "Send them away . . . for they have nothing to eat" (v. 36). Rather than do that, Jesus sat the people down in groups of fifty and one hundred and performed yet another one of His miracles—He fed five thousand people with five loaves of bread and two fish. It was a marvelous time of fellowship, a wonderful picnic, and a great conclusion to a special day of enlightenment filled with positive surprises and fun.

Conclusion: When Jesus related to the needs of people, He consistently reflected the traits of a High I. He communicated through parables (word pictures) and consistently projected a shepherd's heart in offering hope to the multitudes of people, who were living in a time of misery and despair.

JESUS AS A LOW I

Whereas the High I prefers to work with people, the Low I is very comfortable working alone. In addition, a Low I is skilled in focusing on the facts of issues, whereas the High I is influenced by social pressure. Key traits: Under stress, withdraws to be alone; when alone, has a tendency to spend the time in reassessing objectives, goals, and direction; is the master of his emotions; is able to back off from the emotions of the moment and to keep sight of his goals and objectives.

Following the miracle of the feeding of the five thousand, the people, with the support of the disciples, decided to make Jesus their king (John 6:14-15). They reasoned that He would be able to meet their physical needs continually and free them from the oppression of the Romans.

Jesus understood their motives and quickly dispatched the disciples into a boat and dismissed the people (v. 15; see also

Matthew 14:22). He discerned that this mob action left unchecked would only serve to thwart His true mission. What was needed was to reassess the situation in private. When everyone was gone, He, too, departed to the mountain to pray and be alone with the Father (Matthew 14:23).

The following are the elements of the environment He created in dismissing the people:

1. Allowed for a cooling down of the emotional high experienced by the people, the disciples, and Jesus (for the record, the positive affirmation of the crowd would fulfill a High I's greatest fantasy yet would get him into serious trouble)
2. Allowed Himself to commune alone with the Father to formulate a better plan of action and communicate clearly who He was and the purpose of His mission (Matthew 14:23-33; 16:13-21)

Conclusion: When Jesus had to respond to issues involving His mission on earth, He was consistently dependent on the Father rather than being influenced by people. He continually spent time alone with the Father to insure that they were together on a plan of action. Behaviorally, this best reflects the traits of a Low I.

JESUS AS A HIGH S

The High S is characteristic of an individual possessing incredible patience and constancy. Even in adversity, the High S has the tendency to be extremely loyal to the members of his team. Key traits: Steady, patient, loyal, committed to creating harmony, good at follow-through, yet willing to make allowance for mistakes.

On the night of the Last Supper, following the singing of a hymn, Jesus gave the disciples insight into what was about to happen: that night He would be arrested and they would be scattered. He also assured the disciples that He would meet them again in Galilee (Mark 14:26-31; Luke 22:31-34).

Peter attempted to convince Jesus that He was wrong and that he was willing to die for Him: "Even if all are made to stumble, yet I will not be" (Mark 14:29). Jesus patiently told him that this was not so. Satan, Jesus said, had asked permission to sift Peter "as wheat" (Luke 22:31). "Assuredly, I say to you that today, even this night, before the rooster crows twice, you will deny Me three times" (Mark 14:30; Luke 22:34). Peter disagreed with Jesus vehemently. "If I have to die with You, I will not deny You!" (Mark 14:31). All the disciples "said likewise" (v. 31). Jesus listened patiently and reaffirmed what would happen, but He also confirmed that He had personally prayed for Peter, that he would not be broken but would be strengthened through this experience (Luke 22:32; see also vv. 33-34).

As Jesus was being tried before the high priest, Peter remained in the shadows. A servant girl and two others questioned Peter about his association with Jesus. Peter cursed as he denied the Lord a third time. As the cock crowed, the Lord turned and looked at Peter, communicating disappointment but not judgment (Matthew 26:69-75; Mark 14:66-72; Luke 22:54-62). John 21:15-19 records the resolution of the events. Jesus chose to allow Peter to undo his three denials and restored him to a position of leadership in front of his peers. What patience and grace!

Conclusion: When Jesus was dealing with the disciples and, in particular, Peter, He continually projected unbelievable patience. This trait is most common among the High S profiles.

JESUS AS A LOW S

Whereas a High S desires structure and order, a Low S profile desires variety and change. In addition, a Low S is skilled at creatively adapting to the needs of a situation, whereas the High S will tend to respond to the same situation with a more traditional approach. Key traits: Spontaneous, outgoing, unpredictable, good at assessing the needs and resources of the moment and employing them for maximum effect.

Luke 5:1-11 records the events that led Peter, the professional fisherman, to choose to become a follower of Jesus after a seemingly innocuous event in Peter's village. Jesus happened to be there, and a multitude pressed about Him to hear what He had to say about God. Rather than go into the synagogue, Jesus got into one of the boats, which happened to be Simon's, and cast out a short distance so that all could see and hear Him. Then He sat down and began to teach the multitudes from the boat.

When He had stopped speaking, He said casually to Simon Peter, "Launch out into the deep and let down your nets for a catch" (v. 4). Being a Low S also, Peter "answered and said to Him, 'Master, we have toiled all night and caught nothing; nevertheless at Your word I will let down the net.' And when they had done this, they caught a great number of fish"—so great, they called for help (vv. 5-7).

When Simon Peter saw what had happened, he was stunned and "fell down at Jesus' knees, saying, 'Depart from me, for I am a sinful man, O Lord'" (v. 8). Jesus responded by saying to Simon, "Do not be afraid. From now on you will catch men" (v. 10).

So when Peter and his partners, James and John, brought their boats to land, they left their jobs and began to follow Him.

Conclusion: Jesus began with a familiar reference point that Peter understood, *fishing,* and creatively used it to inspire him to consider a new ministry. His flexible style and spontaneous action fit Peter's need perfectly. In this situation, Jesus' behavior best represents Low S traits.

JESUS AS A HIGH C

High C tendencies are characteristic of an individual who is committed to accuracy and quality control. Typically, once a High C takes ownership of a plan of action, compliance is assured down to the smallest detail. Key traits: Perfection, accuracy, courtesy, conscientious model of diplomacy and restraint, absolute commitment to an agreed-upon plan down to the last item.

Matthew 26:37-56 and Luke 22:39-53 record the agony Jesus went through in the garden in anticipation of His arrest, beatings, trials, crucifixion, and separation from the Father, and the moment of arrest itself. As He became sorrowful and deeply distressed, He humbly prayed, "O My Father, if it is possible, let this cup pass from Me; nevertheless, not as I will, but as you will" (Matthew 26:39). Although honestly expressing His inner feelings, Jesus remained totally committed to the Father's will and plan.

While He was still praying, Judas was on his way with soldiers armed with swords and clubs to arrest Him. Jesus was very much aware of their subversive plan and yet courteously addressed Judas as His friend.

However, Peter's response was to cut off the ear of a servant of the high priest. Jesus reacted by touching the servant's ear and healing him. Then He rebuked Peter for his act of violence and commanded him to put his sword away. As He exercised these acts of restraint, Jesus told Peter that He had available to Him more than twelve legions of angels (as many as seventy-two thousand angelic warriors of the Lord). All He had to do was ask the Father, and they would come to His aid immediately—but that was not the plan.

What was agreed upon between the Father and the Son was for the words of the prophets in the Scriptures to be fulfilled. The disciples would all flee, and Jesus would go to the cross alone—and that is what happened.

Conclusion: Facing certain death, Jesus chose to endure the betrayal, arrest, trial, and cross so that the redemption of man would be completed. In human terms, His incredible restraint could best be described as High C.

Jesus as a Low C

Whereas a High C desires procedures and order, a Low C profile prefers a spontaneous approach. In addition, a Low C is skilled in knowing when to challenge the status quo for the purpose of correction. Key traits: Is his "own person," is a nonconformist, can be rebellious, defiant, obstinate, and sarcastic toward individuals he perceives to be hypocritical; has a tendency to be a lightning rod for challenging perceived hypocrisy.

The scribes and Pharisees continually challenged Jesus because, based on their interpretation of the law, He and His disciples flagrantly violated specific parts of it. The scribes and Pharisees felt compelled to bring those errors to His attention. In Matthew 15:1-14, the specific violation of the disciples was neglecting to wash their hands before they ate.

Jesus aggressively countered the accusations of the scribes and Pharisees by asking them why they selectively nullified God's commandments for the sake of their traditions. "For God commanded, saying, 'Honor your father and your mother'; and, 'He who curses father or mother, let him be put to death.' But you say, 'Whoever says to his father or mother, "Whatever profit you might have received from me has been dedicated to the temple"—is released from honoring his father or mother.' Thus you have made the commandment of God of no effect by your tradition" (vv. 4-6). Then Jesus addressed the crowd and publicly called his accusers hypocrites.

His disciples thought that He was coming on a little too strong and tried to reason with Him in an attempt to get Him to tone down His criticism. "Do You know that the Pharisees were offended when they heard this saying?" (v. 12). Jesus replied by stepping up His criticism of the Pharisees, referring to them as "blind leaders of the blind" (v. 14). In Matthew 23 Jesus' criticism of the Pharisees is also particularly strong.

Conclusion: Jesus reserved His greatest criticism for the religious leaders, particularly the Pharisees, the scholars of the Jewish law. His unrelenting attacks best fit the traits of a Low C and/or a High D.

DEFINING GRAPH II: JESUS' CORE BEHAVIOR

Graph II defines a person's instinctive response to pressure situations. It is this profile that generally best describes an individual's core behavior. Another way to say it is this: Graph II most often defines the true self, or who a person really is. Whereas all profiles commonly overextend their strengths un-

Graph II

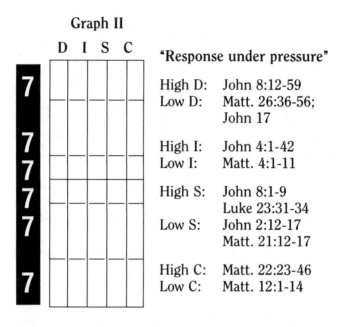

	D	I	S	C

"Response under pressure"

High D:	John 8:12-59
Low D:	Matt. 26:36-56;
	John 17

| High I: | John 4:1-42 |
| Low I: | Matt. 4:1-11 |

High S:	John 8:1-9
	Luke 23:31-34
Low S:	John 2:12-17
	Matt. 21:12-17

| High C: | Matt. 22:23-46 |
| Low C: | Matt. 12:1-14 |

der stress, Jesus appeared to remain in perfect control. Yet the perception of some individuals was that He had to be dysfunctional. Although the range of behavior He expressed is beyond that of a normal man, another plausible explanation is that Jesus is the Son of God. If Jesus was Deity in a human body, His behavioral traits in Graph II, although identifiable with specific styles, would appear to be supernatural. In addition, His behavior would logically cover a great range, but would also have to be correct and perfect. You decide how well Jesus responded to pressure by studying the Scripture references below.

DEFINING GRAPH III: THE DEITY AND HUMANITY OF JESUS

In the DISC system, the third graph provides a description of an individual's self-identity. It is a composite graph that combines the expected behavior of Graph I with the core behavior of Graph II. Based on the evidence recorded in Scripture, it appears that Jesus expressed all the human behavior traits listed on all four DISC scales. What makes Jesus unique is that whatever style He expressed, it was the right one for the specific situation. Behaviorally, the evidence strongly suggests He had to be God. No other conclusion can be rationally supported, based on the range of His behavioral responses.

The individuals who spent the most time with Him came to a similar conclusion. His best friend, John, says, "[The things that Jesus did were] written [and recorded so] that you may believe that Jesus is the Christ, the Son of God, and that believing you may have life in His name" (John 20:30-31).

Although some were confused about who He was, when Jesus asked the disciples what their perceptions were, Peter, the leader of the disciples, responded, "You are the Christ, the Son of the living God" (Matthew 16:16).

God the Father spoke three times in the gospels. Twice He directly confirmed that Jesus was indeed His Son. The first occasion was at Jesus' baptism (Mark 1:11); the second was at Christ's transfiguration (Matthew 17:5).

When the demons encountered Jesus, they always referred to Him as Deity. On one occasion the demons within two possessed men called Him "Jesus, You Son of God" and humbly begged Him not to torment them (Matthew 8:29).

However, the problem still exists: how can the behavior of man be associated with God? The apostle Paul deals with the dual nature of Jesus' humanity and divinity in Philippians 2:5-11. Paul says that Jesus did not demand to remain in the "form" of God but chose to limit His outward expression of His true inward Deity, that is, having two identities. His purpose was to fulfill His mission among mankind, and He took on the outward expression of mere mortal man (human behavior of Graph I). It was in this form that He humbled Himself to die on the cross. However, though the humanity of Jesus was real and true (complete humanity without sin), He remained, at the same time, undiminished Deity (Graph II). When the two graphs are put together to complete Graph III, one has a model of Jesus as 100 percent man and 100 percent God—which fits the theology of the New Testament in its description of the character of Jesus Christ, the Son of Man.

Graph III of Jesus

D I S C

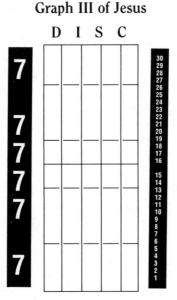

WHAT SHOULD ALL THIS MEAN TO YOU?

By viewing the behavior of a person over an extended period of time, one is able to gain insight into that person's character. As we have looked at the behavior of Jesus during the three and one-half years of His public ministry, we have observed something that can be said of no other person in history. Jesus was able to be flexible in the temperament He projected. However, what made Him unique was that He always selected the behavioral style that was exactly right for the situation. The only way to understand this is to believe what the disciples proclaimed—that He is the Son of God who came to earth to die for the sins of mankind.

John tells us that by receiving Him (as personal Savior) we become God's children (John 1:12). The apostle Paul says that we do this by faith (believing that His death on the cross is sufficient for our forgiveness) and not by our own good works or righteousness (Ephesians 2:8-9). Paul also tells us that every human being is sinful and needs the forgiveness that Jesus Christ offers freely to everyone who will believe and receive it (Romans 3:10, 23; 6:23).

In *Mere Christianity,* C. S. Lewis asserts that Jesus Christ's telling "people that their sins were forgiven . . . makes sense only if He really was the God whose laws are broken and whose love is wounded in every sin."[6] This means that people cannot reject Christ's diety and still regard Him as a moral or sane man. "A man who was merely a man and said the sort of things Jesus said would not be a great moral teacher. He would either be a lunatic—on a level with the man who says he is a poached egg—or else he would be the Devil of Hell. You can shut Him up for a fool, you can spit at Him and kill Him as a demon; or you can fall at His feet and call Him Lord and God. But let us not come with any patronising nonsense about His being a great human teacher. He has not left that open to us. He did not intend to.[7]

Just as the personality of Jesus Christ is supernatural, so is the forgiveness that He offers to us. It takes the supernatural change that comes through faith in Christ to transform our shortcomings in personality. We can become more flexible and useful to God and can strengthen the limitations of our own temperaments only in Jesus Christ. But even more important, we can be forgiven of the sin in our lives and have the assurance of eternity with God by believing in and accepting the One who demonstrated by His behavior that He is truly the eternal Son of God. This belief in Him brings with it an eternal relationship with God (John 3:16). God allows you the free will to decide for yourself whether to believe the gospel of the New Testament and receive the benefits of salvation or to reject the gospel and suffer the consequences of that rejection (1 John 5:12). The choice is yours to make.

6. C. S. Lewis, *Mere Christianity* (New York: Macmillan, 1952), 2:55-56.
7. Ibid.

Jesus Claimed to be God

(JOHN 8:58)

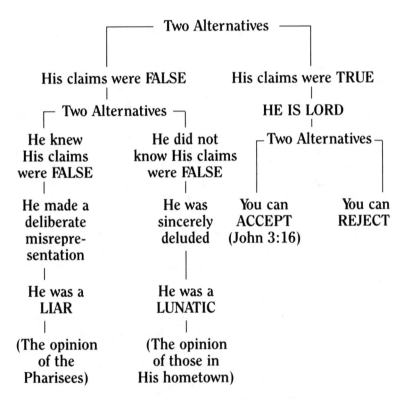

Used by permission of Campus Crusade for Christ.

SMALL GROUP EXERCISES

The following pages contain small group exercises
that apply to the discovering and loving
of the four DISC personality styles.

Discovering the High D

1*a*. If I had to describe my behavior in three phrases, I would choose the following words:

1*b*. I like jobs that have tasks which involve:

1*c*. but would rather delegate tasks that are involved with:

2. If I could select three key elements to incorporate into a loving environment for me, they would be:

3. As I reflect on the environment Jesus creates for Paul in Acts 9, He would also have ministered to me when He:

4. When I am under stress, the most loving thing you can do for me is:

5. In order to develop better relationships with the other profiles, I continually need to work on the following areas of my behavioral style:

In relating to the High I:

In relating to the High S:

In relating to the High C:

Bonus question

6. I have learned to control my personal anger by:

Loving the High D

1. The areas of my life where I need the gifts of the High D are:

2. As I reflect on the most favorable environment for the High D, the most difficult for me to create and communicate is:

3. The one element Jesus uses in Acts 9 in communicating with Paul that I have never used in loving the High D—but am willing to try—is:

4. As I review the differences between my style and that of the High D, I see the greatest potential for conflict to be:

because:

5. In order to build a better personal and working relationship with the High D, I need to be willing to modify my need to/for:

Bonus question

6. If I were planning a date or function for a High D, I would include the following activities:

Discovering the High I

1*a.* If I had to describe my behavior in three phrases, I would choose the following words:

1*b.* I like jobs that have tasks which involve:

1*c.* but would rather delegate tasks that involve:

2. If I could select three elements to incorporate into a loving environment for me, they would be:

3. As I reflect on the environment Jesus creates for Peter in John 21, He would also have ministered to me when He:

4. When I am under stress, the most loving thing you could do for me is:

5. In order to build better relationships with the other profiles, I continually need to work on the following areas of my behavioral style:

In relating to the High D:

In relating to the High S:

In relating to the High C:

Bonus question

6. I have learned to control my need for social recognition by:

Loving the High I

1. The areas of my life where I need the gifts of High I are:

2. As I reflect on the best environment for the High I, the most difficult element for me to create and communicate is:

3. The one element Jesus uses in John 21 I have never tried in loving the High I—but am willing to try—is:

4. As I focus on the differences in my style and that of the High I, I see the greatest potential for conflict to be:

because:

5. In order to build a better working relationship with the High I's, I need to be willing to modify my need to/for:

Bonus question

6. If I were planning a date or party for a High I, I would include the following activities:

Discovering the High S

1a. If I had to describe my behavior in three phrases, I would choose the following words:

1b. I like jobs that have tasks which include:

1c. but would rather delegate tasks that are involved with:

2. If I could select three key elements to incorporate into a loving environment for me, they would be:

3. As I reflect on the environment God created for Abraham, He would also have ministered to me personally when He:

4. When I am under stress, the most loving thing you can do for me is:

5. In order to develop better relationships with the other profiles, I need continually to work on the following areas of my behavioral style:

In relating to the High D:

In relating to the High I:

In relating to the High C:

Bonus question

6. I have learned to overcome my need for status quo by:

Loving the High S

1. The areas of my life where I need the gifts of the High S are:

2. As I reflect on God's style in loving Abraham, the most difficult for me to project is:

3. The one element I have never tried in loving the High S —but will next time—is:

4. As I review the differences between my style and that of the High S, I see the greatest potential for conflict to be:

because:

5. In order to build a better personal and working relationship with the High S, I need to be willing to modify my need for:

Bonus question

6. If I were planning a date or function for a High S, I would include the following activities:

Discovering the High C

1*a*. If I had to describe my behavior in three phrases, I would choose the following words:

1*b*. I like jobs that have tasks which include:

1*c*. but would rather delegate tasks that involve:

2. If I could select three key elements to incorporate into a loving environment for me, they would be:

3. As I reflect on the environment the Lord creates for Moses in Exodus 3-4, He would also have ministered to me when He:

4. When I am under stress, the most loving thing you can do for me is:

5. In order to develop better relationships with the other profiles, I continually need to work on the following areas of my behavioral style:

In relating to the High D:

In relating to the High I:

In relating to the High S:

Bonus question

6. I have learned to handle my high expectations of myself by:

Loving the High C

1. The areas of my life where I need the gifts of the High C are:

2. As I reflect on the best environment for the High C, the most difficult for me to create and communicate is:

3. The one element the Lord uses in Exodus 3-4 that I have never used in loving the High C—but am willing to try—is:

4. As I review the difference in my style and the High C style, I see my greatest potential for conflict to be:

5. In order to build a better personal and working relationship with the High C, I need to be willing to modify my need to/for:

Bonus question

6. If I were planning a date or function for a High C, I would include the following activities:

BIBLIOGRAPHY

RESOURCES

SUPPORT MATERIALS

The Personal DISCernment Inventory. Atlanta, Ga.: Team Resources, 1991.

Voges, Ken, and Ron Braund. *Understanding How Others Misunderstand You Workbook.* Rev. and enl. Chicago: Moody, 1995.

Voges, Ken. *Understanding Jesus.* Chicago: Moody, 1992.

ADDITIONAL RESOURCES

Personality Analysis Work Survey. Gainesville, Ga.: Christian Financial Concepts, 1994, 1995.

Ellis, Lee, and Larry Burkett. *Finding the Career That Fits You.* Chicago: Moody, 1994.

————. *Your Career in Changing Times.* Chicago: Moody, 1994.

LaHaye, Tim. *Understanding the Male Temperament.* Old Tappan, N.J.: Revell, 1977.

Littauer, Florence. *Personality Plus.* Old Tappan, N.J.: Revell, 1983.

MacMillan, Pat. *Hiring Excellence.* Colorado Springs, Colo.: Navpress, 1992.

O'Connor, Mike. *The "DISC" Model: Trainer and Consultant's Reference Encyclopedia.* Bonita Springs, Fla.: Life Associates.

SPECIFIC SUBJECTS

Values vs. Needs materials. Bonita Springs, Fla.: Life Associates.

For all parents:

Boyd, Charles F. *Different Children, Different Needs.* Sisters, Oreg. Multnomah, 1994.

Dobson, James C. *Parenting Isn't for Cowards.* Waco, Tex.: Word, 1987.

For parents of D and I children:

Dobson, James C. *The Strong-Willed Child.* Wheaton, Ill.: Tyndale, 1978.

For parents of S and C children:

Sloat, Don. *The Dangers of Growing Up in a Christian Home.* Nashville: Thomas Nelson, 1986.

How Do Others See You?

WORKBOOK
Foreword by Joe L. Wall

7 PRODUCTS IN 1
A WORKBOOK
PLUS
SIX ASSESSMENTS

Ken Voges & Ron Braund
UNDERSTANDING
HOW OTHERS
MISUNDERSTAND

A Unique
and Proven Plan
for Strengthening
Personal
Relationships

YOU

Understanding How Others
Misunderstand You Workbook

Using the pioneering DISC profile, this book teaches--
in clear terms--how to build closer, more understanding
relationships at home, work and church.

Paperback 0-8024-1106-1